The Millennials

AMERICANS UNDER AGE 25

The Millennials

AMERICANS UNDER AGE 25

1st EDITION

BY THE NEW STRATEGIST EDITORS

New Strategist Publications, Inc.
Ithaca, New York

New Strategist Publications, Inc.
P.O. Box 242, Ithaca, New York 14851
800/848-0841; 607/273-0913
www.newstrategist.com

ISBN 1-885070-40-3

Printed in the United States of America

Table of Contents

Chapter 4. Income

Chapter 5. Labor Force

Chapter 6. Living Arrangements

Chapter 7. Population

Chapter 8. Spending

Tables

Chapter 1. Attitudes and Behavior

Chapter 2. Education

Chapter 3. Health

Chapter 4. Income

Chapter 7. Population

Chapter 8. Spending

Illustrations

Introduction

The millennial generation—America's children, teens, and youngest adults—is the most mysterious of the five generations of living Americans. Literally the new kids in town, the characteristics of millennials are only now beginning to emerge as the oldest enter their twenties. *The Millennials: Americans under Age 25* provides the first comprehensive demographic and socioeconomic profile of the generation. Because millennials are the children of baby boomers, the generation has already attracted the media spotlight. Because of their numbers, business and government have little choice but to heed their wants and needs.

The millennial generation, aged 7 to 24 in 2001, numbers 71 million and accounts for 26 percent of the total population—close to the baby-boom's 28 percent share. For convenience, children under age 7 are also included in the millennial profile in this book. The under-7 age group adds another 27 million, for a total of 97 million people under age 25 in the U.S. in 2001—or 35 percent of the total population. The oldest millennials entirely fill the 18-to-24 age group, accounting for a significant 13 percent of the adult population—a proportion that gets bigger every day.

Population under age 25

(percent of people under age 25 in the population, 1920 to 2020)

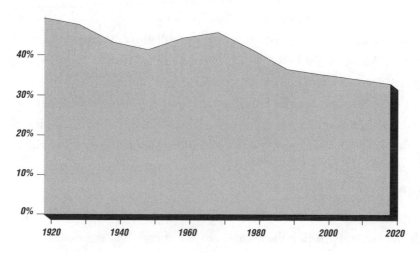

The oldest millennials were born in 1977, when the long anticipated echo boom of births began. In that year, following a 12-year lull, the number of births climbed to 3.3 million. By 1980, annual births had risen to 3.6 million. By 1990, they topped 4 million. Altogether, 68 million babies were born between 1977 and 1994, when births once again dropped below 4 million.

As is every other generation of Americans, millennials are defined by their numbers. And like the large baby boom before them, the millennial generation's entrance is making waves. Public schools are straining with enrollment numbers not seen since boomers filled classrooms. Colleges and universities that had been competing for scarce Gen Xers now enjoy picking and choosing from among the best as applications soar. In time, the housing and labor markets will also be shaped by the large generation embarking on career and family life.

Each generation of Americans is unique, shaped not only by its numbers but also by the historical moment. Millennials are no exception. Already, three distinct characteristics are emerging, characteristics that will reshape American society as millennials mature. One, millennials are racially and ethnically diverse—so diverse, in fact, that in many parts of the country the term "minority" no longer has meaning for their peer group. Two, they are fiercely independent thanks to divorce, day care, single parenthood, latchkey lifestyles, and the technological revolution that has put the joy stick squarely in their hands. Three, millennials feel powerful. Raised by indulgent parents, they have a sense of security not shared by Gen Xers. Optimistic about the future, millennials see opportunity where others see problems.

The Millennials: Americans under Age 25 examines the youth generation from two perspectives. One, as independent individuals establishing themselves in the household and labor market. Many of the tables in the book examine people aged 16 to 24 as workers, householders, parents, and consumers. Because most millennials are not yet independent, the second perspective examines them as children in the home of their parents. Many tables examine the activities and lifestyles of parents—the labor force participation of parents with children under age 18, for example, or the spending of married couples with children under age 6. Together, the two perspectives provide a comprehensive picture of the lifestyles of children, teens, and the youngest adults.

Despite the growing number of Americans under age 25, children and youth will not regain the prominent position they once held in our society. Because of the aging of the U.S. population over the past century, the under-age-25 segment is a much smaller share of the total population than it once was. In 1920, nearly half of Americans were under age 25. By

1950, the figure had fallen to 41 percent. It rose slightly with the birth of the baby-boom generation, reaching 46 percent in 1970. Then the figure plummeted as smaller families became the norm. While the number of children and youth is rising, it is not growing as fast as the older population. In the next two decades, people under age 25 will account for a shrinking share of the total population, declining from 35 percent in 2001 to 33 percent in 2020.

How to Use This Book

We designed *The Millennials: Americans under Age 25* for easy use. Its eight chapters—Attitudes and Behavior, Education, Health, Income, Labor Force, Living Arrangements, Population, and Spending—appear in alphabetical order.

Most of the tables rely on data collected and published by the federal government, in particular the Bureau of the Census, the Bureau of Labor Statistics, the National Center for Education Statistics, the National Center for Health Statistics, and the Centers for Disease Control and Prevention. The federal government continues to be the best source of up-to-date, reliable information about the changing characteristics of Americans.

While the federal government has produced most of the data reported in this book, the tables in *Millennials* are not simply reprints of government spreadsheets—as is the case in many reference books. Instead, New Strategist's editors compiled and created each table individually, the calculations designed to reveal trends and highlight important information. Each chapter of *Millennials* includes the demographic and lifestyle data most important to researchers. Each table tells a story about children, teens, and young adults—a story fleshed out by the accompanying text, which analyzes the data and identifies trends. Should you need even more statistical detail than the tables provide, try plumbing the source listed at the bottom of each table.

The book contains a comprehensive list of tables to help you locate the information you need. For a more detailed search, use the index at the back of the book. The glossary defines the terms and describes the surveys appearing in the tables and text. A list of telephone and Internet contacts also appears at the end of the book, enabling you to access government specialists and web sites.

Each new generation of Americans is unique and surprising in its own way. With *The Millennials: Americans under Age 25* on your bookshelf, you won't be surprised by the unique characteristics of this exciting, new generation of Americans.

1

Attitudes and Behavior

♦ Many parents think work interferes with family life, but most children do not agree. The majority of children think their parents work the right amount, and most believe their parents rarely or never put job before family.

♦ Many teens think their parents do a good job of making them feel important and loved, but fewer than half give their parents an A for "knowing what is really going on in my life."

♦ A substantial minority of teens are risk takers. In the past month, 37 percent of 12th graders have ridden in a car with a driver who had been drinking.

♦ In 1998, 11 percent of high school seniors were threatened by someone with a weapon in school, down from 13 percent in 1986.

♦ Among school-aged children aged 9 to 17, the 53 percent majority use the Internet. The proportion is even higher among 18-to-24-year-olds, 57 percent of whom are Internet users.

♦ Fifty-two percent of 18-to-24-year-olds identify themselves as political independents, a challenge for political parties in the decades ahead.

♦ Among college freshmen, 76 percent of men and 71 percent of women say being very well off financially is essential or very important to them. Raising a family is essential to 73 percent of men and women.

Children Believe Parents Put Family First

Parents are not so sure about how good a job they're doing.

Most children today have working parents, and most think their parents are doing a good job of juggling work and family responsibilities. In fact, they think their parents are doing better than the parents themselves believe.

When children aged 8 to 18 are asked whether they think their parents work too much, only 33 percent say their father does and an even smaller 25 percent think their mother does. In contrast, fully 49 percent of fathers and 46 percent of mothers think they work too much. The majority of children think their parents work the right amount.

When children are asked how well their parents manage work and parenting responsibilities, 69 percent say their father manages "very successfully" and 74 percent say their mother does. In contrast, just 31 to 34 percent of parents say they manage the responsibilities very successfully.

Children believe their parents rarely or never put job before family, but rather, family before job.

♦ While many parents think work interferes with family life, most children do not agree—a finding that should boost the psychological well-being of many mothers and fathers.

Children think their parents manage well

(percent of parents who think they manage work and parenting responsibilities "very successfully," and percent of children who think their parents manage work and parenting responsibilities "very successfully," by sex of parent, 1998)

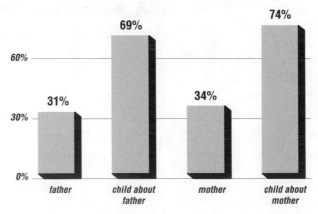

How Parents and Children Feel about Parents' Work, 1998

(percent distribution of employed parents and children aged 8 to 18 by attitude toward how well parent manages work and family, by sex of parent, 1998)

	father	child about father	mother	child about mother
PARENT: Does your child think you work too much, too little, or about the right amount?				
CHILD: Do you think your mother/father works too much, too little, or about the right amount?				
• Too much	49%	33%	46%	25%
• About the right amount	49	64	53	70
• Too little	2	3	1	5
PARENT: How successful are you in managing your work and parenting responsibilities?				
CHILD: How successful is your father/mother in managing work and parenting responsibilities?				
• Very successful	31	69	34	74
• Somewhat successful	65	26	60	21
• Somewhat unsuccessful	3	3	6	3
• Very unsuccessful	0	2	0	2
PARENT: How often do you put your job before your family?				
CHILD: How often do you feel that your father/mother puts his/her job before your family?				
• Very often	14	4	8	4
• Often	19	5	13	3
• Sometimes	32	16	39	9
• Rarely	21	28	26	24
• Never	14	48	14	60
PARENT: How often do you put your family before your job?				
CHILD: How often do you feel that your father/mother puts the family before his/her job?				
• Very often	25	47	25	60
• Often	28	26	26	19
• Sometimes	31	17	34	13
• Rarely	14	5	14	3
• Never	2	5	2	5

Source: Data from pp. 46, 47, 248, 250, 251 from Ask the Children *by Ellen Galinsky; copyright © 1999 by Ellen Galinsky. Reprinted by permission of HarperCollins Publishers, Inc., William Morrow*

Most Teens Think Their Parents Appreciate Them

But few say their parents know what is really going on in their life.

When asked to grade their parents on a variety of parenting skills, many children in 7th through 12th grade give their parents As. But teens are tough graders, and many give their parents lower grades on some skills. Fathers generally earn lower grades than mothers.

Eighty-one percent of teens give their mother an A for "being there when I am sick." Only 52 percent give Dad an A on this item. When asked to grade their parents on "raising me with good values," 75 percent of teens award Mom an A and 69 percent do so for Dad. Sixty-four percent of teens give Mom an A and 57 percent give Dad an A for "making me feel important and loved."

Fewer than half of teens give either parent an A for skills such as "being involved with what is happening to me at school," "being someone I can go to when I am upset," "spending time talking with me," and "knowing what is really going on in my life."

♦ The distance between teens and parents can be difficult to bridge, but most teens think their parents are doing something right.

Teens Grade Their Parents, 1998

(percent of children in 7th through 12th grade who give their parents an A for selected parenting practices, by sex of parent, 1998)

	Mom gets an A:	Dad gets an A:
Being there for me when I am sick	81%	52%
Raising me with good values	75	69
Making me feel important and loved	64	57
Being able to attend important events in my life	64	55
Appreciating me for who I am	64	58
Encouraging me to want to learn and to enjoy learning	59	58
Being involved with what is happening to me at school	46	38
Being someone I can go to when I am upset	46	38
Spending time talking with me	43	43
Establishing family routines and traditions with me	38	41
Knowing what is really going on in my life	35	31
Controlling his/her temper when I do something that makes him/her angry	29	31

Source: Data from pp. 46, 47, 248, 250, 251 from Ask the Children *by Ellen Galinsky; copyright © 1999 by Ellen Galinsky. Reprinted by permission of HarperCollins Publishers, Inc., William Morrow*

Many Teens Are Risk Takers

Not wearing a bicycle helmet is the only "risk" taken by the majority of teens.

When asked whether they have engaged in a variety of risky behaviors, the majority of teens in 9th through 12th grade say no. But a substantial minority of teens are risk takers.

Half of 9th grade boys have been in a physical fight in the past year, as have one-third of 9th grade girls. In the past month, 37 percent of 12th graders have ridden in a car with a driver who had been drinking. Twenty-seven to 29 percent of 9th through 12th graders have felt sad or hopeless almost every day for at least two weeks sometime during the year preceding the survey. Eighteen to 22 percent seriously considered attempting suicide.

Some risk taking declines as students mature. The percentage of boys who have been in a physical fight falls from 50 to 39 percent between 9th and 12th grade. Other risky behavior increases with age. The proportion of students who admit to driving after drinking in the past month rises from just 5 percent among 9th graders (most of whom are too young to drive) to 23 percent among 12th graders. Nearly one-third of 12th grade boys admit to driving after drinking in the past month.

♦ With so many teens engaging in risky behavior, it is difficult for parents to keep their children safe without help from society at large. Teen curfews, stricter driver's license requirements, and more after-school supervision would help reduce the risks children take.

Risk Behavior of 9th Graders by Sex, 1999

(percent of 9th graders engaging in selected risk behaviors, by sex, 1999)

	total	male	female
Rarely/never wear bicycle helmet*	80%	83%	77%
Engaged in physical fight[†]	41	50	33
Rode with driver who had been drinking[‡]	31	30	32
Felt sad or hopeless[§]	27	21	34
Engaged in physical fight on school property[†]	19	24	13
Seriously considered attempting suicide[†]	18	12	24
Carried a weapon[‡]	18	29	7
Rarely/never use seat belts	17	20	14
Threatened or injured with a weapon on school property[†]	11	13	8
Attempted suicide[†]	10	6	14
Forced to have sexual intercourse	8	6	10
Physically hurt by boyfriend/girlfriend on purpose[†]	8	8	8
Carried a weapon on school property[‡]	7	11	3
Felt too unsafe to go to school[‡]	7	6	8
Drove after drinking[‡]	5	6	5
Carried a gun[‡]	5	10	1
Suicide attempt required medical attention[†]	3	3	4

* Of those who rode bicycles in the 12 months preceding the survey.
[†] One or more times in the 12 months preceding the survey.
[‡] On one or more days of the 30 days preceding the survey.
[§] Almost every day for at least two weeks in the 12 months preceding the survey.
Source: Centers for Disease Control and Prevention, Youth Risk Behavior Surveillance—United States, 1999, *Morbidity and Mortality Weekly Report, Vol. 49, No. SS-5, June 9, 2000; Internet site <ftp://ftp.cdc.gov/pub/ Publications/mmwr/SS/SS4905.pdf>*

Risk Behavior of 10th Graders by Sex, 1999

(percent of 10th graders engaging in selected risk behaviors, by sex, 1999)

	total	male	female
Rarely/never wear bicycle helmet*	87%	88%	86%
Engaged in physical fight[†]	38	46	29
Rode with driver who had been drinking[‡]	33	35	32
Felt sad or hopeless[§]	29	20	38
Seriously considered attempting suicide[†]	22	14	30
Carried a weapon[‡]	19	31	7
Engaged in physical fight on school property[†]	17	22	12
Rarely/never use seat belts	15	18	12
Attempted suicide[†]	11	6	15
Drove after drinking[‡]	10	15	5
Forced to have sexual intercourse	9	5	12
Threatened or injured with a weapon on school property[†]	8	11	5
Physically hurt by boyfriend/girlfriend on purpose[†]	8	6	10
Carried a weapon on school property[‡]	7	11	3
Carried a gun[‡]	5	10	1
Felt too unsafe to go to school[‡]	5	4	5
Suicide attempt required medical attention[†]	3	2	4

* Of those who rode bicycles in the 12 months preceding the survey.
[†] One or more times in the 12 months preceding the survey.
[‡] On one or more days of the 30 days preceding the survey.
[§] Almost every day for at least two weeks in the 12 months preceding the survey.
Source: Centers for Disease Control and Prevention, Youth Risk Behavior Surveillance—United States, 1999, Morbidity and Mortality Weekly Report, Vol. 49, No. SS-5, June 9, 2000; Internet site <ftp://ftp.cdc.gov/pub/ Publications/mmwr/SS/SS4905.pdf>

Risk Behavior of 11th Graders by Sex, 1999

(percent of 11th graders engaging in selected risk behaviors, by sex, 1999)

	total	male	female
Rarely/never wear bicycle helmet*	86%	87%	85%
Engaged in physical fight[†]	31	39	23
Rode with driver who had been drinking[‡]	31	33	28
Felt sad or hopeless[§]	27	19	35
Seriously considered attempting suicide[†]	18	14	23
Drove after drinking[‡]	16	21	12
Carried a weapon[‡]	16	27	5
Rarely/never use seat belts	14	18	10
Engaged in physical fight on school property[†]	11	14	7
Forced to have sexual intercourse	10	5	15
Physically hurt by boyfriend/girlfriend on purpose[†]	8	8	9
Carried a weapon on school property[‡]	7	11	3
Threatened or injured with a weapon on school property[†]	6	7	5
Attempted suicide[†]	6	5	8
Felt too unsafe to go to school[‡]	5	5	4
Carried a gun[†]	4	7	1
Suicide attempt required medical attention[†]	3	2	3

* Of those who rode bicycles in the 12 months preceding the survey.
[†] One or more times in the 12 months preceding the survey.
[‡] On one or more days of the 30 days preceding the survey.
[§] Almost every day for at least two weeks in the 12 months preceding the survey.
Source: Centers for Disease Control and Prevention, Youth Risk Behavior Surveillance—United States, 1999, Morbidity and Mortality Weekly Report, Vol. 49, No. SS-5, June 9, 2000; Internet site <ftp://ftp.cdc.gov/pub/ Publications/mmwr/SS/SS4905.pdf>

Risk Behavior of 12th Graders by Sex, 1999

(percent of 12th graders engaging in selected risk behaviors, by sex, 1999)

	total	male	female
Rarely/never wear bicycle helmet*	91%	91%	90%
Rode with driver who had been drinking‡	37	40	35
Engaged in physical fight†	30	39	22
Felt sad or hopeless§	29	25	34
Drove after drinking‡	23	31	14
Rarely/never use seat belts	19	28	10
Seriously considered attempting suicide†	18	16	21
Carried a weapon‡	16	27	5
Physically hurt by boyfriend/girlfriend on purpose†	12	12	11
Forced to have sexual intercourse	9	6	13
Engaged in physical fight on school property†	8	10	6
Carried a weapon on school property‡	6	10	2
Attempted suicide†	6	5	6
Threatened or injured with a weapon on school property†	5	7	4
Carried a gun‡	5	8	1
Felt too unsafe to go to school‡	4	3	5
Suicide attempt required medical attention†	2	2	1

* Of those who rode bicycles in the 12 months preceding the survey.
† One or more times in the 12 months preceding the survey.
‡ On one or more days of the 30 days preceding the survey.
§ Almost every day for at least two weeks in the 12 months preceding the survey.
Source: Centers for Disease Control and Prevention, Youth Risk Behavior Surveillance—United States, 1999,
Morbidity and Mortality Weekly Report, Vol. 49, No. SS-5, June 9, 2000; Internet site <ftp://ftp.cdc.gov/pub/
Publications/mmwr/SS/SS4905.pdf>

Delinquent Behavior Is Not the Norm

Most 12th graders do not engage in delinquent behavior, but a substantial minority cross the line.

Most teenagers follow the rules, but not all. When asked which delinquent behaviors they participated in during the past year, the largest share (31 percent) admitted taking something worth less than $50 that did not belong to them. Thirty percent said they had taken something from a store without paying for it. One-fourth had entered a home or building when they weren't supposed to be there, while 21 percent had taken part in a fight with a group of friends.

Boys are more likely than girls to engage in delinquent behavior. While in the past year more than one in five boys have hurt someone badly enough that the victim needed bandages or a doctor, only 6 percent of girls have done so. Fifteen percent of boys say they have been arrested and taken to a police station in the past year versus 5 percent of girls.

♦ While delinquent behavior is not the norm among teens, it is widespread enough to raise alarm among parents, teachers, and community leaders.

Delinquent Behavior of 12th Graders, 1998

(percent of 12th graders reporting delinquent behavior in the past 12 months, by type of behavior and sex, 1998)

	total	males	females
Taken something not belonging to you worth under $50	31%	39%	25%
Taken something from a store without paying for it	30	34	26
Gone into a house or building when you weren't supposed to be there	25	31	19
Taken part in a fight with a group of friends	21	26	15
Gotten into a serious fight at school or work	17	21	11
Hurt someone badly enough to need bandages or a doctor	14	23	6
Damaged school property on purpose	14	21	8
Taken something not belonging to you worth over $50	12	17	7
Been arrested and taken to a police station	10	15	5
Damaged property at work on purpose	7	13	2
Taken part of a car without permission	5	8	2
Taken a car that didn't belong to someone in your family without permission	5	7	3
Used a knife, gun, or other weapon to get something from someone	4	7	2
Hit an instructor or supervisor	3	5	1
Set fire to someone's property on purpose	3	4	1

Source: Bureau of Justice Statistics, Kathleen Maguire and Ann L. Pastore, eds., Sourcebook of Criminal Justice Statistics 1999, *Internet site <www.albany.edu/sourcebook>*

Many High School Seniors Experience Crime

But in-school crime is less common now than it was in the 1980s.

Among high school seniors, a substantial minority have been the victims of crime in the past year, with many of those crimes occurring at school. Forty-five percent of 12th graders lost something worth less than $50 through theft in the past 12 months. Thirty-two percent had this happen to them at school, down from 37 percent in 1986.

Most types of in-school crime are less common today than in 1986. Outside of school, however, many types of crime are on the rise. Eighteen percent of seniors have been threatened with a weapon, up from 16 percent in 1986. Five percent have been injured with a weapon, about the same proportion as in 1986.

♦ The increased attention to school safety has had an impact on crime statistics, and fewer students are victimized at school.

High School Seniors Victimized by Crime, 1986 and 1998

(percent of high school seniors reporting any and at-school victimization experiences in the past 12 months, by type of victimization, 1986 and 1998; percentage point change, 1986–98)

	any			at school		
	1998	*1986*	*percentage point change*	*1998*	*1986*	*percentage point change*
Had something worth less than $50 stolen	45%	47%	–2	32%	37%	–5
Had property deliberately damaged	33	32	0	25	26	–1
Was threatened by someone without a weapon	29	28	0	21	25	–4
Had something worth more than $50 stolen	27	18	9	18	14	4
Was threatened with a weapon	18	16	2	11	13	–2
Was injured by someone without a weapon	15	16	–1	11	14	–3
Was injured with a weapon	5	5	0	5	5	–1

Source: Bureau of Justice Statistics, Kathleen Maguire and Ann L. Pastore, eds., Sourcebook of Criminal Justice Statistics 1999, *Internet site <www.albany.edu/sourcebook; calculations by New Strategist*

Boys Experience More Crime Than Girls

Blacks are more likely than whites to be threatened with a weapon.

Among 12th graders, boys are more likely to experience crime than girls are. While the majority of boys have had something worth less than $50 stolen from them in the past year, the figure is only 41 percent among girls. Fully 37 percent of boys have been threatened by someone without a weapon versus 20 percent of girls. One in four boys has been threatened with a weapon versus 11 percent of girls.

Blacks are more likely than whites to have had things stolen from them—both at school and outside of school. But whites are more likely than blacks to be threatened or injured by someone without a weapon. Blacks are more likely than whites to be threatened or injured with a weapon. Seven percent of black high school seniors were injured with a weapon at school in 1998.

◆ There are few times in life when people are more vulnerable than in their teens because of their own risk taking as well as that of their peers.

Many 12th grade boys must cope with crime

(percent of 12th grade boys who have experienced selected crimes in the past 12 months, 1998)

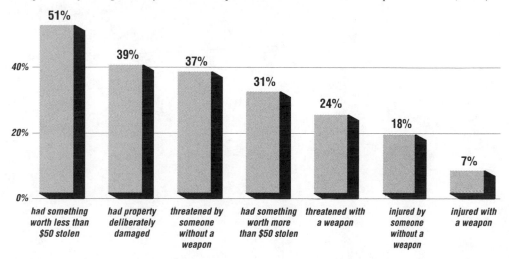

High School Seniors Victimized by Crime by Sex, 1998

(percent of high school seniors reporting any and at-school victimization experiences in the past 12 months, by type of victimization and sex, 1998)

	any		at school	
	male	*female*	*male*	*female*
Had something worth less than $50 stolen	51%	41%	37%	28%
Had property deliberately damaged	39	27	28	22
Was threatened by someone without a weapon	37	20	29	13
Had something worth more than $50 stolen	31	22	24	13
Was threatened with a weapon	24	11	17	6
Was injured by someone without a weapon	18	11	14	8
Was injured with a weapon	7	3	8	2

Source: Bureau of Justice Statistics, Kathleen Maguire and Ann L. Pastore, eds., Sourcebook of Criminal Justice Statistics 1999, *Internet site <www.albany.edu/sourcebook>; calculations by New Strategist*

High School Seniors Victimized by Crime by Race, 1998

(percent of high school seniors reporting any and at-school victimization experiences in the past 12 months, by type of victimization and race, 1998)

	any		at school	
	black	*white*	*black*	*white*
Had something worth less than $50 stolen	51%	43%	34%	32%
Had something worth more than $50 stolen	33	24	23	17
Had property deliberately damaged	32	32	22	25
Was threatened by someone without a weapon	24	30	22	21
Was threatened with a weapon	21	16	14	11
Was injured by someone without a weapon	12	14	11	11
Was injured with a weapon	6	4	7	4

Source: Bureau of Justice Statistics, Kathleen Maguire and Ann L. Pastore, eds., Sourcebook of Criminal Justice Statistics 1999, *Internet site <www.albany.edu/sourcebook>; calculations by New Strategist*

Children Are Big Users of the Internet

More than half of those aged 9 or older are online.

Among children aged 9 to 17, the 53 percent majority use the Internet. The proportion is even higher among young adults aged 18 to 24, 57 percent of whom are Internet users.

Internet use is slightly greater for females than males. Non-Hispanic whites and Asians are more likely to use the Internet than blacks and Hispanics. Among 18-to-24-year-olds, 73 percent of Asians are Internet users versus only 32 percent of Hispanics.

Internet use by children and young adults rises sharply with household income. Among 3-to-8-year-olds, 22 percent of those living in households with incomes of $75,000 or more are online compared with just 5 percent of those living in households with incomes below $15,000. Among 9-to-17-year-olds, 75 percent of those with the highest incomes are online versus 29 percent of those with the lowest incomes.

♦ As the cost of computers and Internet access falls, children's Internet use will rise.

Internet use varies sharply by race and Hispanic origin

(percent of 9-to-17-year-olds who use the Internet, by race and Hispanic origin, 2000)

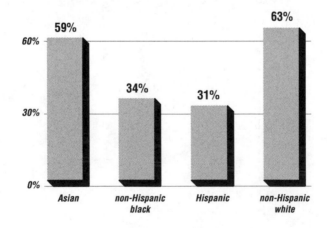

Internet Users under Age 25, 2000

(percent of people aged 3 or older and aged 3 to 24 who use the Internet by selected characteristics, 2000)

	total, 3 or older	3 to 8	9 to 17	18 to 24
Total people	44%	15%	53%	57%
Sex				
Female	44	16	54	60
Male	45	15	53	54
Race and Hispanic origin				
Asian	49	14	59	73
Black, non-Hispanic	29	10	34	42
Hispanic	24	9	31	32
White, non-Hispanic	50	19	63	65
Household income				
Under $15,000	19	5	29	42
$15,000 to $24,999	26	10	36	44
$25,000 to $34,999	36	13	46	52
$35,000 to $49,999	47	17	55	59
$50,000 to $74,999	58	19	64	67
$75,000 or more	70	22	75	78

Source: National Telecommunications and Information Administration, Falling through the Net: Toward Digital Inclusion—A Report on Americans' Access to Technology Tools, *October 2000*

Young Adults Differ from the Average American

The attitudes of 18-to-24-year-olds contrast with those of older Americans on many issues.

Young adults are not as happy as older Americans, but they find life more exciting. They are less trusting than older people, but more optimistic about their children's future. They are more independent—both in politics and religion—than the average person.

Some of the differences between young adults and older people are due to their lifestages. Fewer 18-to-24-year-olds are "pretty well satisfied" with their finances, for example, because most are in entry-level jobs with low earnings. As they establish careers, their satisfaction is likely to rise. Similarly, as they settle down, life may become a little less exciting—which may boost happiness.

But some of the differences between 18-to-24-year-olds and older people suggest changes are in store for America as a whole. The political and religious independence of young adults will challenge political parties and traditional religious institutions. The distrust young adults feel toward others isn't likely to diminish with experience, making it harder to unite them behind any cause or belief.

♦ The much greater diversity of the young, combined with their political independence, will revolutionize the political landscape in the decades ahead.

Attitudes of People Aged 18 to 24, 1998

(responses of people aged 18 or older and aged 18 to 24 to selected statements, in percent, 1998)

	total people	people aged 18 to 24
How would you say things are these days? Would you say that you are very happy, pretty happy, or not too happy?		
• Very happy	32%	23%
In general, do you find life exciting, pretty routine, or dull?		
• Exciting	45	51
Would you say that most people can be trusted or that you can't be too careful in dealing with people?		
• Most people can be trusted	38	20
Do you think most people would try to take advantage of you if they got a chance, or would they try to be fair?		
• Most people try to be fair	52	38
Would you say that most of the time people try to be helpful, or that they are mostly just looking out for themselves?		
• People try to be helpful	48	34
Are you pretty well satisfied with your present financial situation, more or less satisfied, or not satisfied at all?		
• Pretty well satisfied	30	24
Given the chance, would your change your present type of work for something different?		
• Yes	40	57
Compared to your parents when they were the age you are now, do you think your own standard of living now is much better, somewhat better, about the same, somewhat worse, or much worse than theirs was?		
• Much/somewhat better	64	59
When your children are at the age you are now, do you think their standard of living will be much better, somewhat better, about the same, somewhat worse, or much worse than yours is now?		
• Much/somewhat better	60	69
On a seven-point scale from extremely liberal to extremely conservative, where would you place yourself?		
• Liberal	27	34
• Moderate	35	34
• Conservative	33	25

(continued)

(continued from previous page)

	total people	people aged 18 to 24
Do you usually think of yourself as a Republican, Democrat, or independent?		
• Democrat	34%	28%
• Independent	38	52
• Republican	26	19
Believe in God without any doubt	63	54
What is your religious preference?		
• Protestant	54	43
• Catholic	25	24
• Jewish	2	1
• Other	4	6
• None	14	25

Source: 1998 General Social Survey, National Opinion Research Center, University of Chicago; calculations by New Strategist

Most College Freshmen Have Attended Religious Services

Few have discussed politics, however.

Every year for more than 30 years, the Higher Education Research Institute of UCLA has asked the nation's college freshmen a battery of questions about their attitudes, experiences, college plans, and life objectives. Over the decades, the answers reveal the character of each generation of Americans. Based on the answers supplied by college freshmen in 2000, it's apparent that the Millennial generation is not only wired, but also connected to their community. More than 80 percent of male and female college freshmen have attended a religious service in the past 12 months. At least three out of four have performed volunteer work. Another three out of four have attended a public recital or concert. Sixty-five to 70 percent have socialized with someone of another racial or ethnic group. Most have also used a personal computer, gone online to do homework or research, and communicated via e-mail.

Only 14 percent of women and 20 percent of men have discussed politics in the past 12 months—one of the least common experiences. A much larger share (43 to 47 percent) participated in an organized demonstration, suggesting that many demonstrators participate for social more than political reasons.

Women freshmen are more likely to have volunteered in the past 12 months, while their male counterparts are more likely to have drunk beer. Women are twice as likely as men to have felt overwhelmed by all they had to do (36 percent of women versus 18 percent of men).

♦ The Millennial generation already has a reputation for being more optimistic and civic minded than Generation X. Whether this reputation is deserved remains to be seen.

Experiences of College Freshmen by Sex, 2000

(percent of college freshmen who have participated in selected activities in the past year, by sex, 2000)

	men	women	difference between men and women
Attended religious service	80%	85%	–5
Used personal computer	80	78	2
Performed volunteer work	76	85	–9
Attended public recital or concert	75	83	–8
Used Internet for research or homework	66	69	–3
Socialized with someone of another racial/ethnic group	65	70	–5
Communicated via e–mail	62	69	–6
Visited art gallery or museum	56	62	–7
Drank wine or liquor	53	54	–1
Drank beer	53	44	9
Participated in organized demonstrations	43	47	–4
Played musical instrument	42	41	1
Discussed religion	28	32	–4
Participated in Internet chat rooms	23	17	6
Voted in student election	22	24	–2
Discussed politics	20	14	6
Felt overwhelmed by all I had to do	18	36	–19
Smoked cigarettes	10	10	–1
Felt depressed	6	10	–4

Source: Linda J. Sax, Alexander W. Astin, William S. Korn, and Kathryn M. Mahoney, The American Freshman: National Norms for Fall 2000 *(Higher Education Research Institute, UCLA, 2001); calculations by New Strategist*

Men Rate Themselves More Highly Than Most Women Do

The gap is especially large for computer skills and physical health.

When college freshmen are asked to rate their abilities, men give themselves much higher marks on most measures than women do, according to UCLA's Higher Education Research Institute. When asked about their academic ability, fully 71 percent of men believe they are above average compared with a smaller 65 percent of women who feel that way. Fully 69 percent of men believe they are above average in intellectual self-confidence compared with just 53 percent of women.

The biggest gap between men and women is in the self-evaluation of computer skills. Forty-six percent of men believe their computer skills place them above average, twice the 23 percent of women who feel that way. The gap is almost as large for physical health. While 68 percent of men believe their physical health is above average, only 47 percent of women feel that way. Women score themselves slightly higher than men on understanding of others, writing ability, spirituality, and drive to achieve. Perhaps seeing themselves as the underdog, women know they have to work harder to get ahead.

♦ Women freshmen lag far behind their males counterparts in how they rate themselves on a variety of measures. Rather than lacking self-confidence, women may be more realistic about their relative standing among peers.

Student Ability Rating by Sex, 2000

(percentage of college freshmen who rate themselves above average for selected abilities, by sex, 2000)

	men	women	difference between men and women
Academic ability	71%	65%	6
Drive to achieve	69	72	–2
Intellectual self-confidence	69	53	16
Physical health	68	47	21
Leadership ability	64	58	6
Understanding of others	63	68	–5
Self-understanding	62	53	8
Emotional health	60	49	12
Social self-confidence	57	48	10
Popularity	49	34	14
Computer skills	46	23	23
Writing ability	44	47	–3
Spirituality	43	46	–3
Public speaking ability	40	35	5
Artistic ability	30	29	1

Source: Linda J. Sax, Alexander W. Astin, William S. Korn, and Kathryn M. Mahoney, The American Freshman: National Norms for Fall 2000 *(Higher Education Research Institute, UCLA, 2001); calculations by New Strategist*

College Freshmen Are a Mix of Liberal and Conservative

Their top objectives are to make a lot of money and raise a family.

The overwhelming majority of college freshmen believe in gun control, but they also believe the courts are too concerned with the rights of criminals, according to UCLA's Higher Education Research Institute. They think colleges should prohibit racist and sexist speech, but many also think affirmative action should be abolished. They support legal abortion, but not the legalization of marijuana.

Women are far more liberal than men on most issues including gun control, affirmative action, women's roles, and homosexuality. The 63 percent majority of freshmen women versus only 47 percent of their male counterparts believe same-sex couples should have the legal right to marry. Just 17 percent of women versus 29 percent of men believe the activities of married women are best confined to the home and family.

Both men and women want to make a lot of money, however. Fully 76 percent of men and 71 percent of women say that being very well off financially is essential or very important to them. Seventy-three percent of both men and women say raising a family is essential or very important. Women are more likely than men to want to help others in difficulty, while men are more likely than women to want to be successful in their own business.

♦ The large differences in the opinions of young men and women—particularly men's more conservative views toward the role of women—may cause problems in their romantic relationships.

Attitudes of College Freshmen by Sex, 2000

(percent of college freshmen who somewhat or strongly agree with selected statements, by sex, 2000)

	men	women	difference between men and women
Federal government should do more to control the sale of handguns	73%	90%	−17
There is too much concern in the courts for the rights of criminals	68	66	2
Colleges should prohibit racist and sexist speech on campus	56	66	−10
Affirmative action in college admissions should be abolished	56	45	12
Abortion should be legal	55	54	1
Wealthy people should pay a larger share of taxes than they do now	53	52	2
Same-sex couples should have the right to legal marital status	47	63	−16
If two people really like each other, it's OK to have sex even if they've known each other for a short time	55	31	24
Marijuana should be legalized	40	29	11
It is important to have laws prohibiting homosexual relations	36	20	16
Realistically, an individual can do little to bring about change in our society	32	24	8
The activities of married women are best confined to the home and family	29	17	12
People have a right to know about the personal lives of public figures	29	25	4
The death penalty should be abolished	27	34	−7
Racial discrimination is no longer a major problem in America	24	17	7

Source: Linda J. Sax, Alexander W. Astin, William S. Korn, and Kathryn M. Mahoney, The American Freshman: National Norms for Fall 2000 *(Higher Education Research Institute, UCLA, 2001); calculations by New Strategist*

Objectives of College Freshmen by Sex, 2000

(percent of college freshmen who say given objectives are essential or very important, by sex, 2000)

	men	women	difference between men and women
Being very well off financially	76%	71%	5
Raising a family	73	73	–1
Becoming an authority in one's field	62	58	4
Helping others who are in difficulty	53	69	–16
Being successful in a business of one's own	45	35	11
Developing a meaningful philosophy of life	43	42	1
Integrating spirituality into one's life	41	48	–7
Influencing social values	34	41	–7
Keeping up to date with political affairs	32	25	7
Becoming a community leader	31	30	1
Helping to promote racial understanding	28	33	–5
Influencing the political structure	20	15	5
Making a theoretical contribution to science	19	14	5
Participating in a community action program	19	26	–8
Becoming involved in programs to clean up the environment	17	18	0
Writing original works	15	14	1
Creating artistic work	14	16	–2

Source: Linda J. Sax, Alexander W. Astin, William S. Korn, and Kathryn M. Mahoney, The American Freshman: National Norms for Fall 2000 *(Higher Education Research Institute, UCLA, 2001); calculations by New Strategist*

Most Students Depend on Family to Pay the Bills

Many also have grants or loans.

Eighty-three percent of students are paying for tuition, room, and board using money from their parents, other relatives, or friends, according to UCLA's Higher Education Research Institute. Sixty-three percent of students are receiving $1,500 or more from this source.

Nearly half (49 percent) of freshmen use savings from summer work, the second biggest source of funds for college students, to pay for tuition, room, and board. Only 10 percent say this source is contributing $1,500 or more towards college costs, however. Thirty-three percent are depending on a college grant or scholarship, 23 percent receiving at least $1,500 from this source. Nineteen percent are receiving at least $1,500 from a Stafford loan, while 11 percent are receiving that much from a state scholarship or grant.

Paying for college is a big worry for many students. Only 36 percent of college freshmen have no concerns about their ability to finance their college education. The 52 percent majority have "some" concerns but they probably will have enough funds. Twelve percent have major concerns, not knowing whether they will have enough to pay for school.

♦ More federal and state help in paying for college, tied to school performance, would allow more students to go to school and increase the seriousness with which they apply themselves to their studies.

How Students Will Pay for College, 2000

(percent of college freshmen who expect to pay for tuition, room, and board using money from selected sources, by amount of money expected from source, 2000)

	any amount	$1,500 or more
Parents, other relatives, or friends	83%	63%
Savings from summer work	49	10
College grant or scholarship other than those listed below	33	23
Other savings	32	9
Stafford loan (GSL)	26	19
Part-time job on campus	26	4
Part-time job off campus	22	3
State scholarship or grant	22	11
Pell grant	17	9
College work-study grant	13	4
Other private grant	12	5
Other college loan	11	8
Perkins loan	10	5
Other loan	8	6
Supplemental Educational Opportunity grant	6	2
Other government aid (ROTC, GI/military benefits, etc.)	3	2
Full-time job while in college	3	1

Source: Linda J. Sax, Alexander W. Astin, William S. Korn, and Kathryn M. Mahoney, The American Freshman: National Norms for Fall 2000 *(Higher Education Research Institute, UCLA, 2001); calculations by New Strategist*

Education

♦ The oldest members of the Millennial generation are finishing high school and going to college. Their educational attainment is rising rapidly.

♦ Among people aged 15 to 24, non-Hispanic Asian women have the highest level of education by far. Sixty percent are high school graduates and 12 percent already have a bachelor's degree.

♦ Among householders with children aged 0 to 13, 77 percent are satisfied with the elementary school in their area. Only 7 percent are not satisfied.

♦ Enrollment in kindergarten through 12th grade is projected to increase just 0.1 percent between 2000 and 2010. There should be a small decline in enrollment in grades K through 8, and a 4 percent increase in grades 9 through 12.

♦ Going to college is no longer an elite privilege, but the norm. Today, 64 percent of young women and 61 percent of young men enroll in college after graduating from high school.

♦ As the large Millennial generation replaces the much smaller Generation X on college campuses, the student body is growing younger. In 2000, 59 percent of college students were under age 25. The figure should rise to 61 percent by 2010.

Millennials Are Finishing High School

More than half of 20-to-24-year-olds have college experience.

The oldest members of the Millennial generation are in the process of finishing high school and going to college. Their educational attainment, therefore, is rising rapidly. Among men aged 18 and 19, 52 percent are high school graduates. The figure is a much higher 84 percent among men aged 20 to 24. Women are further along than men. Sixty percent of 18- and 19-year-old women and 87 percent of those aged 20 to 24 are high school graduates.

Among women aged 20 to 24, 13 percent are college graduates. The figure is a smaller 9 percent for their male counterparts. Since it takes, on average, six years to get a bachelor's degree today, it's little wonder so few Americans in their early twenties have earned a college degree. More will do so since many are currently in school.

♦ Millennial women appear to be more serious about getting an education than their male counterparts. This could narrow the income gap between men and women in the years ahead.

Among 20-to-24-year-olds, women are better educated than men

(percent distribution of people aged 20 to 24 by educational attainment and sex, 2000)

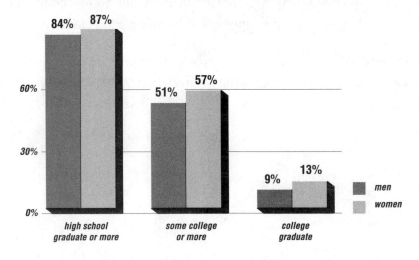

Educational Attainment of Men Aged 15 to 24, 2000

(number and percent distribution of men aged 15 or older and aged 15 to 24 by highest level of education, 2000; numbers in thousands)

	total	15 to 24	15 to 17	18 to 19	20 to 24
Total men	**103,114**	**19,502**	**6,212**	**4,082**	**9,208**
Not a high school graduate	22,812	9,596	6,132	1,961	1,503
High school graduate	30,859	4,208	69	1,145	2,994
Some college, no degree	18,927	4,387	7	954	3,426
Associate's degree	6,460	508	0	18	490
Bachelor's degree or more	24,056	804	4	4	796
High school graduate or more	80,302	9,907	80	2,121	7,706
Some college or more	49,443	5,699	11	976	4,712
Bachelor's degree or more	24,056	804	4	4	796
Total men	**100.0%**	**100.0%**	**100.0%**	**100.0%**	**100.0%**
Not a high school graduate	22.1	49.2	98.7	48.0	16.3
High school graduate	29.9	21.6	1.1	28.0	32.5
Some college, no degree	18.4	22.5	0.1	23.4	37.2
Associate's degree	6.3	2.6	0.0	0.4	5.3
Bachelor's degree or more	23.3	4.1	0.1	0.1	8.6
High school graduate or more	77.9	50.8	1.3	52.0	83.7
Some college or more	47.9	29.2	0.2	23.9	51.2
Bachelor's degree or more	23.3	4.1	0.1	0.1	8.6

Source: Bureau of the Census, Educational Attainment in the United States: March 2000, *detailed tables from Current Population Report P20-536, 2000; Internet site <www.census.gov/population/www/socdemo/education/ p20-536.html>; calculations by New Strategist*

Educational Attainment of Women Aged 15 to 24, 2000

(number and percent distribution of women aged 15 or older and aged 15 to 24 by highest level of education, 2000; numbers in thousands)

	total	15 to 24	15 to 17	18 to 19	20 to 24
Total women	**110,660**	**19,040**	**5,798**	**4,009**	**9,233**
Not a high school graduate	23,113	8,476	5,704	1,602	1,170
High school graduate	35,415	3,980	64	1,149	2,767
Some college, no degree	21,048	4,834	28	1,247	3,559
Associate's degree	8,255	516	0	7	509
Bachelor's degree or more	22,829	1,234	0	4	1,230
High school graduate or more	87,547	10,564	92	2,407	8,065
Some college or more	52,132	6,584	28	1,258	5,298
Bachelor's degree or more	22,829	1,234	0	4	1,230
Total women	**100.0%**	**100.0%**	**100.0%**	**100.0%**	**100.0%**
Not a high school graduate	20.9	44.5	98.4	40.0	12.7
High school graduate	32.0	20.9	1.1	28.7	30.0
Some college, no degree	19.0	25.4	0.5	31.1	38.5
Associate's degree	7.5	2.7	0.0	0.2	5.5
Bachelor's degree or more	20.6	6.5	0.0	0.1	13.3
High school graduate or more	79.1	55.5	1.6	60.0	87.3
Some college or more	47.1	34.6	0.5	31.4	57.4
Bachelor's degree or more	20.6	6.5	0.0	0.1	13.3

Source: Bureau of the Census, Educational Attainment in the United States: March 2000, *detailed tables from Current Population Report P20-536, 2000; Internet site <www.census.gov/population/www/socdemo/education/ p20-536.html>; calculations by New Strategist*

Asian Women Are the Best Educated Millennials

Hispanic men are the least educated.

Among people aged 15 to 24, non-Hispanic Asian women have the highest level of education by far. Sixty percent are high school graduates and 12 percent already have a bachelor's degree. Non-Hispanic white women rank second in educational attainment along with non-Hispanic Asian men. Non-Hispanic white women are more likely than non-Hispanic Asian men to be high school graduates, but they're less likely to be college graduates.

The least educated 15-to-24-year-olds are Hispanic men. Only 38 percent are high school graduates and just 1 percent have a college degree. Hispanic women are only slightly better educated. Many Hispanics are immigrants from countries that offer little schooling.

♦ The educational attainment of 15-to-24-year-olds will rise as more of them complete high school and go to college. The gaps in educational attainment by race and Hispanic origin will persist, however, leading to income differences throughout life.

Educational Attainment of Men Aged 15 to 24 by Race and Hispanic Origin, 2000

(number and percent distribution of men aged 15 to 24 by educational attainment, race, and Hispanic origin, 2000; numbers in thousands)

		non-Hispanic		
	Asian	*black*	*white*	*Hispanic*
Total men	**901**	**2,722**	**12,715**	**2,962**
Not a high school graduate	409	1,504	5,705	1,833
High school graduate	136	614	2,779	651
Some college, no degree	255	479	3,210	411
Associate's degree	20	59	395	35
Bachelor's degree or more	80	65	624	31
High school graduate or more	491	1,217	7,008	1,128
Some college or more	355	603	4,229	477
Bachelor's degree or more	80	65	624	31
Total men	**100.0%**	**100.0%**	**100.0%**	**100.0%**
Not a high school graduate	45.4	55.3	44.9	61.9
High school graduate	15.1	22.6	21.9	22.0
Some college, no degree	28.3	17.6	25.2	13.9
Associate's degree	2.2	2.2	3.1	1.2
Bachelor's degree	8.9	2.4	4.9	1.0
High school graduate or more	54.5	44.7	55.1	38.1
Some college or more	39.4	22.2	33.3	16.1
Bachelor's degree or more	8.9	2.4	4.9	1.0

Source: Bureau of the Census, Educational Attainment in the United States: March 2000, *detailed tables from Current Population Report P20-536, 2000; Internet site <www.census.gov/population/www/socdemo/education/p20-536.html>; calculations by New Strategist*

Educational Attainment of Women Aged 15 to 24 by Race and Hispanic Origin, 2000

(number and percent distribution of women aged 15 to 24 by educational attainment, race, and Hispanic origin, 2000; numbers in thousands)

		non-Hispanic		
	Asian	*black*	*white*	*Hispanic*
Total women	**846**	**2,935**	**12,422**	**2,681**
Not a high school graduate	340	1,380	5,144	1,541
High school graduate	104	730	2,562	542
Some college, no degree	265	658	3,389	478
Associate's degree	34	60	354	66
Bachelor's degree or more	105	104	971	53
High school graduate or more	508	1,552	7,276	1,139
Some college or more	404	822	4,714	597
Bachelor's degree or more	105	104	971	53
Total women	**100.0%**	**100.0%**	**100.0%**	**100.0%**
Not a high school graduate	40.2	47.0	41.4	57.5
High school graduate	12.3	24.9	20.6	20.2
Some college, no degree	31.3	22.4	27.3	17.8
Associate's degree	4.0	2.0	2.8	2.5
Bachelor's degree	12.4	3.5	7.8	2.0
High school graduate or more	60.0	52.9	58.6	42.5
Some college or more	47.8	28.0	37.9	22.3
Bachelor's degree or more	12.4	3.5	7.8	2.0

Source: Bureau of the Census, Educational Attainment in the United States: March 2000, *detailed tables from Current Population Report P20-536, 2000; Internet site <www.census.gov/population/www/socdemo/education/p20-536.html>; calculations by New Strategist*

Most Millennials Are Students

More than three out of four people under age 25 are in school.

Among the nation's 72 million students, 66 million—or 92 percent—are under age 25. More than 90 percent of children aged 5 to 17 are in school. The share falls with age, but remains above 50 percent through age 19. Only 19 percent of 24-year-olds are in school.

Education begins at a younger age for millennials than for any previous generation. The 54 percent majority of 3- and 4-year-olds are in school today, up from only 5 percent in the 1960s. Among kindergarteners, fully 58 percent attend for the full day, up from only 11 percent in 1969.

The number of students enrolled in elementary and high school in 1999 equalled the all-time high of 49 million (33 million in grades 1 through 8, and 16 million in grades 9 through 12). This ties the record set in 1970, when the baby-boom generation was in school.

♦ School enrollments will continue to rise as the population grows. Communities will have to invest even more in facilities, teachers, and supplies.

School Enrollment by Age, 1999

(number of people aged 3 or older, and number and percent enrolled in school, by age, fall 1999; numbers in thousands)

	total	enrolled	
		number	percent
Total people	**260,936**	**72,395**	**27.7%**
Under age 25	86,627	66,368	76.6
Aged 3	3,862	1,505	39.0
Aged 4	4,021	2,769	68.9
Aged 5	4,037	3,804	94.2
Aged 6	4,060	3,971	97.8
Aged 7	4,083	4,027	98.6
Aged 8	4,016	3,955	98.5
Aged 9	4,339	4,269	98.4
Aged 10	4,121	4,053	98.4
Aged 11	4,077	4,042	99.1
Aged 12	3,968	3,925	98.9
Aged 13	3,982	3,937	98.9
Aged 14	3,971	3,903	98.3
Aged 15	3,916	3,838	98.0
Aged 16	3,995	3,844	96.2
Aged 17	4,137	3,767	91.1
Aged 18	3,870	2,610	67.5
Aged 19	4,121	2,230	54.1
Aged 20	3,709	1,832	49.4
Aged 21	3,487	1,424	40.8
Aged 22	3,634	1,059	29.1
Aged 23	3,628	911	25.1
Aged 24	3,593	693	19.3
Aged 25 or older	174,310	6,027	3.5

Source: Bureau of the Census, School Enrollment—Social and Economic Characteristics of Students: October 1999, *detailed tables for Current Population Report P20-533, 2001; Internet site <www.census.gov/population/ www/socdemo/school/p20-533.html>; calculations by New Strategist*

Enrollment in Nursery School through 12th Grade, 1999

(number and percent distribution of people attending nursery school through 12th grade, fall 1999; numbers in thousands)

	number	percent
Total students	**57,193**	**100.0%**
Nursery school	**4,578**	**8.0**
Kindergarten	**3,825**	**6.7**
Elementary	**32,874**	**57.5**
1st grade	4,326	7.6
2nd grade	3,927	6.9
3rd grade	4,335	7.6
4th grade	4,207	7.4
5th grade	4,148	7.3
6th grade	4,019	7.0
7th grade	3,905	6.8
8th grade	4,007	7.0
High school	**15,916**	**27.8**
9th grade	4,172	7.3
10th grade	3,861	6.8
11th grade	3,850	6.7
12th grade	4,033	7.1

Source: Bureau of the Census, School Enrollment—Social and Economic Characteristics of Students: October 1999, *detailed tables for Current Population Report P20-533, 2001; Internet site <www.census.gov/population/ www/socdemo/school/p20-533.html>; calculations by New Strategist*

Most Parents Are Satisfied with the Local Elementary School

But some are so bothered by their school that they want to move.

Complaints about public schools have become commonplace, but few households with elementary-school-aged children are dissatisfied with the local elementary school. Among households with children aged 0 to 13, 77 percent are satisfied with the elementary school in their area. Only 7 percent are not satisfied. Three percent of households are so bothered by the local school that they want to move. Renters are slightly more likely than homeowners to be dissatisfied with the local school.

Among households with children aged 5 to 15, 86 percent send at least one child to public school. A substantial 12 percent send a child to private school. Only 1 percent home-school their children. Homeowners are more than twice as likely as renters to send a child to private school, 14 versus 6 percent.

♦ While the great majority of parents are satisfied with the local elementary school, a significant proportion are not. The more than 2 million dissatisfied parents are one of the pressure points for educational reform.

Satisfaction with Local Elementary School by Homeownership Status, 1999

(number and percent distribution of households with children aged 5 to 15 by type of school attended and opinion of local elementary school, by homeownership status, 1999; numbers in thousands)

	total	owner	renter
Total households with children aged 5 to 15	**26,676**	**18,480**	**8,197**
Attend public school, K–12	22,811	15,443	7,369
Attend private school, K–12	3,094	2,562	532
Attend ungraded school, preschool	337	187	150
Home-schooled or no school	298	230	68
Households with children aged 0 to 13	**30,803**	**20,236**	**10,567**
Satisfactory public elementary school	23,740	16,046	7,694
Unsatisfactory public elementary school	2,110	1,439	671
So bothered by school they want to move	790	438	351
Percent distribution			
Total households with children aged 5 to 15	**100.0%**	**100.0%**	**100.0%**
Attend public school, K–12	85.5	83.6	89.9
Attend private school, K–12	11.6	13.9	6.5
Attend ungraded school, preschool	1.3	1.0	1.8
Home schooled or no school	1.1	1.2	0.8
Households with children aged 0 to 13	**100.0**	**100.0**	**100.0**
Satisfactory public elementary school	77.1	79.3	72.8
Unsatisfactory public elementary school	6.8	7.1	6.3
So bothered by school they want to move	2.6	2.2	3.3

Note: Numbers will not add to total because not reported is not shown.
Source: Bureau of the Census, American Housing Survey for the United States in 1999; calculations by New Strategist

Little Change Forecast in School Enrollment

The number of high school graduates should increase 10 percent, however.

School enrollment is projected to remain relatively unchanged for the coming decade now that the large Millennial generation (born from 1977 through 1994) is in school. Overall, enrollment in kindergarten through 12th grade is projected to increase just 0.1 percent. The National Center for Education Statistics foresees a small decline in enrollment in grades K through 8, and a 4 percent increase in grades 9 through 12. Private schools account for 11 percent of K through 12 enrollment, a proportion that is projected to remain unchanged.

The number of high school graduates will rise as the Millennial generation finishes high school. The number of high school graduates is projected to climb 10 percent between 2000 and 2010, from 2.8 million to 3.1 million. The projected growth rate is the same for graduates from both public and private school.

♦ Colleges are already benefiting from the growing number of high school graduates as applications increase and competition stiffens among potential students.

More high school graduates are on the way

(number of high school graduates, 2000 to 2010; in millions)

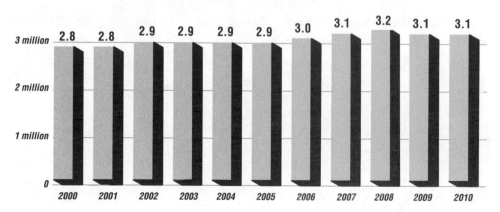

Projected Enrollment in Kindergarten through 12th Grade, 2000 to 2010

(number of people enrolled in kindergarten through 12th grade by control of institution, fall 2000 to 2010; percent change, 2000–10; numbers in thousands)

	total			public			private		
	total	*K–8th*	*9th–12th*	*total*	*K–8th*	*9th–12th*	*total*	*K–8th*	*9th–12th*
2000	52,989	38,132	14,857	47,026	33,521	13,505	5,963	4,611	1,352
2001	53,155	38,172	14,982	47,176	33,557	13,619	5,979	4,616	1,363
2002	53,287	38,157	15,130	47,296	33,543	13,753	5,991	4,614	1,377
2003	53,367	38,042	15,325	47,373	33,442	13,931	5,995	4,600	1,395
2004	53,429	37,809	15,620	47,436	33,237	14,199	5,993	4,572	1,422
2005	53,465	37,598	15,868	47,475	33,051	14,423	5,990	4,546	1,444
2006	53,435	37,442	15,992	47,452	32,915	14,537	5,983	4,527	1,455
2007	53,336	37,352	15,985	47,365	32,835	14,530	5,971	4,517	1,455
2008	53,174	37,340	15,834	47,218	32,825	14,393	5,956	4,515	1,441
2009	53,056	37,399	15,657	47,109	32,877	14,232	5,947	4,522	1,425
2010	53,016	37,538	15,478	47,068	32,999	14,069	5,948	4,539	1,409

Percent change

2000 to 2010	0.1%	−1.6%	4.2%	0.1%	−1.6%	4.2%	−0.3%	−1.6%	4.2%

Source: National Center for Education Statistics, Projections of Education Statistics to 2010, *NCES 2000071, 2000; calculations by New Strategist*

Projections of High School Graduates, 2000 to 2010

(number of people graduating from high school by control of institution, 2000 to 2010; percent change 2000–10; numbers in thousands)

	total	public	private
2000	2,820	2,526	294
2001	2,838	2,542	296
2002	2,886	2,585	301
2003	2,929	2,624	305
2004	2,936	2,630	306
2005	2,944	2,637	307
2006	2,998	2,685	312
2007	3,069	2,750	320
2008	3,153	2,825	328
2009	3,146	2,818	328
2010	3,115	2,791	324

Percent change

2000 to 2010	10.5%	10.5%	10.2%

Source: National Center for Education Statistics, Projections of Education Statistics to 2010, NCES 2000071, 2000; calculations by New Strategist

SAT Scores Rise

Most demographic segments have made gains.

The number of high school students who take the Scholastic Assessment Test (or SAT) expanded enormously over the past few decades. Once limited to the elite, the SAT has been embraced by the masses—as have the nation's college campuses. As larger numbers of "average" students take the test, overall SAT scores have fallen in some years.

Most demographic segments have achieved higher test scores during the past decade, however. While the average verbal score fell 2 points overall between 1986-87 and 1999-00, verbal scores rose for all racial and ethnic groups but Mexican Americans. Math scores rose 13 points between 1986-87 and 1999-00, including double-digit gains for all groups but Mexican Americans.

♦ Overall SAT scores are likely to show slow improvement in the years ahead as minority scores continue to rise.

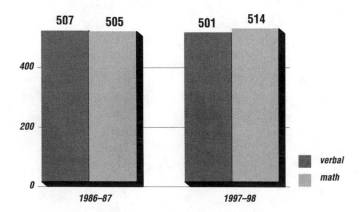

Verbal down, math up

(average verbal and math SAT scores, 1986–87 and 1997–98)

Scholastic Assessment Test Scores by Sex, Race, and Hispanic Origin, 1986–87 and 1999–2000

(average SAT scores and change in scores by sex, race, and Hispanic origin of student, 1986–87 and 1999–2000)

	1999–2000	1986–87	change
VERBAL			
Total students	**505**	**507**	**–2**
Male	507	512	–5
Female	504	502	2
White	528	524	4
Black	434	428	6
Hispanic or Latino	461	464	–3
Mexican American	453	457	–4
Puerto Rican	456	436	20
Asian American	499	479	20
American Indian	482	471	11
Other	508	480	28
MATH			
Total students	**514**	**501**	**13**
Male	533	523	10
Female	498	481	17
White	530	514	16
Black	426	411	15
Hispanic or Latino	467	462	5
Mexican American	460	455	5
Puerto Rican	451	432	19
Asian American	565	541	24
American Indian	481	463	18
Other	514	482	32

Source: National Center for Education Statistics, Digest of Education Statistics 2000; NCES 2001034, 2001; calculations by New Strategist

Most Children from Affluent Families Go to College

The majority of families with children aged 18 to 24 and incomes of $50,000 or more have at least one child in college.

It is no surprise that family income is one of the best predictors of whether children have the opportunity to go to college. Among the nation's 11 million families with children aged 18 to 24, 47 percent have at least one child in college full-time. The proportion rises with income to a high of 67 percent of families with incomes of $75,000 or more.

Among families with children aged 18 to 24 whose income is below $20,000, only 24 percent have a child in college full-time.

♦ Children of the affluent can devote full attention to their studies because their parents are paying the bills. Many children from less affluent families attend school part-time because they must work to support themselves.

College attendance rises with family income

(percentage of families with children aged 18 to 24 that have at least one child attending college full-time, by household income, 1999)

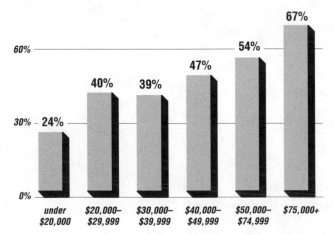

Families with Children in College, 1999

(total number of families, number with children aged 18 to 24, and number and percent with children aged 18 to 24 attending college full-time by household income, 1999; numbers in thousands)

| | | | with one or more children attending college full-time | | |
	total	with children aged 18–24	number	percent of total families	percent of families with children 18-24
Total families	**72,921**	**10,608**	**5,017**	**6.9%**	**47.3%**
Under $20,000	11,570	1,447	354	3.1	24.5
$20,000 to $29,999	9,286	1,117	444	4.8	39.7
$30,000 to $39,999	8,282	1,063	416	5.0	39.1
$40,000 to $49,999	6,834	971	455	6.7	46.9
$50,000 to $74,999	12,932	2,022	1,087	8.4	53.8
$75,000 or more	13,765	2,497	1,671	12.1	66.9

Note: Numbers will not add to total because "not reported" is not shown.
Source: Bureau of the Census, School Enrollment—Social and Economic Characteristics of Students: October 1999, detailed tables for Current Population Report P20-533, 2001; Internet site <www.census.gov/population/www/socdemo/school/p20-533.html>; calculations by New Strategist

A Growing Share of High School Grads Go to College

Going to college is no longer an elite privilege, but the norm.

Most high school graduates continue their education in college. Forty years ago, male high school graduates were much more likely to go to college than female graduates—54 versus 38 percent. Today, the opposite is the case, as 64 percent of girls and a smaller 61 percent of boys continue their education past high school.

Whites and blacks are almost equally likely to go to college today—63 percent of whites attend college within 12 months of graduating from high school as do 59 percent of blacks. Blacks and whites were equally likely to enroll in college in 1977 as well, but then the rate rose for whites while it declined for blacks. Since the mid-1990s, however, blacks have been catching up to whites once again.

Hispanics have a far lower college enrollment rate, 52 percent in 1999. The Hispanic rate has barely changed since 1977.

♦ More financial aid would boost the college enrollment rate of blacks and Hispanics.

Blacks are closing the gap with whites

(percent of people aged 16 to 24 who graduated from high school in the previous 12 months and had enrolled in college as of October of each year, by race, 1977 to 1999)

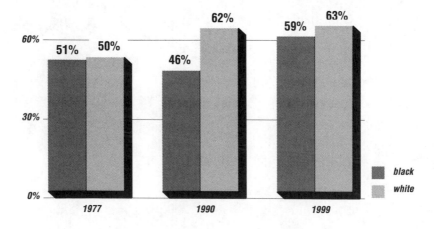

College Enrollment Rate by Sex, 1960 to 1999

(percent of people aged 16 to 24 who graduated from high school in the previous 12 months and were enrolled in college as of October of each year, by sex; percentage point difference in enrollment rates of men and women, 1960–99)

	men	women	percentage point difference
1999	61.4%	64.4%	–3.0
1998	62.4	69.1	–6.7
1997	63.5	70.3	–6.8
1996	60.1	69.7	–9.6
1995	62.6	61.4	1.2
1994	60.6	63.2	–2.6
1993	59.7	65.4	–5.7
1992	59.6	63.8	–4.2
1991	57.6	67.1	–9.5
1990	57.8	62.0	–4.2
1989	57.6	61.6	–4.0
1988	57.0	60.8	–3.8
1987	58.4	55.3	3.1
1986	55.9	51.9	4.0
1985	58.6	56.9	1.7
1980	46.7	51.8	–5.1
1975	52.6	49.0	3.6
1970	55.2	48.5	6.7
1965	57.3	45.3	12.0
1960	54.0	37.9	16.1

Source: National Center for Education Statistics, Digest of Education Statistics 2000, NCES 2001034, 2001; calculations by New Strategist

College Enrollment Rate by Race and Hispanic Origin, 1977 to 1999

(percent of people aged 16 to 24 graduating from high school in the previous 12 months who were enrolled in college as of October of each year, by race and Hispanic origin, 1977–99)

	white	black	Hispanic
1999	62.8%	59.2%	–
1998	65.8	62.1	51.7%
1997	67.5	59.6	54.6
1996	65.8	55.3	55.0
1995	62.6	51.4	51.1
1994	63.6	50.9	55.1
1993	62.8	55.6	55.4
1992	63.4	47.9	58.1
1991	64.6	45.6	53.1
1990	61.5	46.3	53.3
1989	60.4	52.8	53.2
1988	60.7	45.0	48.6
1987	56.6	51.9	45.0
1986	56.0	36.5	43.0
1985	59.4	42.3	46.6
1980	49.9	41.8	49.9
1977	50.7	49.6	48.9

Note: The Hispanic enrollment rate is a three-year moving average. (–) means data not available.
Source: National Center for Education Statistics, Digest of Education Statistics 2000, *NCES 2001034, 2001; calculations by New Strategist*

Millennials Are the Majority of Full-Time College Students

Most college students under age 25 attend school full-time.

Among the nation's 15 million college students in 1999, 9 million were under age 25. Eighty-five percent of college students under age 25 attend school full-time. The percentage of students attending school full-time falls with age, from more than 90 percent of those under age 20 to 75 percent of those aged 22 to 24. Among college students aged 25 or older, only 37 percent go to school full-time.

Men are slightly more likely than women to attend college full-time. Among students under age 25, 87 percent of men and a smaller 83 percent of women are full-time students. The gap is largest among students aged 22 to 24, in which group 80 percent of men but only 71 percent of women attend full-time.

♦ As millennials head to college, many middle-aged parents anxiously face the enormous costs of a college education today. This worry is why politicians are talking about tax breaks for college tuition payments.

Full-timers outnumber part-timers

(percent distribution of college students under age 25 by attendance status, 1999)

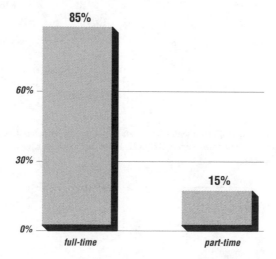

College Students by Sex, Age, and Attendance Status, 1999

(number of people aged 15 or older enrolled in institutions of higher education by sex, age, and attendance status, 1999; numbers in thousands)

| | total | full-time | | part-time | |
		number	percent	number	percent
Total students	**15,202**	**10,111**	**66.5%**	**5,091**	**33.5%**
Under age 25	9,410	7,985	84.9	1,425	15.1
Aged 15 to 17	151	144	95.4	6	4.0
Aged 18 to 19	3,520	3,173	90.1	347	9.9
Aged 20 to 21	3,119	2,696	86.4	425	13.6
Aged 22 to 24	2,620	1,972	75.3	647	24.7
Aged 25 or older	5,794	2,126	36.7	3,666	63.3
Male students	**6,956**	**4,842**	**69.6**	**2,113**	**30.4**
Under age 25	4,475	3,877	86.6	599	13.4
Aged 15 to 17	78	74	94.9	4	5.1
Aged 18 to 19	1,648	1,482	89.9	167	10.1
Aged 20 to 21	1,525	1,344	88.1	180	11.8
Aged 22 to 24	1,224	977	79.8	248	20.3
Aged 25 or older	2,482	965	38.9	1,514	61.0
Female students	**8,247**	**5,270**	**63.9**	**2,976**	**36.1**
Under age 25	4,936	4,111	83.3	826	16.7
Aged 15 to 17	73	70	95.9	3	4.1
Aged 18 to 19	1,872	1,693	90.4	179	9.6
Aged 20 to 21	1,595	1,351	84.7	243	15.2
Aged 22 to 24	1,396	997	71.4	401	28.7
Aged 25 or older	3,312	1,159	35.0	2,150	64.9

Source: Bureau of the Census, School Enrollment—Social and Economic Characteristics of Students: October 1999, *detailed tables for Current Population Report P20-533, 2001; Internet site <www.census.gov/population/ www/socdemo/school/p20-533.html>*

College Students Are Getting Younger

The growing majority of college students are under age 25.

As the large Millennial generation replaces the much smaller Generation X on college campuses over the next decade, the student body will become younger. In 2000, 59 percent of college students were under age 25. The figure should rise to 61 percent by 2010. While the number of college students aged 18 to 24 is projected to grow 20 percent during the decade, the number of students aged 25 or older will increase just 8 percent.

Female college students are older than their male counterparts, but both male and female student bodies will grow younger during the next decade. The proportion of male college students under age 25 will grow from 64 to 66 percent. Among female college students, the proportion under age 25 will climb from 55 to 58 percent between 2000 and 2010. Women will continue to outnumber men on college campuses, as the female share of students rises slightly from 57 to 58 percent between 2000 and 2010.

◆ With students getting younger, colleges will be asked to take on more parental responsibility such as providing more housing and greater supervision of student activities.

Projections of College Enrollment by Sex and Age, 2000 and 2010

(number and percent distribution of people enrolled in institutions of higher education by sex and age, 2000 and 2010; percent change in number, 2000–10; numbers in thousands)

	2000		2010		percent change 2000–10
	number	percent	number	percent	
Total people	**15,136**	**100.0%**	**17,491**	**100.0%**	**15.6%**
Aged 14 to 17	204	1.3	258	1.5	26.5
Aged 18 to 19	3,409	22.5	4,077	23.3	19.6
Aged 20 to 21	2,954	19.5	3,569	20.4	20.8
Aged 22 to 24	2,341	15.5	2,831	16.2	20.9
Aged 25 or older	6,228	41.1	6,756	38.6	8.5
Total men	**6,482**	**100.0**	**7,320**	**100.0**	**12.9**
Aged 14 to 17	98	1.5	113	1.5	15.3
Aged 18 to 19	1,519	23.4	1,761	24.1	15.9
Aged 20 to 21	1,373	21.2	1,607	21.0	17.0
Aged 22 to 24	1,132	17.5	1,342	18.3	18.6
Aged 25 or older	2,360	36.4	2,497	34.1	5.8
Total women	**8,654**	**100.0**	**10,170**	**100.0**	**17.5**
Aged 14 to 17	106	1.2	145	1.4	36.8
Aged 18 to 19	1,890	21.8	2,316	22.8	22.5
Aged 20 to 21	1,581	18.3	1,962	19.3	24.1
Aged 22 to 24	1,209	13.0	1,488	14.6	23.1
Aged 25 or older	3,868	44.7	4,259	41.9	10.1

Source: National Center for Education Statistics, Projections of Education Statistics to 2010, *NCES 2000071, 2000; calculations by New Strategist*

Teens and Young Adults Are Most Likely to Participate in Adult Education

The share of 16-to-24-year-olds who take adult education courses is rising.

As Americans gain in education, they become more appreciative of education. Teens and young adults are no exception. Fifty-two percent of people aged 16 to 24 participated in adult education in 1999, up 5 percentage points from 1995. And that lofty figure does not include full-time college students.

Young adults are more likely than their elders to participate in adult education, primarily because they need training to further their careers. As people grow older, their reasons for participating in adult education shift to more personal ones.

♦ Young adults hesitant to invest years in getting a college degree will be eager customers of adult education courses designed to give them skills to boost their earnings.

Participation in adult education is highest among teens and young adults

(percent of people aged 16 or older participating in adult education, by age, 1999)

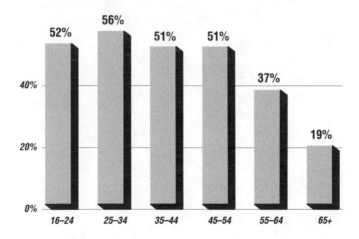

Participation in Adult Education by Age, 1995 and 1999

(percent of people aged 16 or older participating in adult education activities, by age, 1995 and 1999; percentage point change, 1995–99)

	1999	*1995*	*percentage point change*
Total people	**46%**	**40%**	**6**
Aged 16 to 24	52	47	5
Aged 25 to 34	56	48	8
Aged 35 to 44	51	49	2
Aged 45 to 54	51	46	5
Aged 55 to 64	37	28	9
Aged 65 or older	19	15	4

Note: Adult education activities include apprenticeships, courses for basic skills, personal development, English as a second language, work-related courses, and credential programs in organizations other than postsecondary institutions. Excludes full-time participation in postsecondary institutions leading to a college degree, diploma, or certificate.
Source: National Center for Education Statistics, unpublished data from the National Household Education Survey, 1999; and Statistical Abstract of the United States, *1999; calculations by New Strategist*

3

Health

♦ No one is more likely to eat candy on a given day than children aged 6 to 11. Twenty-nine percent of boys and girls aged 6 to 11 ate candy "yesterday."

♦ Although only 6 to 10 percent of teenage girls are overweight, more than one in three believes she is overweight. The majority are trying to lose weight.

♦ Most 11th and 12th grade girls and most 10th, 11th, and 12th grade boys have had sexual intercourse. Twenty-one percent of 12th graders have had four or more sexual partners.

♦ The birth rate among women under age 25 has been falling for decades. Nevertheless, a substantial 37 percent of births are to women under age 25.

♦ A survey of teenagers shows widespread and growing drug use. Twelve percent of 8th graders have used an illicit drug in the past month. The figure is 22 percent for 10th graders and 26 percent among 12th graders.

♦ Cigarette smoking has been declining in the population as a whole, but it is on the rise among young adults. More than 40 percent of 19-to-21-year-olds have smoked a cigarette in the past month.

The Nation's Children Are in Good Health

The proportion is lower among 18-to-24-year-olds, however.

While two out of three Americans of all ages report being in "very good" or "excellent" health, according to the National Center for Health Statistics, the proportion is significantly greater among those under age 25. More than 80 percent of people under age 18 are in very good or excellent health. The figure is a smaller 73 percent among those aged 18 to 24. Fewer than 5 percent say their health is "fair" or "poor."

About the same percentages of boys and girls are in excellent or very good health. But among young adults aged 18 to 24, men report being in better health than women. While 77 percent of men aged 18 to 24 say their health is excellent or very good, the proportion is a smaller 70 percent among women. Perhaps women are more conscious of health problems and thus more hesitant to report the very best health.

♦ The growing health consciousness of Americans could mean that today's children will remain feeling very good to excellent well into middle and old age.

The great majority of children feel great

(percent of people under age 25 whose health is very good or excellent, 1996)

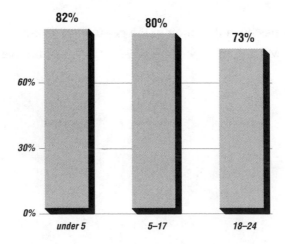

Health Status of People under Age 25, 1996

(respondent or parent-assessed health status of total people and people under age 25, by sex, 1996)

	excellent/ very good	good	fair/poor
Total people	**66.9%**	**23.1%**	**10.0%**
Under age 5	81.9	15.6	2.5
Aged 5 to 17	80.2	17.1	2.6
Aged 18 to 24	73.3	22.3	4.4
Total males	**69.3**	**21.8**	**9.0**
Under age 5	81.4	16.0	2.6
Aged 5 to 17	80.7	16.8	2.5
Aged 18 to 24	76.5	19.9	3.4
Total females	**64.6**	**24.5**	**10.9**
Under age 5	82.4	15.2	2.4
Aged 5 to 17	79.8	17.5	2.8
Aged 18 to 24	70.1	24.6	5.3

Source: National Center for Health Statistics, Current Estimates from the National Health Interview Survey, 1996, *Series 10, No. 200, 1999; calculations by New Strategist*

Kids Love Junk Food

The biggest consumers of candy, soft drinks, and snack foods are children.

No one is more likely to eat candy on a given day than children aged 6 to 11. Twenty-nine percent of boys and girls in the age group ate candy "yesterday." More than half ate cake, cookies, pastries, or pie.

Among 12-to-19-year-olds, candy consumption falls slightly, but this does not mean teenagers eat better than their younger siblings. Rather, soft drinks and other fast-food items replace candy on the menu. More than 60 percent of children aged 12 to 19 have a soft drink on an average day. More than one-third have fried potatoes (French fries).

Getting kids to eat healthy foods has never been more of an an uphill battle, which is one reason why parents appreciate the addition of vitamins and minerals to snack foods. Fewer than one in four children under age 20 drink fruit juice on an average day. Only 4 to 7 percent eat dark-green vegetables.

♦ Children's diets tend to expand and improve with age. But like their parents and grandparents, they will always be tempted by the convenience and taste of junk food.

Food Consumption of Males Aged 6 to 19, 1994–96

(percent of total people and males aged 6 to 19 consuming selected types of food on an average day, 1994–96)

		males	
	total, both sexes	*6 to 11*	*12 to 19*
Grain products	**96.9%**	**98.8%**	**98.2%**
Yeast breads and rolls	66.3	68.3	62.7
Cereals and pastas	46.8	65.0	44.6
Ready-to-eat cereals	28.5	53.3	33.2
Rice	11.0	10.0	10.0
Pasta	7.4	7.9	5.9
Quick breads, pancakes, French toast	22.7	26.0	24.5
Cakes, cookies, pastries, pies	41.2	52.1	41.3
Crackers, popcorn, pretzels, corn chips	27.8	33.8	27.2
Mixtures, mainly grain	35.9	44.8	46.1
Vegetables	**82.8**	**79.6**	**78.2**
White potatoes	44.3	48.8	49.6
Fried	27.0	38.4	38.7
Dark-green vegetables	9.8	6.1	3.6
Deep-yellow vegetables	12.9	12.0	8.1
Tomatoes	38.8	38.0	43.0
Lettuce, lettuce-based salads	24.9	14.2	23.8
Green beans	7.7	6.8	3.5
Corn, green peas, lima beans	11.7	14.0	7.4
Other vegetables	42.5	30.1	33.3
Fruits	**53.7**	**55.9**	**44.5**
Citrus fruits and juices	26.5	24.1	24.8
Juices	20.4	20.6	21.7
Other fruits, mixtures, and juices	39.3	43.8	27.0
Apples	12.2	18.9	8.2
Bananas	13.4	8.1	6.0
Melons and berries	7.8	6.2	4.1
Other fruits and mixtures, mainly fruit	13.7	15.1	7.1
Noncitrus juices and nectars	8.5	11.3	8.1
Milk and milk products	**78.9**	**92.1**	**81.3**
Milk, milk drinks, yogurt	60.5	84.9	65.8
Fluid milk	55.6	79.4	59.5
Whole	19.4	31.3	22.7

(continued)

(continued from previous page)

	total, both sexes	males 6 to 11	12 to 19
Low fat	26.3%	43.1%	30.5%
Skim	11.0	9.8	7.1
Yogurt	4.0	3.5	1.7
Milk desserts	17.4	25.5	13.6
Cheese	32.6	30.0	37.1
Meat, poultry, and fish	**86.2**	**87.1**	**86.9**
Beef	20.9	22.5	24.2
Pork	15.8	12.5	15.8
Frankfurters, sausages, luncheon meats	28.6	35.0	31.8
Poultry	22.6	22.2	20.6
Chicken	19.2	19.6	17.7
Fish and shellfish	8.0	5.6	5.1
Mixtures, mainly meat, poultry, fish	36.2	35.6	38.4
Eggs	19.1	15.4	17.0
Legumes	13.6	9.8	11.0
Nuts and seeds	9.6	15.4	8.7
Fats and oils	54.5	46.5	43.2
Table fats	30.4	27.7	20.8
Salad dressings	29.3	25.2	27.7
Sugars and sweets	53.2	58.5	46.6
Sugars	28.1	12.1	13.4
Candy	15.4	29.1	21.0
Beverages	**86.9**	**74.9**	**87.4**
Alcoholic	12.5	0.0	2.9
Wine	3.5	0.0	0.3
Beer and ale	7.6	0.0	2.3
Nonalcoholic	85.8	74.9	86.8
Coffee	39.5	1.0	6.1
Tea	22.8	9.3	16.3
Fruit drinks and ades	19.7	38.8	28.5
Carbonated soft drinks	50.4	47.6	69.1
Regular	39.3	43.7	66.1
Low calorie	12.8	5.8	5.2

Source: USDA, ARS Food Surveys Research Group, Supplementary Data Tables: USDA's 1994–96 Continuing Survey of Food Intakes by Individuals*; Internet site <www.barc.usda.gov/bhnrc/foodsurvey/home.htm>*

Food Consumption of Females Aged 6 to 19, 1994–96

(percent of total people and females aged 6 to 19 consuming selected types of food on an average day, 1994-96)

		females	
	total, both sexes	6 to 11	12 to 19
Grain products	**96.9%**	**99.3%**	**97.6%**
Yeast breads and rolls	66.3	70.7	60.8
Cereals and pastas	46.8	59.1	45.9
Ready-to-eat cereals	28.5	45.3	30.2
Rice	11.0	9.5	8.6
Pasta	7.4	7.3	9.3
Quick breads, pancakes, French toast	22.7	27.0	19.9
Cakes, cookies, pastries, pies	41.2	54.8	40.7
Crackers, popcorn, pretzels, corn chips	27.8	35.6	30.9
Mixtures, mainly grain	35.9	45.5	46.1
Vegetables	**82.8**	**81.9**	**79.5**
White potatoes	44.3	49.8	46.4
Fried	27.0	38.4	34.6
Dark-green vegetables	9.8	5.5	7.0
Deep-yellow vegetables	12.9	12.2	10.6
Tomatoes	38.8	33.5	35.3
Lettuce, lettuce-based salads	24.9	17.4	25.1
Green beans	7.7	7.8	4.4
Corn, green peas, lima beans	11.7	15.5	7.4
Other vegetables	42.5	30.2	34.5
Fruits	**53.7**	**61.5**	**45.6**
Citrus fruits and juices	26.5	27.2	22.4
Juices	20.4	21.3	18.1
Other fruits, mixtures, and juices	39.3	46.9	30.2
Apples	12.2	16.0	8.2
Bananas	13.4	6.8	4.4
Melons and berries	7.8	7.4	5.9
Other fruits and mixtures, mainly fruit	13.7	18.5	11.4
Noncitrus juices and nectars	8.5	15.0	9.7
Milk and milk products	**78.9**	**90.6**	**75.4**
Milk, milk drinks, yogurt	60.5	82.2	53.9
Fluid milk	55.6	77.0	49.6
Whole	19.4	33.4	17.5

(continued)

(continued from previous page)

	total, both sexes	females 6 to 11	females 12 to 19
Low fat	26.3%	39.1%	23.8%
Skim	11.0	8.1	9.4
Yogurt	4.0	2.9	2.2
Milk desserts	17.4	22.7	17.0
Cheese	32.6	31.0	36.1
Meat, poultry, and fish	**86.2**	**85.8**	**80.2**
Beef	20.9	19.4	22.2
Pork	15.8	10.8	11.3
Frankfurters, sausages, luncheon meats	28.6	31.7	24.5
Poultry	22.6	22.4	21.6
Chicken	19.2	19.4	19.0
Fish and shellfish	8.0	5.9	5.8
Mixtures, mainly meat, poultry, fish	36.2	33.3	33.9
Eggs	19.1	13.8	15.1
Legumes	13.6	11.1	10.7
Nuts and seeds	9.6	16.6	7.8
Fats and oils	54.5	48.3	45.6
Table fats	30.4	30.0	23.9
Salad dressings	29.3	23.0	28.6
Sugars and sweets	53.2	60.8	46.3
Sugars	28.1	13.3	11.9
Candy	15.4	28.5	23.8
Beverages	**86.9**	**72.0**	**86.9**
Alcoholic	12.5	0.2	1.7
Wine	3.5	0.0	0.4
Beer and ale	7.6	0.0	0.9
Nonalcoholic	85.8	72.0	86.7
Coffee	39.5	0.8	3.7
Tea	22.8	11.0	19.2
Fruit drinks and ades	19.7	35.3	27.2
Carbonated soft drinks	50.4	44.4	62.2
Regular	39.3	40.3	56.2
Low calorie	12.8	6.0	8.5

Source: USDA, ARS Food Surveys Research Group, Supplementary Data Tables: USDA's 1994–96 Continuing Survey of Food Intakes by Individuals; *Internet site <www.barc.usda.gov/bhnrc/foodsurvey/home.htm>*

Most Children Eat Away from Home Daily

Many eat at school cafeterias, fast-food restaurants, and other people's houses.

Teen boys are especially likely to eat away from home. Fully 72 percent of boys aged 12 to 19 eat away from home on an average day. Among those eating out, 40 percent eat at a fast-food restaurant, 34 percent in a school cafeteria, 25 percent in a store, and 20 percent at someone else's home. A smaller 64 percent of girls aged 12 to 19 eat out, in part because girls are much less likely to eat at fast-food restaurants than boys.

Eating away from home has become so common that many of even the youngest children eat out on an average day. More than one-third of children aged 1 or 2 ate out "yesterday," 28 percent in a fast-food restaurant and 21 percent in a store. Nineteen percent ate in a day care establishment, while 35 percent ate at someone else's home.

♦ Because eating out has become so common, it's unlikely the Millennial generation will ever bring back home cooking.

People under Age 20 Consuming Food Away from Home by Location, 1994–96

(percent of people under age 20 eating away from home on an average day, and percent distribution of those eating away from home by location, by sex for those aged 6 or older, 1994–96)

	< 1	1–2	3–5	males 6–11	males 12–19	females 6–11	females 12–19
Percent eating away from home	16.2%	36.7%	54.0%	67.5%	72.0%	66.2%	64.3%
Percent distribution by location							
Total eating away from home	100.0	100.0	100.0	100.0	100.0	100.0	100.0
Fast-food restaurant	12.4	27.9	25.6	23.2	40.2	25.9	33.0
Sit-down restaurant	1.0	12.1	13.4	11.5	12.5	8.9	19.5
Store	42.7	20.8	17.4	14.4	24.8	16.2	24.6
Someone else/gift	43.0	35.1	31.5	25.5	20.4	31.5	31.4
School cafeteria	0.0	1.4	15.6	49.6	33.8	49.9	33.6
Other cafeteria	0.0	1.5	0.9	1.4	1.7	1.1	1.0
Day care	4.5	19.4	20.6	3.6	0.4	5.2	0.4
Other	1.4	5.7	8.5	9.6	17.7	9.1	19.6

Note: Numbers will not add to 100 because food may be eaten at more than one location during the day.
Source: USDA, ARS Food Surveys Research Group, Data Tables: Results from USDA's 1994-96 Continuing Survey of Food Intakes by Individuals and 1994-96 Diet and Health Knowledge Survey, 1999; Internet site <www.barc.usda.gov/bhnrc/foodsurvey/home.htm>

Few Teens Take Vitamin and Mineral Supplements

Among children, 3-to-5-year-olds are most likely to take supplements.

Most children will take vitamin and mineral supplements only if encouraged to do so by their parents or at the prodding of a physician. The parents of 3-to-5-year-olds are most successful at supplementing their children's diets, as the 56 percent majority of the age group takes supplements.

Resistance arises during elementary school. Forty-six percent of boys and 42 percent of girls aged 6 to 11 taking a vitamin or mineral supplement. The proportion of supplement takers falls even further in the teenage years. Only 29 percent of boys and 39 percent of girls aged 12 to 19 take vitamin or mineral supplements.

♦ With children resisting vitamin pills as they enter their teens, many parents turn to vitamin and mineral fortified foods to supplement their children's diets.

Vitamin use falls in the teen years

(percent of children aged 6 to 19 who take vitamin/mineral supplements, by sex, 1994–96)

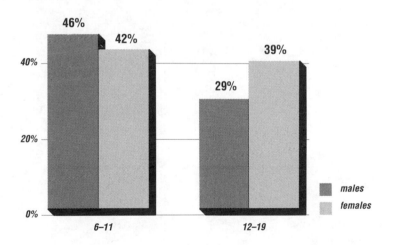

Use of Vitamin and Mineral Supplements by People under Age 20, 1994—96

(percent of people under age 20 taking vitamin/mineral supplements, by type of supplement and sex, 1994–96)

	< 1	1–2	3–5	males 6–11	males 12–19	females 6–11	females 12–19
Any supplement	**15.3%**	**44.9%**	**56.1%**	**46.1%**	**29.2%**	**41.7%**	**39.3%**
Multivitamin	5.6	21.3	27.6	23.9	14.6	20.1	15.7
Multivitamin with iron or other minerals	5.6	19.0	24.3	17.1	7.6	15.7	12.5
Combination of vitamin C with iron	0.2	1.6	2.7	2.4	3.0	2.2	4.0
Single vitamins or minerals	4.3	4.3	4.9	5.6	8.8	6.3	11.8

Source: USDA, ARS Food Surveys Research Group, Supplementary Data Tables: USDA's 1994–96 Continuing Survey of Food Intakes by Individuals; *Internet site <www.barc.usda.gov/bhnrc/foodsurvey/home.htm>*

The Majority of Teen Girls Are Trying to Lose Weight

Few girls are actually overweight, however.

Although only 6 to 10 percent of teenage girls are overweight, more than one in three believes she is overweight. The majority of girls in 9th through 12th grade are trying to lose weight. Skeletally thin models and movie stars have distorted young women's ideal body image, sometimes with troublesome consequences. From 9 to 14 percent of girls in 9th through 12th grade have taken diet pills, powders, or liquids to lose or avoid gaining weight. Seven to 9 percent have taken laxatives or vomited to lose or avoid gaining weight.

Teen boys are more likely to be overweight than girls, but fewer than 30 percent are attempting to lose weight. Boys get more of an opportunity to maintain their weight by playing sports. The majority of boys play on a sports team, while the share of girls on a sports team falls from the 53 percent majority of 9th graders to 42 percent of 12th graders.

♦ For teens, weight is a big concern—whether real or imagined.

Many teen girls believe they are overweight

(percent of girls in 9th to 12th grade who are overweight and who think they are overweight, 1999)

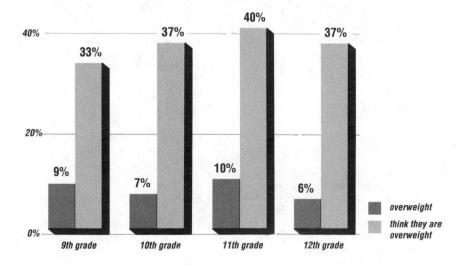

Weight Loss Behavior of 9th to 12th Graders by Sex, 1999

(percent of 9th to 12th graders engaging in selected weight loss activities, by sex, 1999)

	9th grade	10th grade	11th grade	12th grade
Females				
Overweight	9.0%	6.9%	9.8%	5.7%
Think they are overweight	32.5	36.8	40.2	36.8
Are attempting to lose weight	56.5	60.2	59.2	62.7
Exercised to lose/avoid gaining weight*	69.3	68.5	65.5	65.9
Ate less food or foods low in fat to lose/avoid gaining weight*	53.7	58.3	55.0	58.2
Fasted to lose/avoid gaining weight*	19.8	20.2	16.4	18.3
Took diet pills, powders, or liquids to lose/avoid gaining weight*	9.0	10.6	10.5	14.2
Took laxatives or vomited to lose/avoid gaining weight*	6.7	7.8	6.8	9.2
Played on a sports team**	53.4	50.9	45.8	42.3
Males				
Overweight	12.6	13.8	11.6	9.1
Think they are overweight	26.7	23.7	24.0	19.6
Are attempting to lose weight	29.7	27.5	25.6	19.9
Exercised to lose/avoid gaining weight*	54.2	48.5	47.5	46.8
Ate less food or foods low in fat to lose/avoid gaining weight*	25.5	24.0	25.7	24.4
Fasted to lose/avoid gaining weight*	8.1	6.0	5.1	6.0
Took diet pills, powders, or liquids to lose/avoid gaining weight*	4.4	4.0	4.8	4.7
Took laxatives or vomited to lose/avoid gaining weight*	2.3	2.3	2.0	2.1
Played on a sports team**	63.9	62.3	58.8	60.7

* On one or more days of the 30 days preceding the survey.
** During the 12 months preceding the survey.
Note: Overweight is defined as greater than or equal to the 95th percentile in body mass index for age/sex group.
Source: Centers for Disease Control and Prevention, Youth Risk Behavior Surveillance—United States, 1999, *Morbidity and Mortality Weekly Report, Vol. 49, No. SS-5, June 9, 2000; Internet site <ftp://ftp.cdc.gov/pub/ Publications/mmwr/SS/SS4905.pdf>*

Bicycling Is the Most Popular Recreational Activity

Basketball is a close second among children.

Many of the ten most popular recreational activities among children aged 6 to 17 require plenty of physical activity. The number one activity is bicycling. Fully 11 million 6-to-17-year-olds bicycle on more than 52 days a year. A close second in popularity is basketball, with nearly 11 million children playing basketball on 25 or more days per year.

Swimming is third in popularity, with 8 million 6-to-17-year-olds going swimming once a week, on average. Other popular activities that require plenty of exertion are inline skating, soccer, baseball, and touch football.

Walking, calisthenics, and running—which are popular with adults—round out the top ten list of the most popular recreational activities among children.

♦ As children enter adulthood, they are likely to adopt more sedentary recreational activities.

Recreational Activities among Children Aged 6 to 17, 2000

(ten most popular recreational activities among people aged 6 to 17, 2000; ranked by number participating frequently; numbers in thousands)

1.	Bicycling (recreational, 52 or more days/year)	11,454
2.	Basketball (25 or more days/year)	10,702
3.	Swimming (recreational, 52 or more days/year)	8,244
4.	Inline skating (25 or more days/year)	6,992
5.	Soccer (25 or more days/year)	6,572
6.	Baseball (25 or more days/year)	5,261
7.	Walking (recreational, 52 or more days/year)	4,491
8.	Calisthenics (100 or more days/year)	3,720
9.	Running/jogging (100 or more days/year)	3,368
10.	Football, touch (25 or more days/year)	3,345

Source: Sporting Goods Manufacturers Association, Internet site <www.sgma.com/press_room/2000_releases>

The Majority of 11th and 12th Graders Have Had Sex

One in five 12th graders has had four or more sexual partners.

If teenagers are to be believed, then most 11th and 12th grade girls and most 10th, 11th, and 12th grade boys have had sexual intercourse. Twenty-one percent of 12th graders have had four or more sexual partners in their lifetime.

Fewer than half the boys in 9th to 12th grade and girls in 9th to 11th grade are currently sexually active—meaning they've had sexual intercourse during the past three months. From 20 to 37 percent of 9th to 12th graders are currently abstinent—meaning they've had sexual intercourse at some point but not during the past three months.

Birth control use is widespread among teens, and 56 to 70 percent of 9th to 12th grade boys used a condom during their most recent sexual intercourse. From 5 to 14 percent of 9th to 12th grade girls have been pregnant, while 4 to 7 percent of boys have gotten someone pregnant.

♦ With teenagers so sexually active, the prevention of pregnancy and sexually transmitted diseases is of prime concern to parents and schools.

Sexual activity increases with age

(percent of 9th to 12th graders who have had sexual intercourse, by sex, 1999)

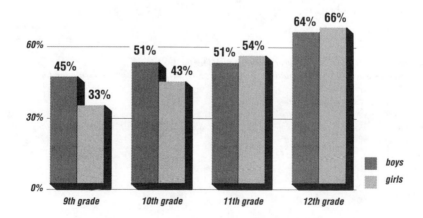

Sexual Behavior of 9th to 12th Graders by Sex, 1999

(percent of 9th to 12th graders engaging in selected sexual activities, by sex, 1999)

	9th grade	10th grade	11th grade	12th grade
Females				
Ever had sexual intercourse	32.5%	42.6%	53.8%	65.8%
Four or more sex partners during lifetime	7.9	10.1	15.1	20.6
Currently sexually active*	24.0	32.0	39.5	53.0
Currently abstinent**	26.7	24.8	26.5	19.5
Condom used during last sexual intercourse***	63.1	55.3	50.0	41.1
Birth control pill used before last sexual intercourse***	12.8	12.8	18.4	31.4
Alcohol or drug use at last sexual intercourse***	20.0	17.7	20.0	17.0
Have been pregnant	4.8	4.9	8.1	13.8
Were taught about HIV/AIDS in school	89.2	90.3	93.7	93.5
Males				
Ever had sexual intercourse	44.5	51.1	51.4	63.9
Four or more sex partners during lifetime	15.6	21.4	19.4	20.6
Currently sexually active*	29.1	33.9	35.4	48.1
Currently abstinent**	34.7	33.1	30.9	24.6
Condom used during last sexual intercourse***	69.5	70.0	69.3	55.9
Birth control pill used before last sexual intercourse***	11.3	5.9	11.6	17.3
Alcohol or drug use at last sexual intercourse***	30.0	28.7	38.2	27.9
Have gotten someone pregnant	4.2	5.5	3.7	6.7
Were taught about HIV/AIDS in school	87.2	90.9	90.9	90.1

* Sexual intercourse during the three months preceding the survey.
** Among those who have ever had sexual intercourse, no sexual intercourse during the three months preceding the survey.
*** Among currently sexually active students.
Source: Centers for Disease Control and Prevention, Youth Risk Behavior Surveillance—United States, 1999, *Morbidity and Mortality Weekly Report, Vol. 49, No. SS-5, June 9, 2000; Internet site <ftp://ftp.cdc.gov/pub/ Publications/mmwr/SS/SS4905.pdf>*

Millennial Generation Accounts for More Than One-Third of Births

Over 1 million babies were born to women under age 25 in 1999.

The birth rate among women under age 25 has been falling for decades. Nevertheless, a substantial 37 percent of births in 1999 were to women under age 25. The 20-to-24 age group ranks second only to the 25-to-29 age group in number of births.

Non-Hispanic whites accounted for fewer than half the babies born to women under age 25 in 1999. Fully 24 percent of young mothers were Hispanic, while another 22 percent were black. The younger the mother, the smaller the percentage of non-Hispanic whites. Among babies born to girls under age 15, only 22 percent were non-Hispanic white.

The 56 percent majority of women under age 25 who gave birth in 1999 were having their first child. Among babies born to women aged 20 to 24, however, the 54 percent majority were second or higher-order births.

While 33 percent of babies were born were out of wedlock in 1999, the proportion was 58 percent among those born to women under age 25. The proportion of new mothers who are unmarried falls with age, from 97 percent of those under age 15 to 48 percent among those aged 20 to 24.

♦ The millennial generation now accounts for a much larger share of births than the baby-boom generation does. In a few years, the majority of the nation's newborns will have millennial generation mothers.

Over one-third of births are to women under age 25

(percent distribution of births by age of mother, 1999)

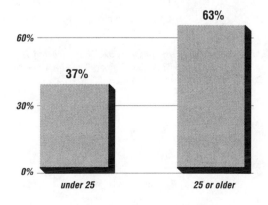

Births to Women under Age 25 by Race and Hispanic Origin, 1999

(number and percent distribution of births by age, race, and Hispanic origin of mother, 1999)

	total	race white	black	Asian	Native American	Hispanic origin Hispanic	non-Hispanic white
Total births	**3,957,829**	**3,130,100**	**606,720**	**180,993**	**40,015**	**762,364**	**2,349,536**
Under age 25	1,466,001	1,089,263	318,726	36,700	21,311	357,955	730,295
Under age 15	9,049	4,723	3,981	142	203	2,721	2,046
Aged 15 to 17	163,559	111,481	45,979	3,119	2,980	48,127	63,659
Aged 18 to 19	312,186	225,842	75,283	6,135	4,925	76,226	149,564
Aged 20 to 24	981,207	747,217	193,483	27,304	13,203	230,881	515,026
Aged 25 or older	2,491,828	2,040,837	287,994	144,293	18,704	404,409	1,619,241

Percent distribution by race and Hispanic origin

	total	white	black	Asian	Native American	Hispanic	non-Hispanic white
Total births	**100.0%**	**79.1%**	**15.3%**	**4.6%**	**1.0%**	**19.3%**	**59.4%**
Under age 25	100.0	74.3	21.7	2.5	1.5	24.4	49.8
Under age 15	100.0	52.2	44.0	1.6	2.2	30.1	22.6
Aged 15 to 17	100.0	68.2	28.1	1.9	1.8	29.4	38.9
Aged 18 to 19	100.0	72.3	24.1	2.0	1.6	24.4	47.9
Aged 20 to 24	100.0	76.2	19.7	2.8	1.3	23.5	52.5
Aged 25 or older	100.0	81.9	11.6	5.8	0.8	16.2	65.0

Percent distribution by age

	total	white	black	Asian	Native American	Hispanic	non-Hispanic white
Total births	**100.0%**	**100.0%**	**100.0%**	**100.0%**	**100.0%**	**100.0%**	**100.0%**
Under age 25	37.0	34.8	52.5	20.3	53.3	47.0	31.1
Under age 15	0.2	0.2	0.7	0.1	0.5	0.4	0.1
Aged 15 to 17	4.1	3.6	7.6	1.7	7.4	6.3	2.7
Aged 18 to 19	7.9	7.2	12.4	3.4	12.3	10.0	6.4
Aged 20 to 24	24.8	23.9	31.9	15.1	33.0	30.3	21.9
Aged 25 or older	63.0	65.2	47.5	79.7	46.7	53.0	68.9

Note: Numbers will not add to total because Hispanics may be of any race and "not stated" is not shown.
Source: National Center for Health Statistics, Births: Preliminary Data for 1999, *National Vital Statistics Reports, Vol. 48, No. 14, 2000; calculations by New Strategist*

Births to Women under Age 25 by Birth Order, 1999

(number and percent distribution of births by age of mother and birth order, 1999)

	total births	first child	second or later child
Total births	**3,957,829**	**1,587,971**	**2,351,366**
Under age 25	1,466,001	827,669	631,129
Under age 15	9,049	8,818	169
Aged 15 to 19	475,745	370,749	102,246
Aged 20 to 24	981,207	448,102	528,714
Aged 25 or older	2,491,828	760,302	1,720,237
Percent distribution by birth order			
Total births	**100.0%**	**40.1%**	**59.4%**
Under age 25	100.0	56.5	43.1
Under age 15	100.0	97.4	1.9
Aged 15 to 19	100.0	77.9	21.5
Aged 20 to 24	100.0	45.7	53.9
Aged 25 or older	100.0	30.5	69.0
Percent distribution by age			
Total births	**100.0%**	**100.0%**	**100.0%**
Under age 25	37.0	52.1	26.8
Under age 15	0.2	0.6	0.0
Aged 15 to 19	12.0	23.3	4.3
Aged 20 to 24	24.8	28.2	22.5
Aged 25 or older	63.0	47.9	73.2

Note: Numbers will not add to total because "not stated" is not shown.
Source: National Center for Health Statistics, Births: Preliminary Data for 1999, National Vital Statistics Reports, Vol. 48, No. 14, 2000; calculations by New Strategist

Births to Women under Age 25 by Marital Status, 1998

(total number of births and number and percent to unmarried women under age 25, by race and Hispanic origin of mother, 1998)

		race		Hispanic origin	
	total	white	black	non-Hispanic white	Hispanic
Total births	**3,941,553**	**3,118,727**	**609,902**	**2,361,462**	**734,661**
Under age 25	1,459,479	1,082,159	320,314	732,402	347,217
Under age 15	9,462	4,801	4,289	2,132	2,716
Aged 15 to 19	484,895	340,694	126,937	219,169	121,388
Aged 20 to 24	965,122	736,664	189,088	511,101	223,113
Aged 25 or older	2,482,074	2,036,568	289,588	1,629,060	387,444
Births to unmarried women					
Total births	**1,293,567**	**821,441**	**421,383**	**517,153**	**305,442**
Under age 25	850,372	542,023	277,631	345,546	197,065
Under age 15	9,137	4,514	4,270	2,044	2,516
Aged 15 to 19	380,868	245,832	121,458	157,517	88,529
Aged 20 to 24	460,367	291,677	151,903	185,985	106,020
Aged 25 or older	443,195	279,418	143,752	171,607	108,377
Percent of births to unmarried women					
Total births	**32.8%**	**26.3%**	**69.1%**	**21.9%**	**41.6%**
Under age 25	58.3	50.1	86.7	47.2	56.8
Under age 15	96.6	94.0	99.6	95.9	92.6
Aged 15 to 19	78.5	72.2	95.7	71.9	72.9
Aged 20 to 24	47.7	39.6	80.3	36.4	47.5
Aged 25 or older	17.9	13.7	49.6	10.5	28.0

Note: Births by race and Hispanic origin will not add to total because Hispanics may be of any race, not all races are shown, and "not stated" is not shown.
Source: National Center for Health Statistics, Births: Final Data for 1998, *National Vital Statistics Report, Vol. 48, No. 3, 2000, calculations by New Strategist*

Cigarette Smoking Is above Average among Millennials

More than 40 percent of 19-to-21-year-olds have smoked cigarettes in the past month.

Cigarette smoking has been declining in the population as a whole, but among young adults it is on the rise. Either antismoking campaigns are backfiring, or Hollywood's cigarette-smoking role models are overcoming the warnings about the dangers of cigarettes.

Overall, 26 percent of people aged 12 or older smoked cigarettes in the month before a 1999 survey was taken. The proportion surpasses 20 percent among 16-year-olds and peaks at 44 percent among 20-year-olds.

One reason for the growing popularity of cigarettes among teens and young adults may be that their peers are less likely to disapprove of them today than in the early 1990s. Surveys of 8th, 10th, and 12th graders show a smaller percentage disapproving or strongly disapproving of cigarettes in 1999 than in 1991. At the same time, however, the percentage of those who believe cigarette smoking presents a "great" physical risk is up. The figure ranges from 55 percent among 8th graders to 71 percent among 12th graders.

♦ Cigarette smoking still looks "cool" to many teens and young adults, making them difficult to reach with anti-smoking messages.

Many teens and young adults smoke cigarettes

(percent of people who have smoked cigarettes in the past month, by age, 1999)

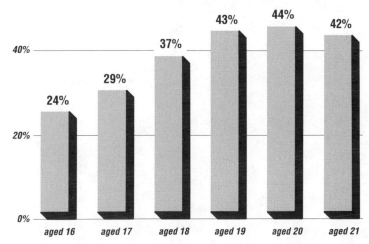

Cigarette Smoking by People under Age 25, 1999

(percent of people aged 12 or older and aged 12 to 24 reporting any, past year, and past month use of cigarettes, 1999)

	any time	*past year*	*past month*
Total people	**68.2%**	**30.1%**	**25.8%**
Aged 12	11.3	5.2	2.2
Aged 13	21.9	13.3	5.8
Aged 14	34.6	21.0	11.3
Aged 15	44.0	27.5	17.4
Aged 16	51.6	33.5	23.7
Aged 17	58.0	39.7	28.7
Aged 18	63.4	47.0	37.4
Aged 19	69.9	51.1	42.5
Aged 20	69.2	52.2	43.5
Aged 21	70.6	49.2	42.1
Aged 22	70.0	45.9	37.2
Aged 23	71.8	48.5	42.1
Aged 24	69.3	44.6	37.9

Source: U.S. Substance Abuse and Mental Health Services Administrations, National Household Survey on Drug Abuse, *1999; Internet site <www.samhsa.gov/NHSDA.htm>*

Attitudes toward Cigarette Smoking by 8th, 10th, and 12th Graders, 1991 and 1999

(percent of 8th, 10th, and 12th graders who think cigarettes present a "great" physical risk, and percent who "disapprove" or "strongly disapprove" of cigarette smoking, 1991 and 1999; percentage point change, 1991–99)

	1999	1991	percentage point change
Great risk			
8th graders	54.8%	51.6%	3.2
10th graders	62.7	60.3	2.4
12th graders	70.8	69.4	1.4
Disapprove			
8th graders	81.4	82.8	−1.4
10th graders	76.1	79.4	−3.3
12th graders	69.5	71.4	−1.9

Source: Institute for Social Research, University of Michigan, Monitoring the Future—National Results on Adolescent Drug Use, Summary of Key Findings, *1999*

Most Teens Don't Wait for Legal Drinking Age

The majority of 19- and 20-year-olds have had an alcoholic beverage in the past month.

Nearly half of Americans aged 12 or older have had an alcoholic beverage in the past month. The figure climbs above 50 percent among 19-year-olds although the legal drinking age is 21.

Many teens and young adults take part in binge drinking, meaning they have had five or more drinks on one occasion in the past month. At least one in ten 18-to-24-year-olds is a heavy drinker—meaning he or she has participated in binge drinking at least five times in the past month.

Full-time college students aged 18 to 22 are more likely to drink alcohol than other 18-to-22-year-olds. Sixty-three percent of college students have drunk alcohol in the past month, and 43 percent have been on a binge. College students are less likely to use tobacco than other 18-to-22-year-olds. Thirty-four percent of college students have smoked cigarettes in the past month versus 44 percent of other 18-to-22-year-olds.

♦ Heavy drinking is a problem on many college campuses. As nearly half of students aged 18-to-22 take part in binge drinking, campus authorities have a deeply entrenched problem to address.

Alcohol Use by People under Age 25, 1999

(percent of people aged 12 or older and aged 12 to 24 who drank alcoholic beverages during the past month, by level of alcohol use, 1998)

	any time	binge	heavy
Total people	**47.3%**	**20.2%**	**5.6%**
Aged 12	3.9	1.7	0.1
Aged 13	8.5	3.7	0.4
Aged 14	14.6	7.3	1.2
Aged 15	21.2	12.1	2.2
Aged 16	28.8	18.1	4.4
Aged 17	34.5	22.4	6.5
Aged 18	43.7	30.5	10.0
Aged 19	53.0	36.6	13.5
Aged 20	54.7	38.7	15.8
Aged 21	66.6	45.6	17.4
Aged 22	65.1	42.5	14.6
Aged 23	64.2	40.0	13.5
Aged 24	61.5	38.3	12.4

Note: Binge drinking is defined as having had five or more drinks on the same occasion on at least one day in the 30 days prior to the survey. Heavy drinking is having had five or more drinks on the same occasion on each of five or more days in 30 days prior to the survey.
Source: U.S. Substance Abuse and Mental Health Services Administrations, National Household Survey on Drug Abuse, *1999; Internet site <www.samhsa.gov/NHSDA.htm>*

Cigarette and Alcohol Use by College Enrollment Status, 1999

(percent of people aged 18 to 22 who have used tobacco or consumed alcohol in the past month, by college enrollment status, 1999)

	full-time undergraduates	*others*
Any tobacco	**39.6%**	**48.5%**
Cigarettes	33.8	44.1
Smokeless tobacco	5.4	6.2
Cigars	11.4	13.1
Pipes	1.4	1.6
Any alcohol	**63.2**	**52.1**
Binge drinking	43.1	35.9
Heavy drinking	18.1	12.0

Note: Binge drinking is defined as having had five or more drinks on the same occasion on at least one day in the 30 days prior to the survey. Heavy drinking is having had five or more drinks on the same occasion on each of five or more days in 30 days prior to the survey.
Source: U.S. Substance Abuse and Mental Health Services Administrations, National Household Survey on Drug Abuse, 1999; Internet site <www.samhsa.gov/NHSDA.htm>

Drug Use Is Prevalent among Teens and Young Adults

More than one in five 18-to-20-year-olds has used an illicit drug in the past month.

Among Americans aged 12 or older, only 7 percent have used an illicit drug in the past month. Young adults are much more likely to be current drug users than the average person. From 10 to 21 percent of 15-to-24-year-olds have used an illicit drug in the past month.

A survey of teenagers shows widespread and growing drug use. Twelve percent of 8th graders have used an illicit drug in the past month, more than double the percentage in 1991. The figure rises to 22 percent in 10th grade and to 26 percent in 12th grade. The most commonly used drug is marijuana. Nearly half of 12th graders have used marijuana at some time in their lives, as have 41 percent of 10th graders and 22 percent of 8th graders.

Behind these shockingly high rates of drug use are changing attitudes among teens. Between 1975 and 1991, a growing share of 12th graders believed illicit drug use presented a "great" physical risk and disapproved of it. Since 1991, however, the percentage of those who believe drugs present great risk or who disapprove of drugs has fallen sharply.

♦ The greater acceptance of drug use among teens may be a result of the ambivalence of their baby-boom parents toward drugs.

Drug Use by People under Age 25, 1999

(percent of people aged 12 or older and aged 12 to 24 reporting any, past year, and past month use of illicit drugs, 1999)

	any time	past year	past month
Total people	**39.7%**	**11.9%**	**6.7%**
Aged 12	10.3	7.4	4.1
Aged 13	15.9	11.0	5.9
Aged 14	25.0	17.2	9.2
Aged 15	31.6	24.1	12.4
Aged 16	38.8	29.4	16.1
Aged 17	43.7	32.8	17.5
Aged 18	48.7	34.0	20.2
Aged 19	53.0	34.3	20.7
Aged 20	54.5	34.2	20.8
Aged 21	54.9	30.6	17.8
Aged 22	53.3	28.9	16.8
Aged 23	54.9	28.0	15.0
Aged 24	53.4	22.7	12.3

Note: "Any time" indicates use at least once of marijuana/hashish, cocaine (including crack), inhalants, hallucinogens (including PCP and LSD), heroin, or any prescription-type psychotherapeutic used nonmedically.
Source: U.S. Substance Abuse and Mental Health Services Administrations, National Household Survey on Drug Abuse, 1999; Internet site <www.samhsa.gov/NHSDA.htm>

Lifetime Drug Use by 8th, 10th, and 12th Graders, 1991 and 1999

(percent of 8th, 10th, and 12th graders who have ever used illicit drugs by type of drug, 1991 and 1999; percentage point change, 1991–99)

	1999	1991	percentage point change
8th graders			
Any illicit drug	**28.3%**	**18.7%**	**9.6**
Marijuana	22.0	10.2	11.8
Inhalants	19.7	17.6	2.1
Hallucinogens	4.8	3.2	1.6
Cocaine	4.7	2.3	2.4
Heroin	2.3	1.2	1.1
Amphetamines	10.7	10.5	0.2
Steroids	2.7	1.9	0.8
10th graders			
Any illicit drug	**46.2**	**30.6**	**15.6**
Marijuana	40.9	23.4	17.5
Inhalants	17.0	15.7	1.3
Hallucinogens	9.7	6.1	3.6
Cocaine	7.7	4.1	3.6
Heroin	2.3	1.2	1.1
Amphetamines	15.7	13.2	2.5
Steroids	2.7	1.8	0.9
12th graders			
Any illicit drug	**54.7**	**44.1**	**10.6**
Marijuana	49.7	36.7	13.0
Inhalants	15.4	17.6	–2.2
Hallucinogens	13.7	9.6	4.1
Cocaine	9.8	7.8	2.0
Heroin	2.0	0.9	1.1
Amphetamines	16.3	15.4	0.9
Steroids	2.9	2.1	0.8

Source: Institute for Social Research, University of Michigan, Monitoring the Future—National Results on Adolescent Drug Use, Summary of Key Findings, *1999; calculations by New Strategist*

Past Month Drug Use by 8th, 10th, and 12th Graders, 1991 and 1999

(percent of 8th, 10th, and 12th graders who have used illicit drugs in the past 30 days, by type of drug, 1991 and 1999; percentage point change, 1991–99)

	1999	1991	percentage point change
8th graders			
Any illicit drug	**12.2%**	**5.7%**	**6.5**
Marijuana	9.7	3.2	6.5
Inhalants	5.0	4.4	0.6
Hallucinogens	1.3	0.8	0.5
Cocaine	1.3	0.5	0.8
Heroin	0.6	0.3	0.3
Amphetamines	3.4	2.6	0.8
Steroids	0.7	0.4	0.3
10th graders			
Any illicit drug	**22.1**	**11.6**	**10.5**
Marijuana	19.4	8.7	10.7
Inhalants	2.6	2.7	–0.1
Hallucinogens	2.9	1.6	1.3
Cocaine	1.8	0.7	1.1
Heroin	0.7	0.2	0.5
Amphetamines	5.0	3.3	1.7
Steroids	0.9	0.6	0.3
12th graders			
Any illicit drug	**25.9**	**16.4**	**9.5**
Marijuana	23.1	13.8	9.3
Inhalants	2.0	2.4	–0.4
Hallucinogens	3.5	2.2	1.3
Cocaine	2.6	1.4	1.2
Heroin	0.5	0.2	0.3
Amphetamines	4.5	3.2	1.3
Steroids	0.9	0.8	0.1

Source: Institute for Social Research, University of Michigan, Monitoring the Future—National Results on Adolescent Drug Use, Summary of Key Findings, *1999; calculations by New Strategist*

Attitudes toward Drug Use among 12th Graders, 1975 and 1999

(percent of high school seniors who think the use of illicit drugs is a "great" physical risk and percent who "disapprove" or "strongly disapprove" of drug use by people aged 18 or older, by type of use, 1975 and 1999; percentage point change, 1975–91 and 1991–99)

| | 1999 | 1991 | 1975 | percentage point change | |
				1991–99	1975–91
Great risk					
Try marijuana once or twice	15.7%	27.1%	15.1%	–11.4	0.6
Smoke marijuana occasionally	23.9	40.6	18.1	–16.7	5.8
Smoke marijuana regularly	57.4	78.6	43.3	–21.2	14.1
Try cocaine once or twice	52.1	59.4	42.6	–7.3	9.5
Take cocaine regularly	85.8	90.4	73.1	–4.6	12.7
Take one or two drinks nearly every day	21.8	32.7	21.5	–10.9	0.3
Smoke one or more packs of cigarettes per day	70.8	69.4	51.3	1.4	19.5
Disapprove					
Try marijuana once or twice	48.8	68.7	47.0	–19.9	1.8
Smoke marijuana occasionally	62.5	79.4	54.8	–16.9	7.7
Smoke marijuana regularly	78.6	89.3	71.9	–10.7	6.7
Try cocaine once or twice	89.1	93.6	81.3	–4.5	7.8
Take cocaine regularly	94.9	97.3	93.3	–2.4	1.6
Take one or two drinks nearly every day	67.2	76.5	67.6	–9.3	–0.4
Smoke one or more packs of cigarettes per day	69.5	71.4	67.5	–1.9	2.0

Source: Institute for Social Research, University of Michigan, Monitoring the Future—National Results on Adolescent Drug Use, Summary of Key Findings, *1999; calculations by New Strategist*

Children under Age 18 Account for One-Fourth of the Uninsured

More than 10 million children do not have health insurance.

Among all Americans, 43 million lacked health insurance in 1999—or 16 percent of the population. The figure is slightly lower among children under age 18, at 14 percent. It is much higher among 18-to-24-year-olds, at 29 percent—a larger share than in any other age group. People under age 25 account for fully 42 percent of the uninsured.

One in four Americans is covered by government health insurance. Among children under age 18, the proportion is almost as high. One in five children under age 18 is covered by Medicaid, the health insurance program for low-income families. Another 3 percent of children are covered by military health insurance. Ten percent of 18-to-24-year-olds are covered by Medicaid, while 3 percent have military insurance.

For 63 percent of the population, an employer provides health insurance. Among 18-to-24-year-olds, the figure stands at just 51 percent.

◆ Because many young adults are part-time workers, their employers do not provide them with health insurance. The lack of insurance makes them vulnerable to financial catastrophe in the event of major illness or injury.

Many young adults are without health insurance

(percent of people who do not have health insurance, by age, 1999)

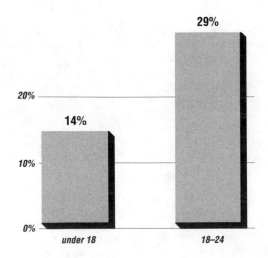

Health Insurance Coverage of People under Age 25, 1999

(number and percent distribution of total people and people under age 25 by health insurance coverage status, 1999; numbers in thousands)

| | | covered by private or government health insurance | | | | | | | |
| | | private health insurance | | | government health insurance | | | | |
	total	total	total	employ-ment based	total	Medicaid	Medicare	military	not covered
Total	274,087	231,533	194,599	172,023	66,176	27,890	36,066	8,530	42,554
Under 18	72,325	62,302	49,822	46,594	16,579	14,479	355	2,080	10,023
18 to 24	26,532	18,844	16,438	13,535	3,450	2,643	152	798	7,688

Percent distribution by type of coverage

Total	100.0%	84.5%	71.0%	62.8%	24.1%	10.2%	13.2%	3.1%	15.5%
Under 18	100.0	86.1	68.9	64.4	22.9	20.0	0.5	2.9	13.9
18 to 24	100.0	71.0	62.0	51.0	13.0	10.0	0.6	3.0	29.0

Percent distribution by age

Total	100.0%	100.0%	100.0%	100.0%	100.0%	100.0%	100.0%	100.0%	100.0%
Under 18	26.4	26.9	25.6	27.1	25.1	51.9	1.0	24.4	23.6
18 to 24	9.7	8.1	8.4	7.9	5.2	9.5	0.4	9.4	18.1

Note: Numbers may not add to total because some people have more than one type of health insurance coverage.
Source: Bureau of the Census, unpublished tables from the 2000 Current Population Survey, Internet site <www.census.gov/hhes/hlthins/historic/hihistt2.html>; calculations by New Strategist

The Common Cold Is the Biggest Health Problem among Children

One in four reports having had a cold in the past two weeks.

As any parent knows, children's noses always seem to be dripping. So it's no surprise to discover that 26 percent of children under age 18 reported having had a cold in the past two weeks. The second most common health problem among children is also well known to parents—21 percent of kids reported minor cuts and scratches in the past two weeks.

The list of common health problems experienced by children is one with which every parent is familiar—at least one in ten children had lip problems, bruises, diarrhea, upset stomach, or teeth problems in the past two weeks. Less common among children are the problems that plague adults: anxiety, fatigue, eating too much, and trouble sleeping.

♦ The pharmaceutical industry has profited enormously from the common cold, offering parents all sorts of remedies to ease their children's symptoms.

Health Problems in an Average Two-Week Period: Children

(percent of people under age 18 self-reporting or parent-reporting health problems during the past two weeks, by type of problem; ranked by percent reporting problem, 1992)

	percent reporting
Common cold	26%
Minor cuts/scratches	21
Lip problems	19
Bruises	16
Diarrhea	12
Upset stomach	10
Teeth problems	10
Sore throat not associated with a cold	8
Headache	7
Sinus problems	7
Acne/pimples	6
Eye problems	6
Painful dry skin	5
Constipation	5
Hay fever	5
Muscle aches/pains	4
Overweight problems	4
Sleep problems	4
Overindulgence of food	2
Fatigue	1
Back problems	1
Anxiety	1

Note: (–) means not applicable or sample too small to make a reliable estimate.
Source: Consumer Healthcare Products Association, Self-Medication in the '90s: Practices and Perceptions, *1992*

People under Age 25 Account for Nearly Half of Acute Conditions

Children and young adults account for 53 percent of common colds.

But for a few exceptions, acute conditions afflict the young more than the old. As people age, they build immunity through exposure to a wide variety of viruses, reducing the incidence of many respiratory and gastrointestinal illnesses. Injuries also decline with age as people learn to be more careful.

In 1996, 49 percent of children under age 5 experienced a cold bad enough to send them to a doctor or keep them in bed for at least half a day, according to the National Center for Health Statistics. Fifty-four percent were sick with the flu. Among 5-to-17-year-olds, a smaller 34 percent had a bad cold while 44 percent had the flu. The figures are even lower among 18-to-24-year-olds, with 24 percent getting a bad cold and 41 percent experiencing the flu.

Fifty percent of children under age 5 had an ear infection that sent them to the doctor or kept them in bed for at least half a day. Children outgrow ear infections with age. Only 30 percent of 5-to-17-year-olds reported an ear infection in 1996.

♦ Acute illnesses among young children are rarely life threatening, but they do disrupt the work routines of parents, many of whom must use personal days to care for sick children.

Acute Health Conditions Experienced by People under Age 25, 1996

(total number of acute conditions, number and rate per 100 people under age 25, and share of total acute conditions accounted for by age group, by type of condition, 1996; numbers in thousands)

	total	under age 5			aged 5 to 17			aged 18 to 24		
		number	rate	share of total	number	rate	share of total	number	rate	share of total
Total acute conditions	**432,001**	**63,866**	**317.9**	**14.8%**	**104,842**	**204.4**	**24.3%**	**45,272**	**184.2**	**10.5%**
Infective and parasitic diseases	54,192	11,447	57.0	21.1	19,018	37.1	35.1	5,695	23.2	10.5
Common childhood diseases	3,118	1,369	6.8	43.9	1,203	2.3	38.6	221	0.9	7.1
Intestinal virus	15,980	2,861	14.2	17.9	5,313	10.4	33.2	1,530	6.2	9.6
Viral infections	15,067	4,533	22.6	30.1	4,929	9.6	32.7	688	2.8	4.6
Other	20,027	2,684	13.4	13.4	7,573	14.8	37.8	3,256	13.2	16.3
Respiratory conditions	**208,623**	**25,991**	**129.4**	**12.5**	**52,088**	**101.5**	**25.0**	**21,150**	**86.0**	**10.1**
Common cold	62,251	9,756	48.6	15.7	17,318	33.8	27.8	5,839	23.8	9.4
Other acute upper respiratory infections	29,866	2,635	13.1	8.8	7,690	15.0	25.7	3,961	16.1	13.3
Influenza	95,049	10,780	53.7	11.3	22,744	44.3	23.9	9,946	40.5	10.5
Acute bronchitis	12,116	1,446	7.2	11.9	2,214	4.3	18.3	947	3.9	7.8
Pneumonia	4,791	783	3.9	16.3	883	1.7	18.4	347	1.4	7.2
Other respiratory conditions	4,550	590	2.9	13.0	1,238	2.4	27.2	110	0.4	2.4
Digestive system conditions	**17,646**	**1,931**	**9.6**	**10.9**	**5,030**	**9.8**	**28.5**	**1,584**	**6.4**	**9.0**
Dental conditions	2,970	720	3.6	24.2	537	1.0	18.1	274	1.1	9.2
Indigestion, nausea, and vomiting	7,963	457	2.3	5.7	3,786	7.4	47.5	617	2.5	7.7
Other digestive conditions	6,713	754	3.8	11.2	706	1.4	10.5	693	2.8	10.3

(continued)

(continued from previous page)

	total	under age 5			aged 5 to 17			aged 18 to 24		
		number	rate	share of total	number	rate	share of total	number	rate	share of total
Injuries	**57,279**	**4,597**	**22.9**	**8.0%**	**10,952**	**21.4**	**19.1%**	**7,736**	**31.5**	**13.5%**
Fractures and dislocations	8,465	246	1.2	2.9	3,019	5.9	35.7	736	3.0	8.7
Sprains and strains	12,977	100	0.5	0.8	1,794	3.5	13.8	1,790	7.3	13.8
Open wounds and lacerations	9,027	1,375	6.8	15.2	1,008	2.0	11.2	1,634	6.6	18.1
Contusions and superficial injuries	9,979	715	3.6	7.2	2,004	3.9	20.1	1,433	5.8	14.4
Other current injuries	16,832	2,161	10.8	12.8	3,127	6.1	18.6	2,143	8.7	12.7
Selected other acute conditions	**63,090**	**16,055**	**79.9**	**25.4**	**12,521**	**24.4**	**19.8**	**6,243**	**25.4**	**9.9**
Eye conditions	3,478	760	3.8	21.9	339	0.7	9.7	384	1.6	11.0
Acute ear infections	21,766	11,038	55.0	50.7	6,385	12.4	29.3	937	3.8	4.3
Other ear conditions	3,833	596	3.0	15.5	1,151	2.2	30.0	185	0.8	4.8
Acute urinary conditions	8,405	477	2.4	5.7	1,013	2.0	12.1	707	2.9	8.4
Disorders of menstruation	839	–	–	–	133	0.3	15.9	169	0.7	20.1
Other disorders of female genital tract	1,597	–	–	–	38	0.1	2.4	446	1.8	27.9
Delivery and other conditions of pregnancy	3,279	–	–	–	311	0.6	9.5	1,096	4.5	33.4
Skin conditions	4,986	572	2.8	11.5	739	1.4	14.8	493	2.0	9.9
Acute musculoskeletal conditions	8,461	603	3.0	7.1	419	0.8	5.0	1,321	5.4	15.6
Headache, excluding migraine	1,738	–	–	–	395	0.8	22.7	282	1.1	16.2
Fever, unspecified	4,708	2,009	10.0	42.7	1,597	3.1	33.9	224	0.9	4.8
Other acute conditions	**31,170**	**3,846**	**19.1**	**12.3**	**5,233**	**10.2**	**16.8**	**2,863**	**11.6**	**9.2**

Note: The acute conditions shown here are those that caused people to seek medical attention or to restrict their activity for at least half a day. (–) means not applicable or sample is too small to make a reliable estimate.

Source: National Center for Health Statistics, Current Estimates from the National Health Interview Survey, 1996, Series 10, No. 200, 1999; Internet site <www.cdc .gov/nchs/data/nvs48_3.pdf>; calculations by New Strategist

Chronic Conditions Are Rare among Children

Respiratory problems are the exception, however.

While children under age 18 account for few chronic conditions, they are well represented among those experiencing respiratory problems. People under age 18 account for 30 percent of Americans suffering from asthma. Hay fever and chronic sinusitis are also common among children. Thirty-five percent of people experiencing chronic acne problems are under age 18, as are 26 percent of those with dermatitis.

Children under age 18 also account for a large share of Americans with speech impairments (43 percent), epilepsy (26 percent), and heart murmurs (25 percent).

♦ As children enter adulthood, they will experience fewer acute illnesses but many more chronic conditions.

Chronic Health Conditions Experienced by People under Age 18, 1996

(total number of chronic conditions, number and rate per 1,000 people under age 18, and share of total chronic conditions accounted for by people under age 18, by type of condition, 1996; numbers in thousands)

		under age 18		
	total	number	rate	share of total
Skin and musculoskeletal conditions				
Arthritis	33,638	136	1.9	0.4%
Gout, including gouty arthritis	2,487	–	–	–
Intervertebral disc disorders	6,700	69	1.0	1.0
Bonespur or tendinitis	2,934	–	–	–
Disorders of bone or cartilage	1,730	34	0.5	2.0
Bunions	2,360	96	1.3	4.1
Bursitis	5,006	55	0.8	1.1
Sebaceous skin cyst	1,190	32	0.4	2.7
Acne	4,952	1,743	24.4	35.2
Psoriasis	2,940	228	3.2	7.8
Dermatitis	8,249	2,175	30.5	26.4
Dry, itching skin	6,627	903	12.7	13.6
Ingrown nails	5,807	374	5.2	6.4
Corns and calluses	3,778	80	1.1	2.1
Impairments				
Visual impairment	8,280	448	6.3	5.4
Color blindness	2,811	283	4.0	10.1
Cataracts	7,022	33	0.5	0.5
Glaucoma	2,595	–	–	–
Hearing impairment	22,044	897	12.6	4.1
Tinnitus	7,866	186	2.6	2.4
Speech impairment	2,720	1,160	16.3	42.6
Absence of extremities	1,285	70	1.0	5.4
Paralysis of extremities	2,138	274	3.8	12.8
Deformity or orthopedic impairment	29,499	1,830	25.6	6.2
Back	16,905	552	7.7	3.3
Upper extremities	4,170	189	2.6	4.5
Lower extremities	12,696	1,339	18.8	10.5

(continued)

(continued from previous page)

	total	under age 18		
		number	rate	share of total
Digestive conditions				
Ulcer	3,709	96	1.3	2.6%
Hernia of abdominal cavity	4,470	122	1.7	2.7
Gastritis or duodenitis	3,729	218	3.1	5.8
Frequent indigestion	6,420	238	3.3	3.7
Enteritis or colitis	1,686	119	1.7	7.1
Spastic colon	2,083	48	0.7	2.3
Diverticula of intestines	2,529	–	–	–
Frequent constipation	3,149	380	5.3	12.1
Genitourinary, nervous, endocrine, metabolic, and blood conditions				
Goiter or other thyroid disorders	4,598	71	1.0	1.5
Diabetes	7,627	89	1.2	1.2
Anemias	3,457	359	5.0	10.4
Epilepsy	1,335	351	4.9	26.3
Migraine headache	11,546	1,084	15.2	9.4
Neuralgia or neuritis, unspecified	353	15	0.2	4.2
Kidney trouble	2,553	168	2.4	6.6
Bladder disorders	3,139	239	3.3	7.6
Diseases of prostate	2,803	–	–	–
Disease of female genital organs	4,420	242	3.4	5.5
Circulatory conditions				
Rheumatic fever	1,759	83	1.2	4.7
Heart disease	20,653	1,688	23.6	8.2
Ischemic heart disease	7,672	–	–	–
Heart rhythm disorders	8,716	1,217	17.0	14.0
Tachycardia or rapid heart	2,310	–	–	–
Heart murmurs	4,783	1,188	16.6	24.8
Other heart rhythm disorders	1,624	29	0.4	1.8
Other selected diseases of heart	4,265	471	6.6	11.0
High blood pressure (hypertension)	28,314	36	0.5	0.1
Cerebrovascular disease	2,999	29	0.4	1.0
Hardening of the arteries	1,556	–	–	–
Varicose veins of lower extremities	7,399	–	–	–
Hemorrhoids	8,231	20	0.3	0.2

(continued)

(continued from previous page)

		under age 18		
	total	*number*	*rate*	*share of total*
Respiratory conditions				
Chronic bronchitis	14,150	4,087	57.3	28.9%
Asthma	14,598	4,429	62.0	30.3
Hay fever or allergic rhinitis	23,721	4,190	58.7	17.7
Chronic sinusitis	33,161	4,559	63.9	13.7
Deviated nasal septum	1,985	122	1.7	6.1
Chronic disease of tonsils and adenoids	2,513	1,444	20.2	57.5
Emphysema	1,821	–	–	–

Note: Chronic conditions are those that last at least three months or belong to a group of conditions that are considered to be chronic regardless of when they begin. (–) means sample is too small to make a reliable estimate. Source: National Center for Health Statistics, Current Estimates from the National Health Interview Survey, 1996, Series 10, No. 200, 1999; Internet site <www.cdc.gov/nchs/data/nvs48_3.pdf>; calculations by New Strategist

More Than 4 Million Children Are Disabled

Fewer than 2 million are severely disabled, however.

Among the nation's 36 million children aged 6 to 14, a substantial 4 million are disabled—or 11 percent. Boys are much more likely than girls to be disabled: 14 percent of boys aged 6 to 14 were classified as disabled in 1997 versus 8 percent of girls. Behind the difference is the greater difficulty boys have in doing school work, which is the most common disability experienced by the age group. Fully 9.0 percent of boys aged 6 to 14 have difficulty doing their regular school work—double the 4.5 percent rate among girls.

Among children under age 6, only 2 to 3 percent have a disability, most of the disabled suffering from developmental delays. Again, boys are more likely than girls to be disabled.

♦ Problems with school work can be the result of children being placed in school at a level beyond their abilities. As children mature, many will outgrow their learning difficulties.

Children under Age 15 with Disabilities, 1997

(number and percent distribution of children under age 15 by disability status, age and sex, 1997; numbers in thousands)

	total		male		female	
	number	percent distribution	number	percent distribution	number	percent distribution
Under age 3	**11,619**	**100.0%**	**5,947**	**100.0%**	**5,671**	**100.0%**
Has no disability	11,386	98.0	5,809	97.7	5,576	98.3
Has disability	233	2.0	138	2.3	95	1.7
Has developmental delay	206	1.8	121	2.0	85	1.5
Has difficulty moving arms or legs	58	0.5	38	0.6	19	0.3
Aged 3 to 5 years	**12,192**	**100.0**	**6,229**	**100.0**	**5,963**	**100.0**
Has no disability	11,782	96.6	5,990	96.2	5,792	97.1
Has disability	410	3.4	239	3.8	171	2.9
Has developmental delay	335	2.7	194	3.1	141	2.4
Has difficulty running or playing	218	1.8	125	2.0	94	1.6
Aged 6 to 14 years	**35,795**	**100.0**	**18,317**	**100.0**	**17,478**	**100.0**
Has no disability	31,777	88.8	15,679	85.6	16,097	92.1
Has disability	4,018	11.2	2,638	14.4	1,381	7.9
Severe	1,715	4.8	1,187	6.5	528	3.0
Not severe	2,303	6.4	1,450	7.9	853	4.9
Has difficulty doing regular school work	2,446	6.8	1,655	9.0	791	4.5
Has difficulty getting along with others	647	1.8	451	2.5	196	1.1
Has one or more selected conditions	2,818	7.9	1,882	10.3	935	5.4
Learning disability	1,867	5.2	1,209	6.6	658	3.8
Mental retardation	307	0.9	185	1.0	122	0.7
Other developmental disability	240	0.7	167	0.9	73	0.4
Other developmental condition	1,314	3.7	900	4.9	414	2.4
Has developmental disability or condition	1,611	4.5	1,109	6.1	503	2.9
Uses wheelchair	70	0.2	30	0.2	40	0.2
Uses cane/crutches/walker	20	0.1	8	0.0	12	0.1
Has used for 6 months or more	12	0.0	6	0.0	6	0.0
Has difficulty seeing words/letters	264	0.7	160	0.9	104	0.6
Severe	45	0.1	23	0.1	22	0.1
Not severe	219	0.6	136	0.7	83	0.5

(continued)

(continued from previous page)

	total		male		female	
	number	percent distribution	number	percent distribution	number	percent distribution
Has difficulty hearing conversation	234	0.7%	141	0.8%	93	0.5%
Severe	57	0.2	37	0.2	20	0.1
Not severe	177	0.5	104	0.6	73	0.4
Has difficulty with speech	752	2.1	546	3.0	205	1.2
Severe	154	0.4	115	0.6	38	0.2
Not severe	598	1.7	431	2.4	167	1.0
Has difficulty walking or running	758	2.1	431	2.4	327	1.9

Note: For the definition of disability, see the glossary.
Source: Bureau of the Census, Americans with Disabilities: 1997, *detailed tables from Current Population Reports P70–73, 2001*

Young Adults Are Least Likely to Go to the Doctor

People aged 15 to 24 visit doctors fewer than two times a year, on average.

In 1998, Americans visited physicians a total of 829 million times. People under age 25 made 26 percent of visits. Children under age 15 visited a doctor nearly 146 million times in 1998 as parents brought them into the office for immunizations as well as treatment for ear infections, colds, and other childhood ailments. Young adults aged 15 to 24 accounted for a small share of doctor visits in 1998, in part because the age group is least likely to be covered by health insurance.

People under age 25 visit a doctor 2.2 times a year, less than the 3.1 visits per year made by the average person. People aged 15 to 24 see a doctor only 1.9 times a year. Women in the age group visit doctors more frequently than men (2.6 visits versus 1.2 visits for men) because of pregnancy and childbirth.

♦ Among children under age 15, boys visit doctors slightly more often than girls do. This is the only age group in which males go to the doctor more frequently than females.

Physician Office Visits by People under Age 25, 1998

(number, percent distribution, and number of physician office visits per person per year for total people and people under age 25, by sex, 1998; numbers in thousands)

	total	percent distribution	average visits per year
Total visits	**829,280**	**100.0%**	**3.1**
Total, under age 25	217,125	26.2	2.2
Under age 15	145,842	17.6	2.4
Aged 15 to 24	71,283	8.6	1.9
Visits by females	**500,365**	**60.3**	**3.6**
Total, under age 25	116,768	14.1	2.4
Under age 15	68,018	8.2	2.3
Aged 15 to 24	48,750	5.9	2.6
Visits by males	**328,916**	**39.7**	**2.5**
Total, under age 25	100,357	12.1	2.2
Under age 15	77,825	9.4	2.5
Aged 15 to 24	22,532	2.7	1.2

Source: National Center for Health Statistics, National Ambulatory Medical Care Survey: 1998 Summary, Advance Data No. 315, 2000; calculations by New Strategist

Among Children and Young Adults, Accidents Are the Leading Cause of Death

Homicide and suicide are important causes of death as well.

Once past infancy, most deaths of people under age 25 are caused by accidents—which means a large portion of deaths in the age group are preventable. Among infants, congenital anomalies and other birth problems are the leading causes of death.

In the 1 to 4 age group, accidents account for more than one-third of deaths, while congenital anomalies rank second. Disturbingly, homicide is the third leading cause of death among preschoolers. Among 5-to-14-year-olds, accidents are the leading cause of death, followed by cancer and homicide. Among 15-to-24-year-olds, accidents, homicide, and suicide are the leading causes of death.

Life expectancy has been rising for decades thanks to the success of medical science at combating the ailments of childhood. In 1998, life expectancy at birth stood at 74 years for males and nearly 80 years for females. At age 25, males and females have more than 50 years of life remaining.

♦ As medical science tamed the ailments that once killed many infants and children, accidents have become a more important cause of death. Only greater diligence by families can significantly cut into accidental deaths.

Leading Causes of Death for Infants, 1998

(number and percent distribution of deaths accounted for by the ten leading causes of death for children under age 1, 1998)

		number	percent distribution
All causes		**28,371**	**100.0%**
1.	Congenital anomalies	6,212	21.9
2.	Disorders relating to short gestation and low birthweight	4,101	14.5
3.	Sudden infant death syndrome	2,822	9.9
4.	Newborn affected by maternal complications of pregnancy	1,343	4.7
5.	Respiratory distress syndrome	1,295	4.6
6.	Newborn affected by complications of placenta, cord, and membranes	961	3.4
7.	Infections specific to the perinatal period	815	2.9
8.	Accidents and adverse effects	754	2.7
9.	Intrauterine hypoxia and birth asphyxia	461	1.6
10.	Pneumonia and influenza	441	1.6
	All other causes	9,166	32.3

Source: National Center for Health Statistics, Deaths: Final Data for 1998, *National Vital Statistics Reports, Vol. 48, No. 11, 2000; calculations by New Strategist*

Leading Causes of Death for Children Aged 1 to 4, 1998

(number and percent distribution of deaths accounted for by the ten leading causes of death for children aged 1 to 4, 1998)

		number	percent distribution
All causes		**5,251**	**100.0%**
1.	Accidents and adverse effects	1,935	36.9
2.	Congenital anomalies	564	10.7
3.	Homicide	399	7.6
4.	Malignant neoplasms	365	7.0
5.	Diseases of heart	214	4.1
6.	Pneumonia and influenza	146	2.8
7.	Septicemia	89	1.7
8.	Certain conditions originating in the perinatal period	75	1.4
9.	Cerebrovascular diseases	57	1.1
10.	Benign neoplasms	53	1.0
	All other causes	1,354	25.8

Source: National Center for Health Statistics, Deaths: Final Data for 1998, *National Vital Statistics Reports, Vol. 48, No. 11, 2000; calculations by New Strategist*

Leading Causes of Death for Children Aged 5 to 14, 1998

(number and percent distribution of deaths accounted for by the ten leading causes of death for children aged 5 to 14, 1998)

		number	percent distribution
	All causes	**7,791**	**100.0%**
1.	Accidents and adverse effects	3,254	41.8
2.	Malignant neoplasms	1,013	13.0
3.	Homicide	460	5.9
4.	Congenital anomalies	371	4.8
5.	Diseases of heart	326	5.9
6.	Suicide	324	4.2
7.	Chronic obstructive pulmonary diseases	152	2.0
8.	Pneumonia and influenza	121	1.6
9.	Benign neoplasms	84	1.1
10.	Cerebrovascular diseases	82	1.1
	All other causes	1,604	20.6

Source: National Center for Health Statistics, Deaths: Final Data for 1998, National Vital Statistics Reports, Vol. 48, No. 11, 2000; calculations by New Strategist

Leading Causes of Death for People Aged 15 to 24, 1998

(number and percent distribution of deaths accounted for by the ten leading causes of death for people aged 15 to 24, 1998)

		number	percent distribution
All causes		**30,627**	**100.0%**
1.	Accidents and adverse effects	13,349	43.6
2.	Homicide	5,506	18.0
3.	Suicide	4,135	13.5
4.	Malignant neoplasms	1,699	5.5
5.	Diseases of the heart	1,057	3.5
6.	Congenital anomalies	450	1.5
7.	Chronic obstructive pulmonary diseases and allied conditions	239	0.8
8.	Pneumonia and influenza	215	0.7
9.	Human immunodeficiency virus infection	194	0.6
10.	Cerebrovascular diseases	178	0.6
	All other causes	3,605	11.8

Source: National Center for Health Statistics, Deaths: Final Data for 1998, *National Vital Statistics Reports, Vol. 48, No. 11, 2000; calculations by New Strategist*

Life Expectancy by Age and Sex, 1998

(years of life remaining at selected ages, by sex, 1998)

	males	females
At birth	73.8	79.5
Aged 1	73.4	79.0
Aged 5	69.5	75.1
Aged 10	64.6	70.2
Aged 15	59.7	65.2
Aged 20	55.0	60.3
Aged 25	50.3	55.5
Aged 30	45.7	50.6
Aged 35	41.0	45.8
Aged 40	36.4	41.1
Aged 45	31.9	36.4
Aged 50	27.6	31.8
Aged 55	23.5	27.4
Aged 60	19.6	23.2
Aged 65	16.0	19.2
Aged 70	12.8	15.5
Aged 75	10.0	12.2
Aged 80	7.5	9.2
Aged 85	5.5	6.7
Aged 90	4.1	4.9
Aged 95	3.0	3.6
Aged 100	2.3	2.7

Source: National Center for Health Statistics, Deaths: Final Data for 1998, *National Vital Statistics Report, Vol. 48, No. 11, 2000; Internet site <www.cdc.gov/nchs/data/nvs48_11.pdf>*

4

Income

♦ The $25,171 median income of householders under age 25 in 1999 was 2 percent lower than in 1980, after adjusting for inflation. During the past 20 years, the median income of young adults fell from 72 to 62 percent of the national median.

♦ Among householders under age 25, blacks have the lowest incomes by far— a median of just $15,576. Non-Hispanic whites have the highest median household income, at $27,237 in 1999.

♦ For most age groups, married couples are the most affluent household type. Among households headed by people under age 25, however, the median income of male-headed families is higher than that of married couples.

♦ Among families with children under age 18 at home, the median income of married couples stood at $60,168 in 1999. This compares with $32,427 for male-headed families and just $19,934 for female-headed families.

♦ The incomes of men and women under age 25 are low, with medians well below $10,000, because few in the age group work full-time.

♦ While 12 percent of all Americans are poor, the poverty rate among people under age 25 is a much larger 17 percent. Fully 52 percent of the nation's poor are under age 25.

Incomes of Young Householders Are below Peak

Young adults have lost ground over the past two decades.

The median income of the average household stood at a record high of $40,816 in 1999. The $25,171 median income of householders under age 25, however, was 2 percent below its 1980 level, after adjusting for inflation. During the past 20 years, the median income of young adults has fallen from 72 to 62 percent of the national median.

Several factors account for the decline in the median income of householders under age 25. First, the minimum wage has failed to keep pace with inflation, hurting the finances of young adults because many are entry-level workers. Second, with more young adults going to college, a growing proportion of householders under age 25 work only part-time, if at all, and thus have lower household incomes. Third, married couples now account for a smaller share of households in every age group. Since couples tend to be the most affluent household type because most are dual-earners, fewer married couples means lower household incomes.

♦ The tight labor market of the 1990s is boosting the incomes of young adults. Many companies are paying more than minimum wage to attract workers, lifting the incomes of young adults.

Young adults made gains in the 1990s

(percent change in median income of total households and households headed by people under age 25, 1990–99; in 1999 dollars)

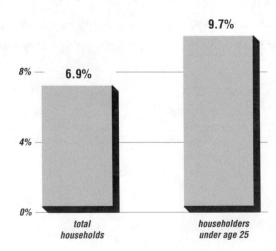

Median Income of Households Headed by People under Age 25, 1980 to 1999

(median income of total households and households headed by people under age 25, and index of under-25 median to total median, 1980–99; percent change for selected years; in 1999 dollars)

	total households	aged 15 to 24	index
1999	$40,816	$25,171	62
1998	39,744	24,084	61
1997	38,411	23,441	61
1996	37,686	22,763	60
1995	37,251	22,934	62
1994	36,270	21,741	60
1993	36,019	22,290	62
1992	36,379	20,974	58
1991	36,850	22,400	61
1990	38,168	22,947	60
1989	38,837	25,075	65
1988	38,341	23,997	63
1987	38,220	24,120	63
1986	37,845	23,272	61
1985	36,568	23,301	64
1984	35,942	22,493	63
1983	34,934	22,417	64
1982	35,152	24,077	68
1981	35,269	24,485	69
1980	35,850	25,731	72

Percent change

1998–1999	2.7%	4.5%	1.8%
1990–1999	6.9	9.7	2.6
1980–1999	13.9	–2.2	–14.1

Note: The index is calculated by dividing the under-25 median by the total median and multiplying by 100.
Source: Bureau of the Census, data from the 2000 Current Population Survey, Internet site <www.census.gov/hhes/income/histinc/h02.html>; calculations by New Strategist

Household Incomes Differ Sharply by Race

Among householders under age 25, blacks have the lowest incomes.

Householders under age 25 had a median income of $25,171 in 1999, well below the $40,816 national median. Within the age group, black householders have the lowest incomes by far—a median of just $15,576. Non-Hispanic whites have the highest median household income, at $27,237. Hispanics are not far behind with a median of $24,268.

Behind the much lower incomes of blacks is household composition. Black households are much less likely than non-Hispanic white or Hispanic households to be headed by married couples—the most affluent household type.

Among the nation's most affluent households—those with incomes of $100,000 or more—householders under age 25 account for a minuscule 1 percent. The youngest adults account for fully one in nine households with incomes below $10,000.

♦ Many young householders are in school and consequently work only part-time. Their investment in education will pay off as their incomes rise when they embark on a career.

Non-Hispanic whites have the highest incomes

(median income of householders under age 25 by race and Hispanic origin, 1999)

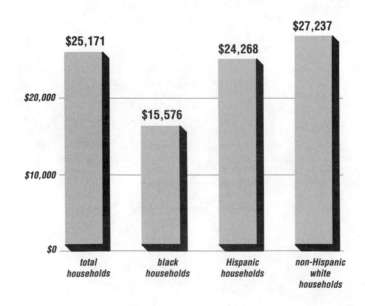

Income Distribution of Households Headed by People under Age 25, 1999: Total Households

(number and percent distribution of total households and households headed by people under age 25, by household income, 1999; households in thousands as of 2000)

	total	aged 15 to 24
Total households	**104,705**	**5,860**
Under $10,000	9,656	1,043
$10,000 to $19,999	15,142	1,239
$20,000 to $29,999	14,128	1,236
$30,000 to $39,999	12,398	799
$40,000 to $49,999	10,524	565
$50,000 to $59,999	8,853	371
$60,000 to $69,999	7,492	202
$70,000 to $79,999	5,830	113
$80,000 to $89,999	4,549	84
$90,000 to $99,999	3,303	53
$100,000 or more	12,831	154
Median income	$40,816	$25,171
Total households	**100.0%**	**100.0%**
Under $10,000	9.2	17.8
$10,000 to $19,999	14.5	21.1
$20,000 to $29,999	13.5	21.1
$30,000 to $39,999	11.8	13.6
$40,000 to $49,999	10.1	9.6
$50,000 to $59,999	8.5	6.3
$60,000 to $69,999	7.2	3.4
$70,000 to $79,999	5.6	1.9
$80,000 to $89,999	4.3	1.4
$90,000 to $99,999	3.2	0.9
$100,000 or more	12.3	2.6

Source: Bureau of the Census, data from the 2000 Current Population Survey, Internet site <http://ferret.bls.census.gov/macro/032000/hhinc/new02_001.htm>; calculations by New Strategist

Income Distribution of Households Headed by People under Age 25, 1999: Black Households

(number and percent distribution of total black households and black households headed by people under age 25, by household income, 1999; households in thousands as of 2000)

	total	aged 15 to 24
Total black households	**12,849**	**1,002**
Under $10,000	2,368	375
$10,000 to $19,999	2,428	196
$20,000 to $29,999	1,973	201
$30,000 to $39,999	1,498	97
$40,000 to $49,999	1,150	47
$50,000 to $59,999	930	46
$60,000 to $69,999	687	14
$70,000 to $79,999	428	5
$80,000 to $89,999	325	0
$90,000 to $99,999	275	17
$100,000 or more	788	3
Median income	$27,910	$15,576
Total black households	**100.0%**	**100.0%**
Under $10,000	18.4	37.4
$10,000 to $19,999	18.9	19.6
$20,000 to $29,999	15.4	20.1
$30,000 to $39,999	11.7	9.7
$40,000 to $49,999	9.0	4.7
$50,000 to $59,999	7.2	4.6
$60,000 to $69,999	5.3	1.4
$70,000 to $79,999	3.3	0.5
$80,000 to $89,999	2.5	0.0
$90,000 to $99,999	2.1	1.7
$100,000 or more	6.1	0.3

Source: Bureau of the Census, data from the 2000 Current Population Survey, Internet site <http://ferret.bls .census.gov/macro/032000/hhinc/new02_003.htm>; calculations by New Strategist

Income Distribution of Households Headed by People under Age 25, 1999: Hispanic Households

(number and percent distribution of total Hispanic households and Hispanic households headed by people under age 25, by household income, 1999; households in thousands as of 2000)

	total	aged 15 to 24
Total Hispanic households	**9,319**	**871**
Under $10,000	1,107	128
$10,000 to $19,999	1,813	226
$20,000 to $29,999	1,617	193
$30,000 to $39,999	1,281	109
$40,000 to $49,999	974	82
$50,000 to $59,999	645	44
$60,000 to $69,999	550	30
$70,000 to $79,999	389	18
$80,000 to $89,999	254	12
$90,000 to $99,999	203	8
$100,000 or more	488	17
Median income	$30,735	$24,268
Total Hispanic households	**100.0%**	**100.0%**
Under $10,000	11.9	14.7
$10,000 to $19,999	19.5	25.9
$20,000 to $29,999	17.4	22.2
$30,000 to $39,999	13.7	12.5
$40,000 to $49,999	10.5	9.4
$50,000 to $59,999	6.9	5.1
$60,000 to $69,999	5.9	3.4
$70,000 to $79,999	4.2	2.1
$80,000 to $89,999	2.7	1.4
$90,000 to $99,999	2.2	0.9
$100,000 or more	5.2	2.0

Source: Bureau of the Census, data from the 2000 Current Population Survey, Internet site <http://ferret.bls .census.gov/macro/032000/hhinc/new02_004.htm>; calculations by New Strategist

Income Distribution of Households Headed by People under Age 25, 1999: White Households

(number and percent distribution of total white households and white households headed by people under age 25, by household income, 1999; households in thousands as of 2000)

	total	aged 15 to 24
Total white households	**87,671**	**4,541**
Under $10,000	6,856	599
$10,000 to $19,999	12,231	968
$20,000 to $29,999	11,701	975
$30,000 to $39,999	10,414	665
$40,000 to $49,999	8,976	495
$50,000 to $59,999	7,576	302
$60,000 to $69,999	6,547	184
$70,000 to $79,999	5,135	105
$80,000 to $89,999	4,039	79
$90,000 to $99,999	2,895	36
$100,000 or more	11,298	135
Median income	$42,504	$26,787
Total white households	**100.0%**	**100.0%**
Under $10,000	7.8	13.2
$10,000 to $19,999	14.0	21.3
$20,000 to $29,999	13.3	21.5
$30,000 to $39,999	11.9	14.6
$40,000 to $49,999	10.2	10.9
$50,000 to $59,999	8.6	6.7
$60,000 to $69,999	7.5	4.1
$70,000 to $79,999	5.9	2.3
$80,000 to $89,999	4.6	1.7
$90,000 to $99,999	3.3	0.8
$100,000 or more	12.9	3.0

Source: Bureau of the Census, data from the 2000 Current Population Survey, Internet site <http://ferret.bls .census.gov/macro/032000/hhinc/new02_002.htm>; calculations by New Strategist

Income Distribution of Households Headed by
People under Age 25, 1999: Non-Hispanic White Households

(number and percent distribution of total non-Hispanic white households and non-Hispanic white households headed by people under age 25, by household income, 1999; households in thousands as of 2000)

	total	aged 15 to 24
Total non-Hispanic white households	**78,819**	**3,721**
Under $10,000	5,813	485
$10,000 to $19,999	10,513	758
$20,000 to $29,999	10,152	785
$30,000 to $39,999	9,179	557
$40,000 to $49,999	8,050	421
$50,000 to $59,999	6,975	262
$60,000 to $69,999	6,025	154
$70,000 to $79,999	4,764	86
$80,000 to $89,999	3,795	66
$90,000 to $99,999	2,714	29
$100,000 or more	10,841	118
Median income	$44,366	$27,237
Total non-Hispanic white households	**100.0%**	**100.0%**
Under $10,000	7.4	13.0
$10,000 to $19,999	13.3	20.4
$20,000 to $29,999	12.9	21.1
$30,000 to $39,999	11.6	15.0
$40,000 to $49,999	10.2	11.3
$50,000 to $59,999	8.8	7.0
$60,000 to $69,999	7.6	4.1
$70,000 to $79,999	6.0	2.3
$80,000 to $89,999	4.8	1.8
$90,000 to $99,999	3.4	0.8
$100,000 or more	13.8	3.2

Source: Bureau of the Census, data from the 2000 Current Population Survey, Internet site <http://ferret.bls .census.gov/macro/032000/hhinc/new02_005.htm>; calculations by New Strategist

Male-Headed Families Are the Most Affluent

Their median income is slightly higher than that of married couples.

For most age groups, married couples are the most affluent household type. Among households headed by people under age 25, however, the $35,692 median income of male-headed families is higher than the $30,399 median of married couples. Female-headed families had a median income of just $16,071, while women who live alone had the lowest incomes with a median of just $14,587.

Behind the higher incomes of male-headed families is the higher number of earners per household. In fully 31 percent of married couples under age 25, only the husband is in the labor force—a larger proportion than in any other age group. Many of these couples have young children, and the mother has chosen not to work. Male-headed families often have more than one working adult in the household, boosting their incomes.

♦ As young wives age into their late twenties and early thirties, a larger share will go to work, making married couples the most affluent household type.

Women who live alone have the lowest incomes

(median income of householders under age 25 by household type, 1999)

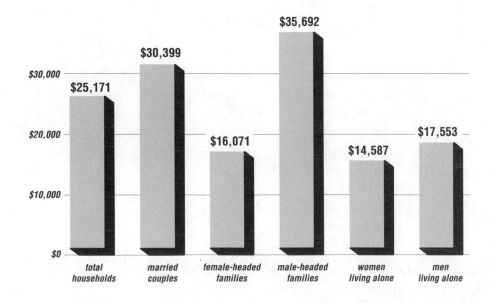

Income Distribution of Households by Household Type, 1999: Aged 15 to 24

(number and percent distribution of households headed by people aged 15 to 24, by household income and household type, 1999; households in thousands as of 2000)

| | | family households | | | nonfamily households | | | |
| | | | | | female householder | | male householder | |
	total	married couples	female hh no spouse present	male hh no spouse present	total	living alone	total	living alone
Total households	5,860	1,450	1,342	560	1,221	587	1,286	556
Under $10,000	1,043	83	468	44	254	204	192	131
$10,000 to $19,999	1,239	249	313	66	297	193	313	184
$20,000 to $29,999	1,236	380	225	108	251	119	272	117
$30,000 to $39,999	799	269	116	103	138	43	173	59
$40,000 to $49,999	565	190	86	74	96	9	119	27
$50,000 to $59,999	371	103	49	53	79	10	89	23
$60,000 to $69,999	202	73	26	31	35	2	37	7
$70,000 to $79,999	113	43	18	11	16	0	24	7
$80,000 to $89,999	84	16	10	19	16	0	22	0
$90,000 to $99,999	53	9	13	21	5	0	6	0
$100,000 or more	154	32	19	30	34	9	40	0
Median income	$25,171	$30,399	$16,071	$35,692	$21,962	$14,587	$24,361	$17,553
Total households	100.0%	100.0%	100.0%	100.0%	100.0%	100.0%	100.0%	100.0%
Under $10,000	17.8	5.7	34.9	7.9	20.8	34.8	14.9	23.6
$10,000 to $19,999	21.1	17.2	23.3	11.8	24.3	32.9	24.3	33.1
$20,000 to $29,999	21.1	26.2	16.8	19.3	20.6	20.3	21.2	21.0
$30,000 to $39,999	13.6	18.6	8.6	18.4	11.3	7.3	13.5	10.6
$40,000 to $49,999	9.6	13.1	6.4	13.2	7.9	1.5	9.3	4.9
$50,000 to $59,999	6.3	7.1	3.7	9.5	6.5	1.7	6.9	4.1
$60,000 to $69,999	3.4	5.0	1.9	5.5	2.9	0.3	2.9	1.3
$70,000 to $79,999	1.9	3.0	1.3	2.0	1.3	0.0	1.9	1.3
$80,000 to $89,999	1.4	1.1	0.7	3.4	1.3	0.0	1.7	0.0
$90,000 to $99,999	0.9	0.6	1.0	3.8	0.4	0.0	0.5	0.0
$100,000 or more	2.6	2.2	1.4	5.4	2.8	1.5	3.1	0.0

Source: Bureau of the Census, data from the 2000 Current Population Survey, Internet site <http://ferret.bls .census.gov/macro/032000/hhinc/new02_000.htm>; calculations by New Strategist

Children in Married-Couple Families Are Better Off

Among families with children, married couples are far more affluent than single parents.

Children with two parents in the household benefit from a second income, which is now the norm for married couples. Among all families with children under age 18 at home, the median income of married couples stood at $60,168 in 1999. It was $32,427 for male-headed families and just $19,934 for female-headed families. Among families with children under age 18, married couples head fully 95 percent of those with incomes of $100,000 or more. Female-headed families account for the majority of those with incomes below $20,000.

Married couples with children aged 6 to 17 have the highest incomes, a median of $64,311 in 1999. More than one in five has an income of $100,000 or more. The incomes of male- and female-headed families with school-aged children also surpass the incomes of those with younger children. Most householders with school-aged children are in their peak earning years, which accounts for their above-average incomes. Female-headed families with preschoolers have the lowest incomes—a median of just $14,755 in 1999.

♦ The financial well-being of children depends largely on the type of household in which they live. Those with married parents fare much better than those in single-parent homes.

Single-parent families have the lowest incomes

(median income of families with children under age 18 at home by family type, 1999)

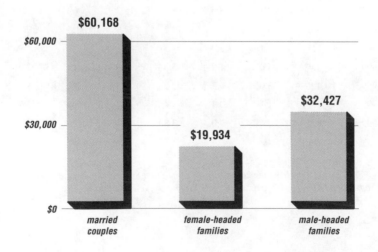

Income Distribution of Households with Children under Age 18 by Family Type, 1999

(number and percent distribution of families with related children under age 18 at home, by household income and family type, 1999; families in thousands as of 2000)

	total families	married couples	female-headed families	male-headed families
Total families	**37,277**	**26,373**	**8,736**	**2,169**
Under $10,000	2,855	499	2,144	213
$10,000 to $19,999	4,143	1,516	2,237	390
$20,000 to $29,999	4,195	2,283	1,549	363
$30,000 to $39,999	4,281	2,939	1,013	329
$40,000 to $49,999	3,868	2,977	643	248
$50,000 to $59,999	3,461	2,912	372	177
$60,000 to $69,999	3,189	2,778	266	145
$70,000 to $79,999	2,520	2,266	180	74
$80,000 to $89,999	1,937	1,791	90	56
$90,000 to $99,999	1,481	1,356	78	47
$100,000 or more	5,345	5,054	166	124
Median income	$47,949	$60,168	$19,934	$32,427

Distribution of families by income

	total families	married couples	female-headed families	male-headed families
Total families	**100.0%**	**100.0%**	**100.0%**	**100.0%**
Under $10,000	7.7	1.9	24.5	9.8
$10,000 to $19,999	11.1	5.7	25.6	18.0
$20,000 to $29,999	11.3	8.7	17.7	16.7
$30,000 to $39,999	11.5	11.1	11.6	15.2
$40,000 to $49,999	10.4	11.3	7.4	11.4
$50,000 to $59,999	9.3	11.0	4.3	8.2
$60,000 to $69,999	8.6	10.5	3.0	6.7
$70,000 to $79,999	6.8	8.6	2.1	3.4
$80,000 to $89,999	5.2	6.8	1.0	2.6
$90,000 to $99,999	4.0	5.1	0.9	2.2
$100,000 or more	14.3	19.2	1.9	5.7

(continued)

(continued from previous page)

	total families	married couples	female-headed families	male-headed families
Distribution of families by family type				
Total families	**100.0%**	**70.7%**	**23.4%**	**5.8%**
Under $10,000	100.0	17.5	75.1	7.5
$10,000 to $19,999	100.0	36.6	54.0	9.4
$20,000 to $29,999	100.0	54.4	36.9	8.7
$30,000 to $39,999	100.0	68.7	23.7	7.7
$40,000 to $49,999	100.0	77.0	16.6	6.4
$50,000 to $59,999	100.0	84.1	10.7	5.1
$60,000 to $69,999	100.0	87.1	8.3	4.5
$70,000 to $79,999	100.0	89.9	7.1	2.9
$80,000 to $89,999	100.0	92.5	4.6	2.9
$90,000 to $99,999	100.0	91.6	5.3	3.2
$100,000 or more	100.0	94.6	3.1	2.3

Source: Bureau of the Census, Money Income in the United States: 1999, Current Population Reports, P60-209, 2000; and Internet sites <http://ferret.bls.census.gov/macro/032000/faminc/new03_016.htm> and <http://ferret.bls.census.gov/macro/032000/faminc/new03_011.htm>; calculations by New Strategist

Income Distribution of Married-Couple Families with Children under Age 18, 1999

(number and percent distribution of total married-couple households and those with related children under age 18 at home, by household income and age of children, 1999; households in thousands as of 2000)

		with one or more children under age 18			
	total	*total*	*all under 6*	*some under 6 some 6 to 17*	*all 6 to 17*
Total couples	**55,315**	**26,373**	**6,340**	**5,875**	**14,157**
Under $10,000	1,328	499	143	112	244
$10,000 to $19,999	4,266	1,516	403	414	699
$20,000 to $29,999	5,868	2,283	645	648	990
$30,000 to $39,999	6,181	2,939	778	813	1,348
$40,000 to $49,999	6,026	2,977	695	740	1,541
$50,000 to $59,999	5,687	2,912	716	687	1,510
$60,000 to $69,999	5,199	2,778	638	583	1,558
$70,000 to $79,999	4,307	2,266	576	455	1,235
$80,000 to $89,999	3,492	1,791	398	287	1,106
$90,000 to $99,999	2,624	1,356	239	256	861
$100,000 or more	10,336	5,054	1,107	883	3,065
Median income	$56,676	$60,168	$56,837	$52,794	$64,311
Total couples	**100.0%**	**100.0%**	**100.0%**	**100.0%**	**100.0%**
Under $10,000	2.4	1.9	2.3	1.9	1.7
$10,000 to $19,999	7.7	5.7	6.4	7.1	4.9
$20,000 to $29,999	10.6	8.7	10.2	11.0	6.0
$30,000 to $39,999	11.2	11.1	12.3	13.8	9.5
$40,000 to $49,999	10.9	11.3	10.0	12.6	10.9
$50,000 to $59,999	10.3	11.0	11.3	11.7	10.7
$60,000 to $69,999	9.4	10.5	10.1	9.9	11.0
$70,000 to $79,999	7.8	8.6	9.1	7.7	8.7
$80,000 to $89,999	6.3	6.8	6.3	4.9	7.8
$90,000 to $99,999	4.7	5.1	3.8	4.4	6.1
$100,000 or more	18.7	19.2	17.5	15.0	21.7

Source: Bureau of the Census, Money Income in the United States: 1999, *Current Population Reports, P60-209, 2000; calculations by New Strategist*

Income Distribution of Female-Headed Families with Children under Age 18, 1999

(number and percent distribution of total female-headed households and those with related children under age 18 at home, by household income and age of children, 1999; households in thousands as of 2000)

	total	with one or more children under age 18			
		total	all under 6	some under 6 some 6 to 17	all 6 to 17
Total female-headed families	**12,687**	**8,736**	**1,874**	**1,686**	**5,176**
Under $10,000	2,502	2,144	657	526	961
$10,000 to $19,999	2,927	2,237	501	478	1,258
$20,000 to $29,999	2,256	1,549	302	296	951
$30,000 to $39,999	1,600	1,013	157	134	721
$40,000 to $49,999	1,167	643	82	110	453
$50,000 to $59,999	687	372	53	37	279
$60,000 to $69,999	543	266	49	35	181
$70,000 to $79,999	338	180	25	24	130
$80,000 to $89,999	200	90	18	7	65
$90,000 to $99,999	161	78	5	14	58
$100,000 or more	306	166	22	26	118
Median income	$23,732	$19,934	$14,755	$15,878	$23,306
Total female-headed families	**100.0%**	**100.0%**	**100.0%**	**100.0%**	**100.0%**
Under $10,000	19.7	24.5	35.1	31.2	18.6
$10,000 to $19,999	23.1	25.6	26.7	28.4	24.3
$20,000 to $29,999	17.8	17.7	16.1	17.6	18.4
$30,000 to $39,999	12.6	11.6	8.4	7.9	13.9
$40,000 to $49,999	9.2	7.4	4.4	6.5	8.8
$50,000 to $59,999	5.4	4.3	2.8	2.2	5.4
$60,000 to $69,999	4.3	3.0	2.6	2.1	3.5
$70,000 to $79,999	2.7	2.1	1.3	1.4	2.5
$80,000 to $89,999	1.6	1.0	1.0	0.4	1.3
$90,000 to $99,999	1.3	0.9	0.3	0.8	1.1
$100,000 or more	2.4	1.9	1.2	1.5	2.3

Source: Bureau of the Census, data from the 2000 Current Population Survey; Internet site <http://ferret.bls .census.gov/macro/032000/faminc/new03_016.htm>; calculations by New Strategist

Income Distribution of Male-Headed Families with Children under Age 18, 1999

(number and percent distribution of total male-headed households and those with related children under age 18 at home, by household income and age of children, 1999; households in thousands as of 2000)

	total	with one or more children under age 18 total	all under 6	some under 6 some 6 to 17	all 6 to 17
Total male-headed families	**4,028**	**2,169**	**591**	**285**	**1,293**
Under $10,000	315	213	69	32	112
$10,000 to $19,999	589	390	167	61	163
$20,000 to $29,999	619	363	115	40	208
$30,000 to $39,999	610	329	86	55	189
$40,000 to $49,999	466	248	54	32	163
$50,000 to $59,999	399	177	26	14	138
$60,000 to $69,999	288	145	23	15	107
$70,000 to $79,999	167	74	15	7	53
$80,000 to $89,999	156	56	10	6	40
$90,000 to $99,999	107	47	8	7	31
$100,000 or more	314	124	18	15	92
Median income	$37,396	$32,427	$25,722	$31,347	$37,758
Total male-headed families	**100.0%**	**100.0%**	**100.0%**	**100.0%**	**100.0%**
Under $10,000	7.8	9.8	11.7	11.2	8.7
$10,000 to $19,999	14.6	18.0	28.3	21.4	12.6
$20,000 to $29,999	15.4	16.7	19.5	14.0	16.1
$30,000 to $39,999	15.1	15.2	14.6	19.3	14.6
$40,000 to $49,999	11.6	11.4	9.1	11.2	12.6
$50,000 to $59,999	9.9	8.2	4.4	4.9	10.7
$60,000 to $69,999	7.1	6.7	3.9	5.3	8.3
$70,000 to $79,999	4.1	3.4	2.5	2.5	4.1
$80,000 to $89,999	3.9	2.6	1.7	2.1	3.1
$90,000 to $99,999	2.7	2.2	1.4	2.5	2.4
$100,000 or more	7.8	5.7	3.0	5.3	7.1

Source: Bureau of the Census, data from the 2000 Current Population Survey; Internet site <http://ferret.bls .census.gov/macro/032000/faminc/new03_011.htm>; calculations by New Strategist

Young Adults Have Seen Little Income Growth

Men's incomes have declined since 1980.

Between 1980 and 1999, men under age 25 saw their median income fall a substantial 11 percent, after adjusting for inflation, while their female counterparts experienced a modest 6 percent increase. Behind this divergence is the long-term decline in wages for entry-level workers and the rising college enrollment rate. As more young adults go to college, fewer have full-time jobs, holding down the median income.

During the 1990s, young adults saw some improvement in their incomes. The median income of men under age 25 grew 3 percent between 1990 and 1999, while women's rose 7 percent. Nevertheless, the median income of young adults remains far below average.

♦ The median income of young adults is low because many are going to school rather than working. In the years ahead, this sacrifice will be rewarded with much higher earnings.

Among young adults, only women's incomes have grown

(percent change in median income of people under age 25, by sex, 1980–99; in 1999 dollars)

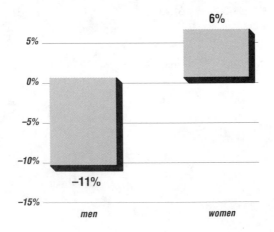

Median Income of Men under Age 25, 1980 to 1999

(median income of men aged 15 or older and aged 15 to 24 with income, 1980 to 1999; percent change for selected years; in 1999 dollars)

	total	men aged 15 to 24
1999	$27,275	$8,302
1998	27,077	8,371
1997	26,171	7,752
1996	25,308	7,391
1995	24,664	7,557
1994	24,417	7,923
1993	24,330	7,412
1992	24,290	7,478
1991	25,038	7,683
1990	25,867	8,055
1989	26,728	8,482
1988	26,627	8,229
1987	26,084	8,003
1986	26,014	8,031
1985	25,255	7,734
1984	25,015	7,551
1983	24,473	7,166
1982	24,310	7,715
1981	24,912	5,681
1980	25,364	9,306
Percent change		
1998–1999	0.7%	–0.8%
1990–1999	5.4	3.1
1980–1999	7.5	–10.8

Source: Bureau of the Census, unpublished data from the Current Population Survey, Internet site <www.census.gov/hhes/income/histinc/p08.html>; calculations by New Strategist

Median Income of Women under Age 25, 1980 to 1999

(median income of women aged 15 or older and aged 15 to 24 with income, 1980 to 1999; percent change for selected years; in 1999 dollars)

	total	women aged 15 to 24
1999	$15,311	$6,689
1998	14,749	6,678
1997	14,223	6,583
1996	13,607	6,245
1995	13,261	5,804
1994	12,890	6,192
1993	12,735	6,169
1992	12,722	6,139
1991	12,814	6,357
1990	12,836	6,248
1989	12,930	6,367
1988	12,511	6,316
1987	12,165	6,465
1986	11,568	6,147
1985	11,174	5,870
1984	11,013	5,787
1983	10,569	5,783
1982	10,259	5,841
1981	10,092	3,691
1980	9,959	6,324
Percent change		
1998–1999	3.8%	0.2%
1990–1999	19.3	7.1
1980–1999	53.7	5.8

Source: Bureau of the Census, unpublished data from the Current Population Survey, Internet site <www .census.gov/hhes/income/histinc/p08.html>; calculations by New Strategist

Incomes of Young Men Are Low

Their incomes are low because few work full-time.

The median income of men under age 25 stood at just $8,302 in 1999. The reason for the low figure is that few men in the age group work full-time—only 23 percent, versus 56 percent of all men aged 16 or older. But even among those who work full-time, median income was $19,515, still well below the $37,574 median of all men who work full-time.

Among men under age 25, Hispanics are most likely to work full-time, and 30 percent do so. Consequently, the median income of young Hispanic men is higher than that of non-Hispanic whites or blacks. But among full-time workers in the age group, non-Hispanic whites have the highest incomes—a median of $20,609 in 1999, compared with $17,176 for blacks and $16,664 for Hispanics.

◆ Young men have low incomes because many are in school and work only part-time. They will be rewarded for their investment in education as they age and advance in their careers.

Among men, non-Hispanic whites have the highest incomes

(median income of men under age 25 who work full-time by race and Hispanic origin, 1999)

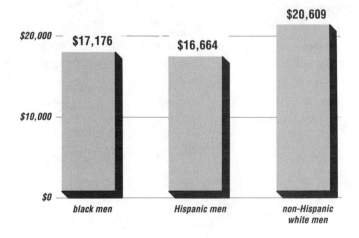

Income Distribution of Men under Age 25, 1999: Total Men

(number and percent distribution of men aged 15 or older and under age 25 by income, 1999; median income by work status, and percent working year-round, full-time; men in thousands as of 2000)

	total	aged 15 to 24
Total men	**103,114**	**19,503**
Without income	7,091	5,075
With income	96,023	14,428
Under $10,000	17,036	7,966
$10,000 to $19,999	18,366	3,585
$20,000 to $29,999	15,982	1,818
$30,000 to $39,999	12,874	630
$40,000 to $49,999	9,345	224
$50,000 to $74,999	12,559	148
$75,000 to $99,999	4,520	41
$100,000 or more	5,346	16
Median income of men with income	$27,275	$8,302
Median income of full-time workers	37,574	19,515
Percent working full-time	55.8%	22.9%
Total men	**100.0%**	**100.0%**
Without income	6.9	26.0
With income	93.1	74.0
Under $10,000	16.5	40.8
$10,000 to $19,999	17.8	18.4
$20,000 to $29,999	15.5	9.3
$30,000 to $39,999	12.5	3.2
$40,000 to $49,999	9.1	1.1
$50,000 to $74,999	12.2	0.8
$75,000 to $99,999	4.4	0.2
$100,000 or more	5.2	0.1

Source: Bureau of the Census, data from the 2000 Current Population Survey, Internet site <http://ferret.bls .census.gov/macro/032000/perinc/new01_000.htm>; calculations by New Strategist

Income Distribution of Men under Age 25, 1999: Black Men

(number and percent distribution of black men aged 15 or older and under age 25 by income, 1999; median income by work status, and percent working year-round, full-time; men in thousands as of 2000)

	total	aged 15 to 24
Total black men	**11,687**	**2,809**
Without income	1,620	1,120
With income	10,067	1,689
Under $10,000	2,621	1,071
$10,000 to $19,999	2,253	354
$20,000 to $29,999	1,817	176
$30,000 to $39,999	1,267	70
$40,000 to $49,999	804	12
$50,000 to $74,999	864	6
$75,000 to $99,999	244	0
$100,000 or more	192	0
Median income of men with income	$20,579	$6,691
Median income of full-time workers	30,297	17,176
Percent working full-time	48.3%	16.6%
Total black men	**100.0%**	**100.0%**
Without income	13.9	39.9
With income	86.1	60.1
Under $10,000	22.4	38.1
$10,000 to $19,999	19.3	12.6
$20,000 to $29,999	15.5	6.3
$30,000 to $39,999	10.8	2.5
$40,000 to $49,999	6.9	0.4
$50,000 to $74,999	7.4	0.2
$75,000 to $99,999	2.1	0.0
$100,000 or more	1.6	0.0

Source: Bureau of the Census, data from the 2000 Current Population Survey, Internet site <http://ferret.bls .census.gov/macro/032000/perinc/new01_000.htm>; calculations by New Strategist

Income Distribution of Men under Age 25, 1999: Hispanic Men

(number and percent distribution of Hispanic men aged 15 or older and under age 25 by income, 1999; median income by work status, and percent working year-round, full-time; men in thousands as of 2000)

	total	aged 15 to 24
Total Hispanic men	**11,327**	**2,962**
Without income	1,282	932
With income	10,045	2,030
Under $10,000	2,189	909
$10,000 to $19,999	3,275	739
$20,000 to $29,999	1,956	263
$30,000 to $39,999	1,096	70
$40,000 to $49,999	625	30
$50,000 to $74,999	616	13
$75,000 to $99,999	158	3
$100,000 or more	129	3
Median income of men with income	$18,234	$11,048
Median income of full-time workers	23,342	16,664
Percent working full-time	57.2%	30.4%
Total Hispanic men	**100.0%**	**100.0%**
Without income	11.3	31.5
With income	88.7	68.5
Under $10,000	19.3	30.7
$10,000 to $19,999	28.9	24.9
$20,000 to $29,999	17.3	8.9
$30,000 to $39,999	9.7	2.4
$40,000 to $49,999	5.5	1.0
$50,000 to $74,999	5.4	0.4
$75,000 to $99,999	1.4	0.1
$100,000 or more	1.1	0.1

Source: Bureau of the Census, data from the 2000 Current Population Survey, Internet site <http://ferret.bls .census.gov/macro/032000/perinc/new01_000.htm>; calculations by New Strategist

Income Distribution of Men under Age 25, 1999: White Men

(number and percent distribution of white men aged 15 or older and under age 25 by income, 1999; median income by work status, and percent working year-round, full-time; men in thousands as of 2000)

	total	aged 15 to 24
Total white men	**86,443**	**15,543**
Without income	4,869	3,520
With income	81,574	12,023
Under $10,000	13,498	6,492
$10,000 to $19,999	15,276	3,057
$20,000 to $29,999	13,493	1,557
$30,000 to $39,999	11,040	536
$40,000 to $49,999	8,202	206
$50,000 to $74,999	11,130	120
$75,000 to $99,999	4,056	41
$100,000 or more	4,876	16
Median income of men with income	$28,564	$8,689
Median income of full-time workers	39,331	19,650
Percent working full-time	56.9%	24.6%
Total white men	**100.0%**	**100.0%**
Without income	5.6	22.6
With income	94.4	77.4
Under $10,000	15.6	41.8
$10,000 to $19,999	17.7	19.7
$20,000 to $29,999	15.6	10.0
$30,000 to $39,999	12.8	3.4
$40,000 to $49,999	9.5	1.3
$50,000 to $74,999	12.9	0.8
$75,000 to $99,999	4.7	0.3
$100,000 or more	5.6	0.1

Source: Bureau of the Census, data from the 2000 Current Population Survey, Internet site <http://ferret.bls .census.gov/macro/032000/perinc/new01_000.htm>; calculations by New Strategist

Income Distribution of Men under Age 25, 1999: Non-Hispanic White Men

(number and percent distribution of non-Hispanic white men aged 15 or older and under age 25 by income, 1999; median income by work status, and percent working year-round, full-time; men in thousands as of 2000)

	total	aged 15 to 24
Total non-Hispanic white men	**75,692**	**12,715**
Without income	3,665	2,635
With income	72,027	10,080
Under $10,000	11,433	5,631
$10,000 to $19,999	12,140	2,345
$20,000 to $29,999	11,635	1,307
$30,000 to $39,999	9,992	467
$40,000 to $49,999	7,615	174
$50,000 to $74,999	10,551	106
$75,000 to $99,999	3,908	38
$100,000 or more	4,752	13
Median income of men with income	$30,594	$8,091
Median income of full-time workers	41,406	20,609
Percent working full-time	56.8%	23.2%
Total non-Hispanic white men	**100.0%**	**100.0%**
Without income	4.8	20.7
With income	95.2	79.3
Under $10,000	15.1	44.3
$10,000 to $19,999	16.0	18.4
$20,000 to $29,999	15.4	10.3
$30,000 to $39,999	13.2	3.7
$40,000 to $49,999	10.1	1.4
$50,000 to $74,999	13.9	0.8
$75,000 to $99,999	5.2	0.3
$100,000 or more	6.3	0.1

Source: Bureau of the Census, data from the 2000 Current Population Survey, Internet site <http://ferret.bls .census.gov/macro/032000/perinc/new01_000.htm>; calculations by New Strategist

Incomes of Young Women Are Low

Fewer than 20 percent of women under age 25 work full-time.

The median income of women under age 25 is even lower than that of their male counter-parts, standing at just $8,302 in 1999. The figures are low for both men and women because few in the age group work full-time. Only 17 percent of women under age 25 work full-time compared with 37 percent of all women aged 16 or older. But even among those who work full-time, median income was $17,851, still well below the $27,370 median of all women who work full-time.

Among women under age 25, non-Hispanic whites are most likely to work full-time, and 22 percent do so. Incomes are highest among black women who work full-time, a median of $18,539. Hispanic women with full-time jobs have the lowest incomes—a median of $15,602 in 1999. The median income of non-Hispanic white women under age 25 who work full-time is $17,699.

♦ Young women are even more likely to be in school than young men, and many work part-time. Their incomes will rise as they gain the credentials to advance in the job market.

Among young women, blacks have the highest incomes

(median income of women under age 25 who work full-time by race and Hispanic origin, 1999)

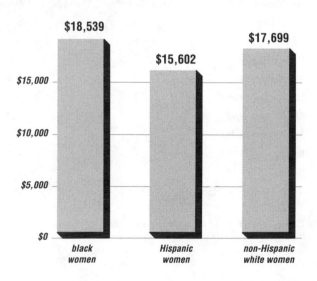

Income Distribution of Women under Age 25, 1999: Total Women

(number and percent distribution of women aged 15 or older and under age 25 by income, 1999; median income by work status, and percent working year-round, full-time; women in thousands as of 2000)

	total	aged 15 to 24
Total women	**110,660**	**19,040**
Without income	11,047	5,083
With income	99,613	13,957
Under $10,000	35,356	8,754
$10,000 to $19,999	24,607	3,322
$20,000 to $29,999	16,038	1,302
$30,000 to $39,999	9,839	377
$40,000 to $49,999	5,632	112
$50,000 to $74,999	5,466	56
$75,000 to $99,999	1,491	12
$100,000 or more	1,185	22
Median income of women with income	$15,311	$6,689
Median income of full-time workers	27,370	17,851
Percent working full-time	36.5%	17.5%
Total women	**100.0%**	**100.0%**
Without income	10.0	26.7
With income	90.0	73.3
Under $10,000	32.0	46.0
$10,000 to $19,999	22.2	17.4
$20,000 to $29,999	14.5	6.8
$30,000 to $39,999	8.9	2.0
$40,000 to $49,999	5.1	0.6
$50,000 to $74,999	4.9	0.3
$75,000 to $99,999	1.3	0.1
$100,000 or more	1.1	0.1

Source: Bureau of the Census, data from the 2000 Current Population Survey, Internet site <http://ferret.bls .census.gov/macro/032000/perinc/new01_000.htm>; calculations by New Strategist

Income Distribution of Women under Age 25, 1999: Black Women

(number and percent distribution of black women aged 15 or older and under age 25 by income, 1999; median income by work status, and percent working year-round, full-time; women in thousands as of 2000)

	total	aged 15 to 24
Total black women	**14,167**	**3,011**
Without income	1,735	995
With income	12,432	2,016
Under $10,000	4,504	1,332
$10,000 to $19,999	3,172	412
$20,000 to $29,999	2,110	188
$30,000 to $39,999	1,289	58
$40,000 to $49,999	623	17
$50,000 to $74,999	542	6
$75,000 to $99,999	99	3
$100,000 or more	91	0
Median income of women with income	$14,771	$6,497
Median income of full-time workers	25,142	18,539
Percent working full-time	41.6%	14.8%
Total black women	**100.0%**	**100.0%**
Without income	12.2	33.0
With income	87.8	67.0
Under $10,000	31.8	44.2
$10,000 to $19,999	22.4	13.7
$20,000 to $29,999	14.9	6.2
$30,000 to $39,999	9.1	1.9
$40,000 to $49,999	4.4	0.6
$50,000 to $74,999	3.8	0.2
$75,000 to $99,999	0.7	0.1
$100,000 or more	0.6	0.0

Source: Bureau of the Census, data from the 2000 Current Population Survey, Internet site <http://ferret.bls .census.gov/macro/032000/perinc/new01_000.htm>; calculations by New Strategist

Income Distribution of Women under Age 25, 1999: Hispanic Women

(number and percent distribution of Hispanic women aged 15 or older and under age 25 by income, 1999; median income by work status, and percent working year-round, full-time; women in thousands as of 2000)

	total	aged 15 to 24
Total Hispanic women	**11,466**	**2,681**
Without income	2,717	1,129
With income	8,749	1,552
Under $10,000	3,901	936
$10,000 to $19,999	2,514	432
$20,000 to $29,999	1,148	137
$30,000 to $39,999	552	28
$40,000 to $49,999	304	10
$50,000 to $74,999	230	5
$75,000 to $99,999	45	2
$100,000 or more	52	3
Median income of women with income	$11,314	$7,189
Median income of full-time workers	20,052	15,602
Percent working full-time	32.9%	17.2%
Total Hispanic women	**100.0%**	**100.0%**
Without income	23.7	42.1
With income	76.3	57.9
Under $10,000	34.0	34.9
$10,000 to $19,999	21.9	16.1
$20,000 to $29,999	10.0	5.1
$30,000 to $39,999	4.8	1.0
$40,000 to $49,999	2.7	0.4
$50,000 to $74,999	2.0	0.2
$75,000 to $99,999	0.4	0.1
$100,000 or more	0.5	0.1

Source: Bureau of the Census, data from the 2000 Current Population Survey, Internet site <http://ferret.bls .census.gov/macro/032000/perinc/new01_000.htm>; calculations by New Strategist

Income Distribution of Women under Age 25, 1999: White Women

(number and percent distribution of white women aged 15 or older and under age 25 by income, 1999; median income by work status, and percent working year-round, full-time; women in thousands as of 2000)

	total	aged 15 to 24
Total white women	**91,138**	**14,971**
Without income	8,357	3,676
With income	82,781	11,295
Under $10,000	29,233	7,028
$10,000 to $19,999	20,486	2,747
$20,000 to $29,999	13,262	1,050
$30,000 to $39,999	8,130	308
$40,000 to $49,999	4,733	93
$50,000 to $74,999	4,591	42
$75,000 to $99,999	1,294	9
$100,000 or more	1,048	17
Median income of women with income	$15,362	$6,723
Median income of full-time workers	28,023	17,699
Percent working full-time	35.7%	18.5%
Total white women	**100.0%**	**100.0%**
Without income	9.2	24.6
With income	90.8	75.4
Under $10,000	32.1	46.9
$10,000 to $19,999	22.5	18.3
$20,000 to $29,999	14.6	7.0
$30,000 to $39,999	8.9	2.1
$40,000 to $49,999	5.2	0.6
$50,000 to $74,999	5.0	0.3
$75,000 to $99,999	1.4	0.1
$100,000 or more	1.1	0.1

Source: Bureau of the Census, data from the 2000 Current Population Survey, Internet site <http://ferret.bls .census.gov/macro/032000/perinc/new01_000.htm>; calculations by New Strategist

Income Distribution of Women under Age 25, 1999: Non-Hispanic White Women

(number and percent distribution of non-Hispanic white women aged 15 or older and under age 25 by income, 1999; median income by work status, and percent working year-round, full-time; women in thousands as of 2000)

	total	aged 15 to 24
Total non-Hispanic white women	**80,228**	**12,422**
Without income	5,732	2,588
With income	74,496	9,834
Under $10,000	25,521	6,147
$10,000 to $19,999	18,121	2,346
$20,000 to $29,999	12,173	920
$30,000 to $39,999	7,608	280
$40,000 to $49,999	4,443	84
$50,000 to $74,999	4,380	37
$75,000 to $99,999	1,251	7
$100,000 or more	1,000	14
Median income of women with income	$15,922	$6,665
Median income of full-time workers	28,023	17,699
Percent working full-time	40.6%	22.3%
Total non-Hispanic white women	**100.0%**	**100.0%**
Without income	7.1	20.8
With income	92.9	79.2
Under $10,000	31.8	49.5
$10,000 to $19,999	22.6	18.9
$20,000 to $29,999	15.2	7.4
$30,000 to $39,999	9.5	2.3
$40,000 to $49,999	5.5	0.7
$50,000 to $74,999	5.5	0.3
$75,000 to $99,999	1.6	0.1
$100,000 or more	1.2	0.1

Source: Bureau of the Census, data from the 2000 Current Population Survey, Internet site <http://ferret.bls.census.gov/macro/032000/perinc/new01_000.htm>; calculations by New Strategist

Children Have the Highest Poverty Rate

The majority of the nation's poor are under age 25.

Children and young adults are much more likely to be poor than older Americans. While 12 percent of all Americans were poor in 1999, the poverty rate among people under age 25 was a much larger 17 percent. Fully 52 percent of the nation's poor are under age 25. Blacks and Hispanics account for the 60 percent majority of poor people under age 18. They account for 45 percent of the poor aged 18 to 24.

Children living in families headed by married couples are much less likely to be poor than those in single-parent families. Only 8 percent of children in married-couple families are poor versus 42 percent of those in female-headed families. The poverty rate is even higher among black and Hispanic children living in single-parent families, where the 52 percent majority is poor.

♦ Poverty rates for children are well above average because many live in female-headed families—the poorest household type. Until single parenthood becomes less common, poverty among the young will remain stubbornly high.

Most of the nation's poor are young

(percent distribution of people living below poverty level by age, 1999)

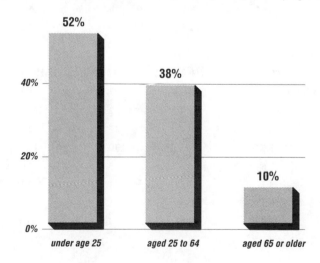

People in Poverty by Age, Race, and Hispanic Origin, 1999

(number, percent, and percent distribution of people with incomes below poverty level by age, race, and Hispanic origin, 1999; people in thousands as of 2000)

	total	black	Hispanic	white	non-Hispanic white
Total people	**32,258**	**8,360**	**7,439**	**21,922**	**14,875**
Under age 18	12,109	3,759	3,506	7,568	4,252
Aged 18 to 24	4,603	1,165	941	3,125	2,236
Aged 25 to 34	3,968	893	1,121	2,792	1,732
Aged 35 to 44	3,733	945	811	2,614	1,845
Aged 45 to 54	2,466	538	422	1,749	1,361
Aged 55 to 59	1,179	231	141	890	750
Aged 60 to 64	1,033	204	140	776	636
Aged 65 or older	3,167	626	358	2,409	2,063
Percent of people in poverty					
Total people	**11.8%**	**23.6%**	**22.8%**	**9.8%**	**7.7%**
Under age 18	16.9	33.1	30.3	13.5	9.4
Aged 18 to 24	17.3	29.3	23.8	14.8	12.9
Aged 25 to 34	10.5	17.3	19.8	9.2	6.9
Aged 35 to 44	8.3	16.6	16.3	7.1	5.7
Aged 45 to 54	6.7	13.1	14.0	5.7	4.9
Aged 55 to 59	9.2	17.9	14.2	8.0	7.4
Aged 60 to 64	9.8	19.8	18.5	8.5	7.6
Aged 65 tor older	9.7	22.7	20.4	8.3	7.6
Percent distribution of poor by age					
Total people	**100.0%**	**100.0%**	**100.0%**	**100.0%**	**100.0%**
Under age 18	37.5	44.0	47.1	34.5	28.6
Aged 18 to 24	14.3	13.9	12.6	14.3	15.0
Aged 25 to 34	12.3	10.7	15.1	12.7	11.6
Aged 35 to 44	11.6	11.3	10.9	11.9	12.4
Aged 45 to 54	7.6	6.4	5.7	7.0	9.1
Aged 55 to 59	3.7	2.8	1.9	4.1	5.0
Aged 60 to 64	3.2	2.4	1.9	3.5	4.3
Aged 65 tor older	9.8	7.5	4.8	10.0	13.9

(continued)

(continued from previous page)

	total	black	Hispanic	white	non-Hispanic white
Percent distribution of poor by race and Hispanic origin					
Total people	**100.0%**	**25.9%**	**23.1%**	**68.0%**	**46.1%**
Under age 18	100.0	31.0	28.0	62.5	35.1
Aged 18 to 24	100.0	25.3	20.4	67.9	48.6
Aged 25 to 34	100.0	22.5	28.3	70.4	43.6
Aged 35 to 44	100.0	25.3	21.7	70.0	49.4
Aged 45 to 54	100.0	21.8	17.1	70.9	55.2
Aged 55 to 59	100.0	19.6	11.0	75.5	63.6
Aged 60 to 64	100.0	19.7	13.6	75.1	61.6
Aged 65 tor older	100.0	19.8	11.3	76.1	65.1

Note: Numbers will not add to total because Hispanics may be of any race and not all races are shown.
Source: Bureau of the Census, Poverty in the United States, *Current Population Reports, P60-210, 2000; calculations by New Strategist*

Children under Age 18 in Poverty by Family Type, 1999

(number, percent, and percent distribution of related children under age 18 in families with incomes below poverty level by family type, race, and Hispanic origin, 1999; people in thousands as of 2000)

	total	black	Hispanic	white	non-Hispanic white
IN MARRIED-COUPLE FAMILIES					
Total poor under age 18	**4,297**	**510**	**1,745**	**3,428**	**1,720**
Under age 6	1,565	146	734	1,331	610
Aged 6 to 17	2,732	365	1,011	2,097	1,110
Percent in poverty					
Total under age 18	**8.4%**	**10.8%**	**22.2%**	**7.9%**	**4.8%**
Under age 6	9.0	10.0	24.0	9.0	5.1
Aged 6 to 17	8.0	11.1	21.1	7.3	4.6
Percent distribution by race and Hispanic origin					
Total under age 18	**100.0%**	**11.9%**	**40.6%**	**79.8%**	**40.0%**
Under age 6	100.0	9.3	46.9	85.0	39.0
Aged 6 to 17	100.0	13.4	37.0	76.8	40.6
IN FEMALE-HEADED FAMILIES					
Total poor under age 18	**6,602**	**2,997**	**1,471**	**3,266**	**1,931**
Under age 6	2,353	1,098	497	1,142	693
Aged 6 to 17	4,249	1,899	974	2,124	1,237
Percent in poverty					
Total under age 18	**41.9%**	**51.7%**	**52.4%**	**35.5%**	**29.0%**
Under age 6	50.3	58.5	54.6	44.4	39.2
Aged 6 to 17	38.3	48.5	51.4	32.0	25.4
Percent distribution by race and Hispanic origin					
Total under age 18	**100.0%**	**45.4%**	**22.3%**	**49.5%**	**29.2%**
Under age 6	100.0	46.7	21.1	48.5	29.5
Aged 6 to 17	100.0	44.7	22.9	50.0	29.1

Note: Numbers will not add to total because Hispanics may be of any race and not all races are shown.
Source: Bureau of the Census, Poverty in the United States: 1999, *Current Population Reports, P60-210, 2000; calculations by New Strategist*

5

Labor Force

♦ Among young adults, men and women are almost equally likely to work. In the 16-to-19 age group, 53 percent of men and 51 percent of women are in the labor force.

♦ Among the nation's 141 million workers, 16 percent are aged 16 to 24. Young adults account for a much larger 37 percent share of the unemployed.

♦ The unemployment rate is much higher for blacks and Hispanics than for whites. Among black men aged 16 to 19 in the labor force, one in four is unemployed.

♦ Workers under age 25 account for 55 percent of salespeople in clothing stores, and for 60 percent of those in shoe stores. They are 44 percent of kitchen workers, and 45 percent of parking lot attendants.

♦ Only 16 percent of all workers have part-time jobs, that is, they work fewer than 35 hours a week. Among workers aged 16 and 17, however, 86 percent work part-time.

♦ For the millennial generation, working parents are the norm. Sixty-four percent of married couples with children under age 18 are dual earners.

More Women Aged 16 to 24 Have Entered the Labor Force

Among young adults, men and women are now almost equally likely to work.

Since 1970, the labor force participation of teenaged and young-adult men has fallen, while participation by their female counterparts has grown. In 2000, the labor force participation rates of men and women aged 16 to 19 were nearly identical. Among those aged 20 to 24, 73 percent of women and 83 percent of men were at work.

In 1970, 56 percent of males aged 16 to 19 were in the labor force. By 2000, the share had fallen to 53 percent. Behind the decline was a rise in the proportion of teenage males who complete high school and go to college, making them less likely to work. Among women aged 16 to 19, a larger share were at work in 2000 than in 1970. Although women are also increasingly likely to finish high school and go to college, their labor force participation rate rose because some work part-time while attending school.

♦ The labor force participation rates of young adults should remain relatively stable for the next decade or so because major shifts in the educational plans of high school students are unlikely.

Labor Force Participation Rate of People under Age 25 by Sex, 1970 to 2000

(civilian labor force participation rate of people aged 16 or older and aged 16 to 24, by sex, 1970 to 2000; percentage point change, 1970–2000)

	2000	1990	1980	1970	percentage point change 1970–2000
Men aged 16 or older	**74.7%**	**76.1%**	**77.4%**	**79.7%**	**–5.0**
Aged 16 to 19	53.0	55.7	60.5	56.1	–3.1
Aged 16 to 17	41.1	43.7	50.1	47.0	–5.9
Aged 18 to 19	65.0	67.0	71.3	66.7	–1.7
Aged 20 to 24	82.6	84.3	85.9	83.3	–0.7
Women aged 16 or older	**60.2**	**57.5**	**51.5**	**43.3**	**13.1**
Aged 16 to 19	51.3	51.8	52.9	44.0	7.3
Aged 16 to 17	41.0	41.9	43.6	34.9	6.1
Aged 18 to 19	61.5	60.5	61.9	53.6	7.9
Aged 20 to 24	73.3	71.6	68.9	57.7	15.6

Sources: Bureau of Labor Statistics, Employment and Earnings, *January 2001 and January 1991; and* Handbook of Labor Statistics, *Bulletin 2340, 1989; calculations by New Strategist*

Unemployment Is Higher Than Average among Young Adults

Young men are slightly more likely than young women to be unemployed.

Among the nation's 141 million workers, 23 million—or 16 percent—are aged 16 to 24. Young adults account for a much larger 37 percent share of the unemployed. While the unemployment rate stood at just 4 percent among all adults in 2000, it was more than twice as high, at 9 percent, among those under age 25.

The unemployment rate peaks at 17 percent among men aged 16 and 17. Women in the age group are slightly less likely to be unemployed, as 14 percent are looking for work. Unemployment falls to 7 percent in the 20-to-24 age group.

♦ Young adults are more likely to be unemployed than older Americans because many are between jobs as they search for more rewarding work.

Employment Status of People Aged 16 to 24 by Sex, 2000

(number and percent of people aged 16 or older and aged 16 to 24 in the civilian labor force by sex and employment status, 2000; numbers in thousands)

| | civilian noninstitutional population | total | civilian labor force | | unemployed | |
			percent of population	employed	number	percent of labor force
Total, aged 16 or older	**209,699**	**140,863**	**67.2%**	**135,208**	**5,655**	**4.0%**
Total, aged 16 to 24	34,453	22,715	65.9	20,597	2,118	9.3
Aged 16 to 19	16,042	8,369	52.2	7,276	1,093	13.1
Aged 16 to 17	8,003	3,284	41.0	2,778	506	15.4
Aged 18 to 19	8,038	5,085	63.3	4,498	587	11.5
Aged 20 to 24	18,411	14,346	77.9	13,321	1,025	7.1
Men, aged 16 or older	**100,731**	**75,247**	**74.7**	**72,293**	**2,954**	**3.9**
Total, aged 16 to 24	17,305	11,875	68.6	10,722	1,153	9.7
Aged 16 to 19	8,151	4,317	53.0	3,713	604	14.0
Aged 16 to 17	4,108	1,688	41.1	1,405	283	16.8
Aged 18 to 19	4,043	2,629	65.0	2,308	321	12.2
Aged 20 to 24	9,154	7,558	82.6	7,009	549	7.3
Women, aged 16 or older	**108,968**	**65,616**	**60.2**	**62,915**	**2,701**	**4.1**
Total, aged 16 to 24	17,147	10,839	63.2	9,875	965	8.9
Aged 16 to 19	7,890	4,051	51.3	3,563	489	12.1
Aged 16 to 17	3,895	1,596	41.0	1,373	223	14.0
Aged 18 to 19	3,995	2,456	61.5	2,190	266	10.8
Aged 20 to 24	9,257	6,788	73.3	6,312	476	7.0

Source: Bureau of Labor Statistics, Employment and Earnings, *January 2001*

Unemployment Is High among Blacks, Hispanics

Young black men are most likely to be unemployed.

Among teenagers, the labor force participation rate is higher for whites than for blacks or Hispanics. While 57 percent of white men aged 16 to 19 are in the labor force, the figure is just 39 percent among blacks and 51 percent among Hispanics. The pattern is the same for women, white teens being more likely to be in the labor force than black or Hispanic teens. The differences are less pronounced in the 20 to 24 age group. In fact, Hispanic men are more likely to be in the labor force than white men.

Minorities are less likely to be in the labor force because more have become discouraged in their job search. The unemployment rate is much higher for blacks and Hispanics than for whites. One in four black men aged 16 to 19 is unemployed—that is, they want a job but cannot find one. In contrast, only 12 percent of white men in the age group are unemployed.

♦ One reason young blacks and Hispanics have difficulty finding jobs even in the midst of a booming economy is that they do not live in areas where jobs are growing.

Minorities face more unemployment

(percent of men aged 16 to 19 who are unemployed, by race and Hispanic origin, 2000)

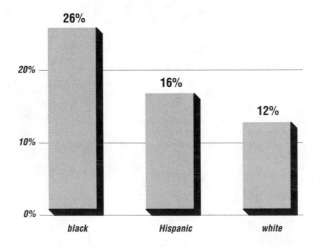

Employment Status of Men Aged 16 to 24 by Race and Hispanic Origin, 2000

(number and percent of men aged 16 or older and aged 16 to 24 in the civilian labor force by race, Hispanic origin, and employment status, 2000; numbers in thousands)

| | civilian noninstitutional population | civilian labor force | | | unemployed | |
		total	percent of population	employed	number	percent of labor force
White men	**84,647**	**63,861**	**75.4%**	**61,696**	**2,165**	**3.4%**
Total, aged 16 to 24	13,916	9,987	71.8	9,166	821	8.2
Aged 16 to 19	6,496	3,679	56.6	3,227	452	12.3
Aged 16 to 17	3,250	1,439	44.3	1,220	219	15.2
Aged 18 to 19	3,246	2,240	69.0	2,007	233	10.4
Aged 20 to 24	7,420	6,308	85.0	5,939	369	5.9
Black men	**11,320**	**7,816**	**69.0**	**7,180**	**636**	**8.1**
Total, aged 16 to 24	2,448	1,379	56.3	1,103	276	20.0
Aged 16 to 19	1,213	473	39.0	348	125	26.4
Aged 16 to 17	626	187	29.9	133	54	28.6
Aged 18 to 19	587	286	48.8	215	71	25.0
Aged 20 to 24	1,235	906	73.4	755	151	16.7
Hispanic men	**11,064**	**8,919**	**80.6**	**8,478**	**441**	**4.9**
Total, aged 16 to 24	2,662	1,912	71.8	1,731	181	9.5
Aged 16 to 19	1,205	613	50.9	517	96	15.7
Aged 16 to 17	575	183	31.8	142	41	22.5
Aged 18 to 19	631	431	68.3	375	55	12.8
Aged 20 to 24	1,457	1,299	89.2	1,214	85	6.5

Source: Bureau of Labor Statistics, Employment and Earnings, *January 2001; calculations by New Strategist*

Employment Status of Women Aged 16 to 24 by Race and Hispanic Origin, 2000

(number and percent of women aged 16 or older and aged 16 to 24 in the civilian labor force by race, Hispanic origin, and employment status, 2000; numbers in thousands)

	civilian noninstitutional population	civilian labor force			unemployed	
		total	percent of population	employed	number	percent of labor force
White women	**89,781**	**53,714**	**59.8%**	**51,780**	**1,934**	**3.6%**
Total, aged 16 to 24	13,511	8,851	65.5	8,183	668	7.5
Aged 16 to 19	6,211	3,396	54.7	3,043	353	10.4
Aged 16 to 17	3,062	1,360	44.4	1,191	170	12.5
Aged 18 to 19	3,149	2,035	64.6	1,852	183	9.0
Aged 20 to 24	7,300	5,455	74.7	5,140	315	5.8
Black women	**13,898**	**8,787**	**63.2**	**8,154**	**633**	**7.2**
Total, aged 16 to 24	2,710	1,520	56.1	1,267	253	16.6
Aged 16 to 19	1,255	494	39.4	380	114	23.0
Aged 16 to 17	620	179	28.8	133	46	25.7
Aged 18 to 19	634	315	49.7	247	68	21.5
Aged 20 to 24	1,455	1,026	70.5	887	139	13.5
Hispanic women	**11,329**	**6,449**	**56.9**	**6,014**	**435**	**6.7**
Total, aged 16 to 24	2,455	1,326	54.0	1,165	162	12.2
Aged 16 to 19	1,136	470	41.4	385	85	18.1
Aged 16 to 17	545	155	28.5	120	36	22.9
Aged 18 to 19	590	315	53.3	265	49	15.7
Aged 20 to 24	1,319	856	64.9	780	77	8.9

Source: Bureau of Labor Statistics, Employment and Earnings, *January 2001; calculations by New Strategist*

The Youngest Workers Dominate Many Entry-Level Positions

They account for the majority of child care workers.

Among the 135 million employed Americans in 2000, only 21 million were under age 25—or 15 percent. In some occupations, however, workers under age 25 account for a disproportionate share. While people aged 16 to 24 are only 6 percent of the nation's managers and professionals, they are a much larger 22 percent of sales workers and 26 percent of service workers.

Within the sales category, 16-to-24-year-olds account for 55 percent of those selling clothes and 60 percent of those selling shoes. Within the service category, they account for 44 percent of kitchen workers, 48 percent of attendants at amusement and recreation facilities, and 45 percent of parking lot attendants. Most young adults will move out of these entry-level positions as they earn educational credentials and gain job experience.

♦ Young adults account for a large share of workers in occupations with considerable public contact. Employers should train young adults to relate well to middle aged and older people if they want customers coming back for more.

Occupations of Workers Aged 16 to 24, 2000

(number of employed people aged 16 or older and aged 16 to 24 by occupation, 2000; numbers in thousands)

| | total | aged 16 to 24 | | |
		total	16 to 19	20 to 24
Total employed, aged 16 or older	**135,208**	**20,597**	**7,276**	**13,321**
Managerial and professional specialty	40,887	2,486	346	2,140
Executive, administrative, and managerial	19,774	1,008	121	887
Professional specialty	21,113	1,479	225	1,254
Technical, sales, and administrative support	39,442	7,486	2,731	4,755
Technicians and related support	4,385	583	92	491
Sales	16,340	3,635	1,737	1,898
Administrative support, including clerical	18,717	3,268	902	2,366
Service	18,278	4,760	2,274	2,486
Private household	792	171	83	88
Protective service	2,399	305	89	216
Other service	15,087	4,284	2,102	2,182
Precision production, craft, and repair	14,882	1,709	364	1,345
Mechanics and repairers	4,875	533	97	436
Construction trades	6,120	830	193	637
Extractive occupations	128	10	2	8
Precision production	3,759	336	72	264
Operators, fabricators, and laborers	18,319	3,535	1,279	2,256
Machine operators, assemblers, and inspectors	7,319	1,045	251	794
Transportation and material moving	5,557	623	151	472
Handlers, equip. cleaners, helpers, and laborers	5,443	1,867	877	990
Farming, forestry, and fishing	3,399	619	281	338
Farm operators and managers	1,125	33	8	25
Other agricultural and related occupations	2,115	562	268	294
Forestry and logging	109	15	3	12
Fishers, hunters, and trappers	51	9	2	7

Source: Bureau of Labor Statistics, unpublished data from the 2000 Current Population Survey

Distribution of Workers Aged 16 to 24 by Occupation, 2000

(percent distribution of employed people aged 16 or older and aged 16 to 24 by occupation, 2000)

		aged 16 to 24		
	total	*total*	*16 to 19*	*20 to 24*
Total workers	**100.0%**	**100.0%**	**100.0%**	**100.0%**
Managerial and professional specialty	30.2	12.1	4.8	16.1
Executive, administrative, and managerial	14.6	4.9	1.7	6.7
Professional specialty	15.6	7.2	3.1	9.4
Technical, sales, and administrative support	29.2	36.3	37.5	35.7
Technicians and related support	3.2	2.8	1.3	3.7
Sales	12.1	17.6	23.9	14.2
Administrative support, including clerical	13.8	15.9	12.4	17.8
Service	13.5	23.1	31.3	18.7
Private household	0.6	0.8	1.1	0.7
Protective service	1.8	1.5	1.2	1.6
Other service	11.2	20.8	28.9	16.4
Precision production, craft, and repair	11.0	8.3	5.0	10.1
Mechanics and repairers	3.6	2.6	1.3	3.3
Construction trades	4.5	4.0	2.7	4.8
Extractive occupations	0.1	0.0	0.0	0.1
Precision production	2.8	1.6	1.0	2.0
Operators, fabricators, and laborers	13.5	17.2	17.6	16.9
Machine operators, assemblers, and inspectors	5.4	5.1	3.4	6.0
Transport and material moving	4.1	3.0	2.1	3.5
Handlers, equip. cleaners, helpers, and laborers	4.0	9.1	12.1	7.4
Farming, forestry, and fishing	2.5	3.0	3.9	2.5
Farm operators and managers	0.8	0.2	0.1	0.2
Other agricultural and related occupations	1.6	2.7	3.7	2.2
Forestry and logging	0.1	0.1	0.0	0.1
Fishing, hunters, and trappers	0.0	0.0	0.0	0.1

Source: Bureau of Labor Statistics, unpublished data from the 2000 Current Population Survey; calculations by New Strategist

Share of Workers Aged 16 to 24 by Occupation, 2000

(employed people aged 16 to 24 as a percent of total employed people aged 16 or older by occupation, 2000)

	total	aged 16 to 24		
		total	*16 to 19*	*20 to 24*
Total workers	**100.0%**	**15.2%**	**5.4%**	**9.9%**
Managerial and professional specialty	100.0	6.1	0.8	5.2
Executive, administrative, and managerial	100.0	5.1	0.6	4.5
Professional specialty	100.0	7.0	1.1	5.9
Technical, sales, and administrative support	100.0	19.0	6.9	12.1
Technicians and related support	100.0	13.3	2.1	11.2
Sales	100.0	22.2	10.6	11.6
Administrative support, including clerical	100.0	17.5	4.8	12.6
Service	100.0	26.0	12.4	13.6
Private household	100.0	21.6	10.5	11.1
Protective service	100.0	12.7	3.7	9.0
Other service	100.0	28.4	13.9	14.5
Precision production, craft, and repair	100.0	11.5	2.4	9.0
Mechanics and repairers	100.0	10.9	2.0	8.9
Construction trades	100.0	13.6	3.2	10.4
Extractive occupations	100.0	7.8	1.6	6.3
Precision production	100.0	8.9	1.9	7.0
Operators, fabricators, and laborers	100.0	19.3	7.0	12.3
Machine operators, assemblers, and inspectors	100.0	14.3	3.4	10.8
Transport and material moving	100.0	11.2	2.7	8.5
Handlers, equip. cleaners, helpers, and laborers	100.0	34.3	16.1	18.2
Farming, forestry, and fishing	100.0	18.2	8.3	9.9
Farm operators and managers	100.0	2.9	0.7	2.2
Other agricultural and related occupations	100.0	26.6	12.7	13.9
Forestry and logging	100.0	13.8	2.8	11.0
Fishing, hunters, and trappers	100.0	17.6	3.9	13.7

Source: Bureau of Labor Statistics, unpublished data from the 2000 Current Population Survey; calculations by New Strategist

Workers Aged 16 to 24 by Detailed Occupation, 2000

(number of employed workers aged 16 or older and number and percent aged 16 to 24 by selected detailed occupation; 2000; numbers in thousands)

	total workers	aged 16 to 24	
		number	percent of total
Total workers	**135,208**	**20,597**	**15.2%**
Managers, food service and lodging establishments	1,446	3	0.2
Accountants and auditors	1,592	111	7.0
Computer systems analysts and scientists	1,797	137	7.6
Actors and directors	139	16	11.5
Editors and reporters	288	33	11.5
Public relations specialists	205	20	9.8
Athletes	90	29	32.2
Health technologists and technicians	1,724	203	11.8
Computer programmers	699	90	12.9
Securities and financial services sales	600	50	8.3
Sales workers, apparel	411	227	55.2
Sales workers, shoes	114	68	59.6
Sales workers, radio, TV, and appliances	258	114	44.2
Sales workers, hardware and building supplies	328	76	23.2
Sales counter clerks	185	68	36.8
Cashiers	2,939	1,545	52.6
Computer equipment operators	323	64	19.8
Information clerks	2,071	585	28.2
Receptionists	1,017	320	31.5
File clerks	338	141	41.7
Telephone operators	156	45	28.8
Dispatchers	269	33	12.3
Traffic, shipping, and receiving clerks	661	108	16.3
Insurance adjusters, examiners, and investigators	451	50	11.1
General office clerks	864	227	26.3
Bank tellers	431	172	39.9
Data-entry keyers	749	192	25.6
Child care workers, private household	275	142	51.6
Firefighters	233	15	6.4
Bartenders	365	89	24.4

(continued)

(continued from previous page)

	total workers	aged 16 to 24	
		number	percent of total
Waiters and waitresses	1,440	733	50.9%
Cooks	2,076	692	33.3
Kitchen workers, food preparation	317	141	44.5
Dental assistants	218	50	22.9
Nursing aides, orderlies, attendants	1,983	311	15.7
Hairdressers, cosmetologists	820	103	12.6
Attendants, amusement and recreation facilities	246	119	48.4
Automobile mechanics	860	137	15.9
Data processing equipment repairers	342	62	18.1
Brickmasons and stonemasons	242	45	18.6
Carpenters	1,467	247	16.8
Electricians	860	113	13.1
Painters, construction and maintenance	624	83	13.3
Roofers	215	42	19.5
Butchers and meat cutters	265	37	14.0
Bakers	154	30	19.5
Paint and paint-spraying machine operators	187	32	17.1
Assemblers	1,299	224	17.2
Parking lot attendants	60	27	45.0
Industrial truck and tractor equipment operators	569	109	19.2
Construction laborers	1,015	274	27.0
Garbage collectors	54	8	14.8
Stock handlers and baggers	1,125	590	52.4
Garage and service station-related occupations	184	93	50.5
Vehicle washers and equipment cleaners	313	136	43.5
Laborers, except construction	1,307	318	24.3
Farm workers	768	217	28.3
Groundskeepers and gardeners	870	248	28.5

Source: Bureau of Labor Statistics, unpublished tables from the 2000 Current Population Survey; calculations by New Strategist

The Youngest Workers Are Part-Timers

Most 20-to-24-year-olds, however, work full-time.

Among people aged 16 or older in the civilian labor force, 10 percent of men and 25 percent of women work part-time. Among 16- and 17-year-olds, however, more than 80 percent are part-time workers. Most are high school students with after-school jobs in fast-food restaurants and other entry-level positions.

Among 18- and 19-year-olds in the labor force, full-time work is the norm for men, 57 percent of whom have full-time jobs. Among their female counterparts, only 43 percent are full-time workers. One factor accounting for this difference is that women are more likely to go to college than men, which makes them less likely to work full-time.

Among 20-to-24-year-olds in the labor force, the majority of both men and women work full-time. Nevertheless, a substantial 19 percent of men and 30 percent of women work part-time. Women in the age group are more likely to work part-time than men because many are raising children.

♦ With more high school students going to college, part-time work is becoming increasingly important in the educational plans of young adults.

Part-time work is common among teens

(percent of people aged 16 to 24 in the civilian labor force who work part-time, by sex, 2000)

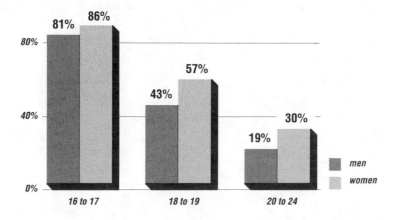

Full- and Part-Time Workers Aged 16 to 24 by Sex, 2000

(number and percent distribution of people aged 16 or older and aged 16 to 24 in the civilian labor force by full- and part-time employment status, by sex, 2000; numbers in thousands)

	men			women		
	total	full-time	part-time	total	full-time	part-time
Total employed	**75,248**	**67,403**	**7,845**	**65,615**	**49,390**	**16,225**
Total, aged 16 to 24	11,876	7,944	3,932	10,840	6,028	4,812
Aged 16 to 17	1,688	319	1,369	1,596	217	1,379
Aged 18 to 19	2,629	1,488	1,141	2,456	1,064	1,392
Aged 20 to 24	7,559	6,137	1,422	6,788	4,747	2,041
Percent distribution by employment status						
Total employed	**100.0%**	**89.6%**	**10.4%**	**100.0%**	**75.3%**	**24.7%**
Total, aged 16 to 24	100.0	66.9	33.1	100.0	55.6	44.4
Aged 16 to 17	100.0	18.9	81.1	100.0	13.6	86.4
Aged 18 to 19	100.0	56.6	43.4	100.0	43.3	56.7
Aged 20 to 24	100.0	81.2	18.8	100.0	69.9	30.1
Percent distribution by age						
Total employed	**100.0%**	**100.0%**	**100.0%**	**100.0%**	**100.0%**	**100.0%**
Total, aged 16 to 24	15.8	11.8	50.1	16.5	12.2	29.7
Aged 16 to 17	2.2	0.5	17.5	2.4	0.4	8.5
Aged 18 to 19	3.5	2.2	14.5	3.7	2.2	8.6
Aged 20 to 24	10.0	9.1	18.1	10.3	9.6	12.6

Source: unpublished data from the Bureau of Labor Statistics; calculations by New Strategist

Young Adults Account for a Large Share of Temp Workers

They account for few independent contractors, however.

Fewer than 2 percent of workers under age 25 are independent contractors—a category that includes most of the nation's self-employed. Among workers of all ages, a larger 6 percent are independent contractors. Self-employment is uncommon among young adults because running a business requires expertise that usually takes years to develop.

Six percent of young adults are in alternative work arrangements, which include independent contracting, on-call work, temping, and work for contract firms. They account for a substantial 27 percent of the nation's temp workers.

♦ Although temp work is often entry-level, it gives young adults the opportunity to experiment with different types of jobs and determine which ones are most satisfying.

Workers Aged 16 to 24 in Alternative Work Arrangements, 1999

(number and percent distribution of employed workers aged 16 or older and aged 16 to 24 by work arrangement, 1999; numbers in thousands)

			alternative workers			
					temporary	workers
			Independent	on-call	help agency	provided by
	total	total	contractors	workers	workers	contract firms
Total employed	**131,494**	**12,236**	**8,247**	**2,032**	**1,188**	**769**
Total, aged 16 to 24	19,124	1,150	328	381	317	124
Aged 16 to 19	6,662	360	76	179	68	37
Aged 20 to 24	12,462	790	252	202	249	87

Percent distribution by alternative work arrangement

Total employed	**100.0%**	**9.3%**	**6.3%**	**1.5%**	**0.9%**	**0.6%**
Total, aged 16 to 24	100.0	6.0	1.7	2.0	1.7	0.6
Aged 16 to 19	100.0	5.4	1.1	2.7	1.0	0.6
Aged 20 to 24	100.0	6.3	2.0	1.6	2.0	0.7

Percent distribution by age

Total employed	**100.0%**	**100.0%**	**100.0%**	**100.0%**	**100.0%**	**100.0%**
Total, aged 16 to 24	14.5	9.4	4.0	18.8	26.7	16.1
Aged 16 to 19	5.1	2.9	0.9	8.8	5.7	4.8
Aged 20 to 24	9.5	6.5	3.1	9.9	21.0	11.3

Note: Independent contractors are workers who obtain customers on their own to provide a product or service, including the self-employed. On-call workers are in a pool of workers who are called to work only as needed, such as substitute teachers and construction workers supplied by a union hiring hall. Temporary help agency workers are those who said they are paid by a temporary help agency. Workers provided by contract firms are employed by a company that provides employees or their services to others under contract, such as for security, landscaping, and computer programming.
Source: Bureau of Labor Statistics, Contingent and Alternative Employment Arrangements, *February 1999, Internet site <www.bls.gov/news.release/conemp.toc.htm>; calculations by New Strategist*

Number of Workers under Age 25 Will Grow Faster Than Average

The Millennial generation will boost the number of teens and young adults in the labor force.

The total number of workers in the labor force is projected to grow 12 percent between 1998 and 2008, according to the Bureau of Labor Statistics. The number of workers under age 25 will grow somewhat faster. The bureau projects a 14 percent gain in the number of working men aged 16 to 19 and a larger 17 percent gain in the number of working women in the age group.

The agency predicts that labor force participation rates will remain about the same for teens and young adults between 1998 and 2008. The bureau projects the participation rate to fall slightly for young men, while it should rise a bit for young women.

♦ The increase in entry-level workers is good news for employers.

More young workers are in the pipeline

(percent increase in total workers and workers aged 16 to 24, by sex and age, 1998 to 2008)

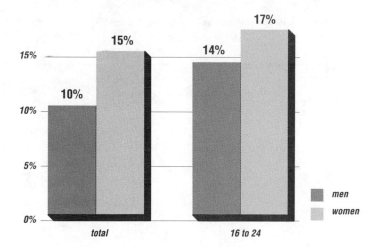

Projections of the Labor Force Aged 16 to 24 by Sex, 1998 to 2008

(number and percent of people aged 16 or older and aged 16 to 24 in the civilian labor force by sex, 1998 and 2008; percent change in number and percentage point change in rate 1998–2008; numbers in thousands)

	number			participation rate		
	1998	2008	percent change 1998–2008	1998	2008	percentage point change 1998–2008
Total labor force	137,673	154,576	12.3%	67.1%	67.6%	0.5
Total men in labor force	73,959	81,132	9.7	74.9	73.7	−1.2
Total, aged 16 to 24	11,465	13,048	13.8	68.4	68.0	−0.4
Aged 16 to 19	4,244	4,769	12.4	53.3	52.9	−0.4
Aged 20 to 24	7,221	8,279	14.7	82.0	81.4	−0.6
Total women in labor force	63,714	73,444	15.3	59.8	61.9	2.1
Total, aged 16 to 24	10,430	12,162	16.6	63.3	64.3	1.0
Aged 16 to 19	4,012	4,627	15.3	52.3	52.4	0.1
Aged 20 to 24	6,418	7,535	17.4	73.0	74.6	1.6

Source: Bureau of Labor Statistics, Internet sites <www.bls.gov/emplt983.htm> and <www.bls.gov/emplt985.htm>

Most Children Have Working Parents

For the millennial generation, working mothers are the norm.

Among women with children under age 18, fully 72 percent are in the labor force. The 52 percent majority of women with children under age 18 work full-time. Even among women with infants, 58 percent are in the labor force—most with full-time jobs.

In 64 percent of married couples with children under age 18, both husband and wife are in the labor force. Seventy-five percent of women heading single-parent families have jobs, as do 86 percent of men who head single-parent families.

Because most parents work, the 53 percent majority of children under age 12 in 1994 (the latest data available) experienced a regular child care arrangement with someone other than an immediate family member. Among children aged 3 to 5 in married-couple families in which both parents work, fully 83 percent had been in child care. They started child care at an average age of 14 months and were cared for an average of 29 hours a week.

♦ With their parents at work, the millennial generation has experienced day care, after-school care, and latch-key care. The health of the next generation depends on the success of these substitutes for stay-at-home moms.

For most children, parents are at work

(percent of families with children under age 18 with parents in the labor force, by type of family, 1999)

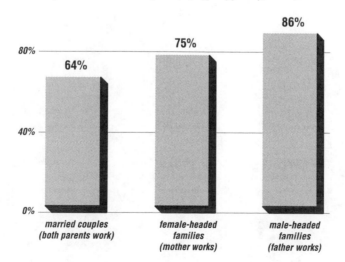

Labor Force Status of Women by Presence of Children, 1999

(labor force status of women by presence and age of own children under age 18, 1999; numbers in thousands)

	civilian population			employed			
		civilian labor force			percent of employed who work		percent of total women who work
	total	number	percent	total	full-time	part-time	full-time
Total women	**108,031**	**64,855**	**60.0%**	**62,042**	**74.7%**	**25.3%**	**42.9%**
No children under 18	72,446	39,169	54.1	37,504	74.8	25.2	38.7
With children under 18	35,585	25,686	72.2	24,538	74.7	25.3	51.5
Children 6 to 17, none younger	19,572	15,311	78.2	14,747	77.5	22.5	58.4
Children under 6	16,014	10,375	64.8	9,791	70.5	29.5	43.1
Children under 3	9,339	5,742	61.4	5,390	68.5	31.5	39.5
Children under 1	3,166	1,792	57.9	1,668	68.2	31.8	35.9

Source: Bureau of Labor Statistics, Internet sites <www.bls.gov/news.release/famee.t05.htm> and <www.bls .gov/news.release/famee.t06.htm>; calculations by New Strategist

Labor Force Status of Parents with Children under Age 18, 1999

(percent distribution of people aged 16 or older with own children under age 18 by family type, labor force status, and age of children, 1999; numbers in thousands)

		with children under age 18	
	total	aged 6 to 17, none younger	under age 6
Married couples	**100.0%**	**100.0%**	**100.0%**
One or both parents employed	97.3	97.1	97.6
Mother employed	68.2	74.6	60.7
Both parents employed	64.1	69.6	57.4
Mother employed, not father	4.2	4.9	3.3
Father employed, not mother	29.1	22.6	36.9
Neither parent employed	2.7	2.9	2.4
Female-headed families	**100.0**	**100.0**	**100.0**
Mother employed	74.7	79.1	67.4
Mother not employed	25.3	20.9	32.6
Male-headed families	**100.0**	**100.0**	**100.0**
Father employed	86.3	84.8	88.5
Father not employed	13.7	15.2	11.5

Source: Bureau of Labor Statistics, Internet site <www.bls.gov/news.release/famee.t04.htm>

Child Care Experiences of Children under Age 12, 1994

(number of children under age 12, percent ever in regular child care with someone other than an immediate family member, average age in months at first child care arrangement, and average hours per week spent in first child care arrangement, by marital and employment status of parents, 1994)

	under 3	3 to 5	6 to 11
Number of children (in 000s)	**8,787**	**9,644**	**19,547**
Percent ever in child care	46.4%	65.1%	50.2%
Average age at first child care arrangement (in months)	5.7	19.7	–
Average time spent in first child care arrangement (hours/week)	29.7	25.6	–
Married couples, both parents work			
Percent ever in child care	71.4	82.7	56.5
Average age at first child care arrangement (in months)	4.8	14.2	–
Average time spent in first child care arrangement (hours/week)	31.5	29.3	–
Married couples, one parent works			
Percent ever in child care	18.0	47.1	39.1
Average age at first child care arrangement (in months)	8.7	29.0	–
Average time spent in first child care arrangement (hours/week)	20.9	16.1	–
Single parent, works			
Percent ever in child care	79.3	90.7	59.4
Average age at first child care arrangement (in months)	5.8	18.6	–
Average time spent in first child care arrangement (hours/week)	33.4	31.3	–

Note: Labor force status of parents is for the month prior to the survey; information about parental employment status at the time of the first child care arrangement is not available. (–) means data not available.
Source: Bureau of the Census, A Child's Day: Home, School, and Play, 1994 (Selected Indicators of Child Well-Being), *Household Economic Studies, Current Population Reports P70-68, 2001*

6

Living Arrangements

♦ People aged 15 to 24 headed fewer than 6 million of the nation's 105 million households in 2000. Young adults today are slow to establish their own households because many are in college and still financially dependent on their parents.

♦ The living arrangements of young adults depend greatly on their race and Hispanic origin. Most households headed by blacks under age 25 are female-headed families, while most headed by non-Hispanic whites are people living with friends.

♦ The majority of young adults go to college after high school, postponing marriage and family until their mid-twenties. Consequently, only a 35 percent minority of householders under age 25 have children in their home.

♦ The majority of households headed by blacks or Hispanics aged 15 to 24 include children under age 18. Just 32 percent of households headed by white young adults have children at home.

♦ Eighty percent of children share their home with a sibling. Twenty-three percent have at least one parent who is a college graduate.

♦ The proportion of young adults who are unmarried has grown enormously in the past three decades as more pursued a college degree. Among women aged 20 to 24, the never-married proportion rose from 36 percent to 70 percent between 1970 and 1998.

The Millennial Generation Heads Few Households

People under age 25 head only 6 percent of households.

People aged 15 to 24 headed fewer than 6 million, or about 6 percent, of the nation's 105 million households in 2000. Young adults today are slow to establish their own households because many are in college and still financially dependent on their parents. In addition, entry-level pay has fallen sharply over the past few decades as the minimum wage has been eroded by inflation. Consequently, few young adults can afford to strike out on their own.

Households headed by young adults are extremely diverse. Married couples account for the 25 percent plurality of households headed by people aged 15 to 24. Not far behind is the 23 percent share held by female-headed families, while 21 and 22 percent are nonfamily households headed by women and men, respectively. Ten percent are male-headed families—the largest share this household type holds among all age groups.

♦ The diversity of young adults' living arrangement makes it difficult for marketers, politicians, or community organizations to reach them.

Households headed by young adults are diverse

(percent distribution of households headed by people aged 15 to 24, by type, 2000)

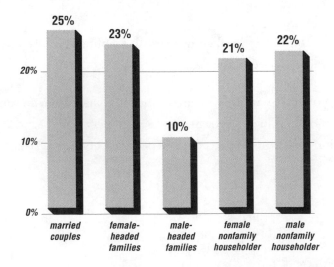

Households Headed by People Aged 15 to 24
by Household Type, 2000: Total Households

(number and percent distribution of total households and households headed by people aged 15 to 24, by household type, 2000; numbers in thousands)

	total	aged 15 to 24
Total households	**104,705**	**5,860**
Family households	**72,025**	**3,353**
Married couples	55,311	1,450
Female householder, no spouse present	12,687	1,342
Male householder, no spouse present	4,028	560
Nonfamily households	**32,680**	**2,508**
Female householder	18,039	1,221
Living alone	15,543	587
Male householder	14,641	1,286
Living alone	11,181	556
Percent distribution by type		
Total households	**100.0%**	**100.0%**
Family households	**68.8**	**57.2**
Married couples	52.8	24.7
Female householder, no spouse present	12.1	22.9
Male householder, no spouse present	3.8	9.6
Nonfamily households	**31.2**	**42.8**
Female householder	17.2	20.8
Living alone	14.8	10.0
Male householder	14.0	21.9
Living alone	10.7	9.5

Source: Bureau of the Census, Internet site <http://ferret.bls.census.gov/macro/03200/hhinc/new02_000.htm>; calculations by New Strategist

Young-Adult Households Vary Sharply by Race and Hispanic Origin

No other age group shows so much diversity in household type.

The living arrangements of young adults depend greatly on their race and Hispanic origin. Fifty percent of black householders aged 15 to 24 are women heading families. In contrast, female-headed families account for only 16 percent of households headed by non-Hispanic whites in the age group.

Married couples account for 36 percent of households headed by young Hispanics, but for only 9 percent of those headed by blacks.

Among young adults, nonfamily households (people who live alone or with nonrelatives) account for half the households headed by non-Hispanic whites. In contrast, they account for only 23 percent of households headed by Hispanics. Twenty-one percent of non-Hispanic white householders under age 25 live alone. Among Hispanics, the comparable figure is just 9 percent.

♦ Young adults have different wants and needs depending on their living arrangement.

Nonfamily households are most common among non-Hispanic whites

(percent of householders aged 15 to 24 who live alone or with nonrelatives, by race and Hispanic origin, 2000)

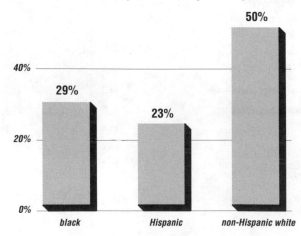

Households Headed by People Aged 15 to 24 by Household Type, 2000: Black Households

(number and percent distribution of total black households and households headed by blacks aged 15 to 24, by household type, 2000; numbers in thousands)

	total	aged 15 to 24
Total black households	**12,849**	**1,002**
Family households	**8,664**	**709**
Married couples	4,144	93
Female householder, no spouse present	3,814	502
Male householder, no spouse present	706	115
Nonfamily households	**4,185**	**293**
Female householder	2,309	190
Living alone	2,025	126
Male householder	1,876	103
Living alone	1,580	76
Percent distribution by type		
Total black households	**100.0%**	**100.0%**
Family households	**67.4**	**70.8**
Married couples	32.3	9.3
Female householder, no spouse present	29.7	50.1
Male householder, no spouse present	5.5	11.5
Nonfamily households	**32.6**	**29.2**
Female householder	18.0	19.0
Living alone	15.8	12.6
Male householder	14.6	10.3
Living alone	12.3	7.6

Source: Bureau of the Census, Internet site <http://ferret.bls.census.gov/macro/03200/hhinc/new02_000.htm>; calculations by New Strategist

Households Headed by People Aged 15 to 24 by Household Type, 2000: Hispanic Households

(number and percent distribution of total Hispanic households and households headed by Hispanics aged 15 to 24, by household type, 2000; numbers in thousands)

	total	aged 15 to 24
Total Hispanic households	**9,319**	**871**
Family households	**7,561**	**671**
Married couples	5,133	315
Female householder, no spouse present	1,769	213
Male householder, no spouse present	658	143
Nonfamily households	**1,758**	**200**
Female householder	783	81
Living alone	630	42
Male householder	974	119
Living alone	666	43
Percent distribution by type		
Total Hispanic households	**100.0%**	**100.0%**
Family households	**81.1**	**77.0**
Married couples	55.1	36.2
Female householder, no spouse present	19.0	24.5
Male householder, no spouse present	7.1	16.4
Nonfamily households	**18.9**	**23.0**
Female householder	8.4	9.3
Living alone	6.8	4.8
Male householder	10.5	13.7
Living alone	7.1	4.9

Source: Bureau of the Census, Internet site <http://ferret.bls.census.gov/macro/03200/hhinc/new02_000.htm>; calculations by New Strategist

Households Headed by People Aged 15 to 24 by Household Type, 2000: White Households

(number and percent distribution of total white households and households headed by whites aged 15 to 24, by household type, 2000; numbers in thousands)

	total	aged 15 to 24
Total white households	**87,671**	**4,541**
Family households	**60,251**	**2,470**
Married couples	48,790	1,298
Female householder, no spouse present	8,380	770
Male householder, no spouse present	3,081	402
Nonfamily households	**27,420**	**2,071**
Female householder	15,215	973
Living alone	13,109	421
Male householder	12,204	1,098
Living alone	9,198	440
Percent distribution by type		
Total white households	**100.0%**	**100.0%**
Family households	**68.7**	**54.4**
Married couples	55.7	28.6
Female householder, no spouse present	9.6	17.0
Male householder, no spouse present	3.5	8.9
Nonfamily households	**31.3**	**45.6**
Female householder	17.4	21.4
Living alone	15.0	9.3
Male householder	13.9	24.2
Living alone	10.5	9.7

Source: Bureau of the Census, Internet site <http://ferret.bls.census.gov/macro/03200/hhinc/new02_000.htm>; calculations by New Strategist

Households Headed by People Aged 15 to 24
by Household Type, 2000: Non-Hispanic White Households

(number and percent distribution of total non-Hispanic white households and households headed by non-Hispanic whites aged 15 to 24, by household type, 2000; numbers in thousands)

	total	aged 15 to 24
Total non-Hispanic white households	**78,819**	**3,721**
Family households	**53,066**	**1,844**
Married couples	43,865	992
Female householder, no spouse present	6,732	587
Male householder, no spouse present	2,468	265
Nonfamily households	**25,753**	**1,878**
Female householder	14,475	897
Living alone	12,508	383
Male householder	11,278	981
Living alone	8,562	399
Percent distribution by type		
Total non-Hispanic white households	**100.0%**	**100.0%**
Family households	**67.3**	**49.6**
Married couples	55.7	26.7
Female householder, no spouse present	8.5	15.8
Male householder, no spouse present	3.1	7.1
Nonfamily households	**32.7**	**50.5**
Female householder	18.4	24.1
Living alone	15.9	10.3
Male householder	14.3	26.4
Living alone	10.9	10.7

Source: Bureau of the Census, Internet site <http://ferret.bls.census.gov/macro/03200/hhinc/new02_000.htm>; calculations by New Strategist

Young-Adult Households Are of Average Size

Between two and three people live in the average household headed by someone under age 25.

Households headed by people aged 15 to 24 are home to an average of 2.5 people, slightly below the national average of 2.6. Householders under age 25 are slightly less likely to live alone than the average householder, 23 versus 26 percent. Two- and three-person households are more common in the age group.

Behind these differences is the fact that many young adults live with friends to share housing costs, particularly while attending college or beginning a career. In addition, female-headed families account for a large share of young-adult households, boosting the number of households with two or three people.

♦ As young adults marry and have children, their household size will rise above average until their children leave home.

Households by Size, 1998

(number and percent distribution of total households and households headed by people aged 15 to 24, by size of household, 1998; numbers in thousands)

	total	aged 15 to 24
Total households	**102,528**	**5,435**
One person	26,327	1,251
Two people	32,965	1,906
Three people	17,331	1,289
Four people	15,358	634
Five people	7,048	247
Six people	2,232	76
Seven or more people	1,267	33
Total households	**100.0%**	**100.0%**
One person	25.7	23.0
Two people	32.2	35.1
Three people	16.9	23.7
Four people	15.0	11.7
Five people	6.9	4.5
Six people	2.2	1.4
Seven or more people	1.2	0.6
Average number of people per household	2.6	2.5

Source: Bureau of the Census, detailed tables from Households and Family Characteristics: March 1998, *Current Population Reports, P20-515, 1998, Internet site <www.census.gov/population/www/socdemo/hh-fam.html>; calculations by New Strategist*

One-Third of Young-Adult Households include Children

Many have preschoolers in the home.

The majority of young adults go to college after high school, postponing marriage and family until their mid-twenties. Consequently, only a 35 percent minority of householders under age 25 have children in their home.

But young-adult households are more likely than the average household to include preschoolers. While 15 percent of all households include children under age 6, the proportion is 32 percent among householders under age 25. Similarly, while only 9 percent of all households include children under age 3, the figure is a much higher 24 percent among young adults.

♦ While most young adults postpone childbearing, others establish independent households because they have children.

Young-adult households are more likely than average to include preschoolers

(percent of total households and households headed by people aged 15 to 24 with children under age 6 at home, 1998)

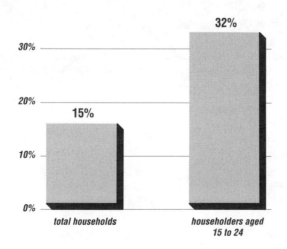

Households Headed by People Aged 15 to 24 by Presence and Age of Children, 1998

(number and percent distribution of total households and households headed by people aged 15 to 24, by presence and age of own children at home, 1998; numbers in thousands)

	total	aged 15 to 24
Total households	**102,528**	**5,435**
With children of any age	**44,979**	**1,880**
Under age 25	40,006	1,879
Under age 18	34,760	1,862
Under age 12	26,030	1,842
Under age 6	15,532	1,751
Under age 3	8,927	1,321
Under age 1	3,160	523
Total households	**100.0%**	**100.0%**
With children of any age	**43.9**	**34.6**
Under age 25	39.0	34.6
Under age 18	33.9	34.3
Under age 12	25.4	33.9
Under age 6	15.1	32.2
Under age 3	8.7	24.3
Under age 1	3.1	9.6

Source: Bureau of the Census, detailed tables from Households and Family Characteristics: March 1998, *Current Population Reports, P20-515, 1998, Internet site <www.census.gov/population/www/socdemo/hh-fam.html>; calculations by New Strategist*

Among 15-to-24-Year-Olds, Most Black and Hispanic Households include Children

Few households headed by whites have children at home.

The 51 percent majority of households headed by blacks aged 15 to 24 include children under age 18. Among Hispanics, the proportion is an even higher 53 percent. Among whites, however, just 32 percent of households headed by young adults have children under age 18 at home.

Regardless of race or Hispanic origin, the majority of young married couples have children. Not surprisingly, the majority of female-headed families also include children. Few male-headed families include children, however, with the figure ranging from 31 percent among blacks to 36 percent among whites.

♦ Most young householders are students or entry-level workers living together while trying to establish themselves financially, but some are young parents struggling to make ends meet.

Householders Aged 15 to 24 by Type of Household and Presence of Children, 1998

(number of total households and households headed by people aged 15 to 24, and number and percent with own children under age 18 at home, by household type, race, and Hispanic origin, 1998; numbers in thousands)

		with own children under age 18	
	total	*number*	*percent*
Total households	**102,528**	**34,760**	**33.9%**
Total aged 15 to 24	5,435	1,862	34.3
Black	935	473	50.6
Hispanic	779	409	52.5
White	4,242	1,345	31.7
Married couples	**54,317**	**25,269**	**46.5**
Total aged 15 to 24	1,373	811	59.1
Black	111	79	71.2
Hispanic	300	215	71.7
White	1,221	712	58.3
Female householders, no spouse present	**12,652**	**7,693**	**60.8**
Total aged 15 to 24	1,095	866	79.1
Black	429	368	85.8
Hispanic	180	142	78.9
White	612	478	78.1
Male householders, no spouse present	**3,911**	**1,798**	**46.0**
Total aged 15 to 24	551	186	33.8
Black	91	28	30.8
Hispanic	147	52	35.4
White	437	156	35.7

Note: Numbers will not add to total because Hispanics may be of any race and not all races are shown.
Source: Bureau of the Census, detailed tables from Households and Family Characteristics: March 1998, *Current Population Reports, P20-515, 1998, Internet site <www.census.gov/population/www/socdemo/hh-fam.html>; calculations by New Strategist*

Most Black Children Live with Mother Only

Fifty-one percent of black children live with only their mother, up from 44 percent in 1980.

Among whites, 74 percent of children live with both parents. Just 18 percent live with their mother only, up from 14 percent in 1980. Among Hispanic children, 64 percent live with both parents while 27 percent live with their mother only—up from 20 percent in 1980.

Few children live with only their father : 5 percent of whites and 4 percent of Hispanics and blacks. Nine percent of black children, 5 percent of Hispanic children, and 3 percent of white children live with someone other than their mother or father, often a grandmother.

♦ While the living arrangements of black children differ from those of white or Hispanic children, the trend is the same for all three groups. A shrinking proportion of children live with two parents.

Most white children live with both parents

(percent of children under age 18 who live with two parents, by race and Hispanic origin, 1998)

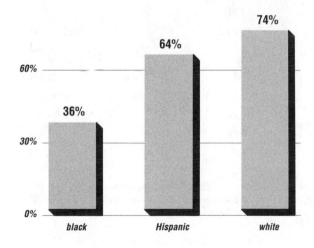

Living Arrangements of Children by Race and Hispanic Origin, 1980 and 1998

(number and percent distribution of children under age 18 by race and Hispanic origin of child and living arrangement, 1980 and 1998; numbers in thousands)

	1998		1980	
	number	*percent*	*number*	*percent*
Total children	**71,377**	**100.0%**	**63,427**	**100.0%**
Both parents	48,642	68.1	48,624	76.7
Mother only	16,634	23.3	11,406	18.0
Father only	3,143	4.4	1,060	1.7
Other	2,959	4.1	2,337	3.7
Black children	**11,414**	**100.0**	**9,375**	**100.0**
Both parents	4,137	36.2	3,956	42.2
Mother only	5,830	51.1	4,117	43.9
Father only	424	3.7	180	1.9
Other	1,015	8.9	1,122	12.0
Hispanic children	**10,863**	**100.0**	**5,459**	**100.0**
Both parents	6,909	63.6	4,116	75.4
Mother only	2,915	26.8	1,069	19.6
Father only	482	4.4	83	1.5
Other	551	5.1	191	3.5
White children	**56,124**	**100.0**	**52,242**	**100.0**
Both parents	41,547	74.0	43,200	82.7
Mother only	10,210	18.2	7,059	13.5
Father only	2,562	4.6	842	1.6
Other	1,799	3.2	1,141	2.2

Note: Numbers will not add to total because Hispanics may be of any race and not all races are shown.
Source: Bureau of the Census, Marital Status and Living Arrangements: March 1998, *Current Population Reports, P20-514, 1998; calculations by New Strategist*

Most Children Have College-Educated Parents

Most also share their home with siblings.

Eighty percent of the nation's 68 million children under age 18 who live with one or both parents share their home with a sibling. Twenty-three percent have at least one parent with a college degree.

Children living in married-couple families tend to have older parents than those living with only their mother, and they have more siblings in the household. Married parents are better educated than single-parents, which leads to higher incomes and more homeownership.

Children aged 6 to 11 are most likely to have siblings at home. Only 13 percent of 6-to-11-year-olds have no siblings compared with 27 percent of preschoolers and 19 percent of 12-to-17-year-olds. Siblings are less common for preschoolers because many are the first child in the family. Siblings are less common among teenagers because many are the youngest child whose older siblings have moved out.

♦ Perhaps no characteristic distinguishes today's children from those in the past more than the high educational level of their parents. Educated parents are more critical and demanding of caregivers, health care providers, schools, and other organizations that cater to children.

Children by Family Characteristics, 1998: Total Children

(number and percent distribution of children under age 18 by selected characteristics of family and type of family, 1998; numbers in thousands)

| | number of children | | | | percent distribution | | | |
	total living with one or both parents	living with both parents	living with mother only	living with father only	total living with one or both parents	living with both parents	living with mother only	living with father only
Total children under age 18	**68,418**	**48,642**	**16,634**	**3,143**	**100.0%**	**100.0%**	**100.0%**	**100.0%**
Age of parent								
Aged 15 to 19	569	100	421	48	0.8	0.2	2.5	1.5
Aged 20 to 24	3,300	1,209	1,829	262	4.8	2.5	11.0	8.3
Aged 25 to 29	7,871	4,694	2,746	432	11.5	9.7	16.5	13.7
Aged 30 to 34	13,978	9,653	3,861	464	20.4	19.8	23.2	14.8
Aged 35 to 39	17,035	12,721	3,656	658	24.9	26.2	22.0	20.9
Aged 40 to 44	14,189	11,093	2,452	644	20.7	22.8	14.7	20.5
Aged 45 to 49	7,373	5,857	1,135	381	10.8	12.0	6.8	12.1
Aged 50 to 54	2,874	2,352	363	159	4.2	4.8	2.2	5.1
Aged 55 to 59	789	614	119	57	1.2	1.3	0.7	1.8
Aged 60 to 64	230	197	17	17	0.3	0.4	0.1	0.5
Aged 65 or older	208	152	33	23	0.3	0.3	0.2	0.7
Education of parent								
Not a high school graduate	11,588	6,718	4,160	709	16.9	13.8	25.0	22.6
High school graduate	22,101	14,693	6,079	1,329	32.3	30.2	36.5	42.3
Some college or associate's degree	18,901	13,265	4,881	755	27.6	27.3	29.3	24.0
College graduate	15,829	13,966	1,514	349	23.1	28.7	9.1	11.1
Number of siblings in household								
None	13,487	7,751	4,529	1,207	19.7	15.9	27.2	38.4
One	27,136	20,251	5,799	1,086	39.7	41.6	34.9	34.6
Two	17,651	13,327	3,748	576	25.8	27.4	22.5	18.3
Three or more	10,145	7,313	2,558	273	14.8	15.0	15.4	8.7

(continued)

(continued from previous page)

	number of children				percent distribution			
	total living with one or both parents	living with both parents	living with mother only	living with father only	total living with one or both parents	living with both parents	living with mother only	living with father only
Homeownership status								
Owner	44,750	36,875	6,216	1,658	65.4%	75.8%	37.4%	52.8%
Renter	23,669	11,786	10,418	1,485	34.6	24.2	62.6	47.2
Median income	42,323	52,553	16,236	29,313	–	–	–	–
Living in poverty	19.0%	9.3%	47.5%	19.9%	–	–	–	–

Note: (–) means not applicable.
Source: Bureau of the Census, detailed tables for Household and Family Characteristics: March 1998, Current Population Reports, P20-515, 1998; calculations by New Strategist

Children by Family Characteristics, 1998: Children under Age 6

(number and percent distribution of children under age 6 by selected characteristics of family and type of family, 1998; numbers in thousands)

	number of children				percent distribution			
	total living with one or both parents	living with both parents	living with mother only	living with father only	total living with one or both parents	living with both parents	living with mother only	living with father only
Total children under age 6	**23,025**	**16,556**	**5,347**	**1,121**	**100.0%**	**100.0%**	**100.0%**	**100.0%**
Age of parent								
Aged 15 to 19	552	98	414	40	2.4	0.6	7.7	3.6
Aged 20 to 24	2,910	1,093	1,576	241	12.6	6.6	29.5	21.5
Aged 25 to 29	5,051	3,280	1,436	335	21.9	19.8	26.9	29.9
Aged 30 to 34	6,359	5,215	933	211	27.6	31.5	17.4	18.8
Aged 35 to 39	4,944	4,124	676	144	21.5	24.9	12.6	12.8
Aged 40 to 44	2,187	1,875	223	89	9.5	11.3	4.2	7.9
Aged 45 to 49	689	593	62	33	3.0	3.6	1.2	2.9
Aged 50 to 54	199	173	7	20	0.9	1.0	0.1	1.8
Aged 55 to 59	73	59	9	5	0.3	0.4	0.2	0.4
Aged 60 to 64	19	13	3	3	0.1	0.1	0.1	0.3
Aged 65 or older	41	33	8	–	0.2	0.2	0.1	–
Education of parent								
Not a high school graduate	3,974	2,139	1,528	306	17.3	12.9	28.6	27.3
High school graduate	7,327	4,868	1,981	478	31.8	29.4	37.0	42.6
Some college or associate's degree	6,303	4,528	1,513	262	27.4	27.3	28.3	23.4
College graduate	5,422	5,021	326	75	23.5	30.3	6.1	6.7
Number of siblings in household								
None	6,289	3,800	1,965	525	27.3	23.0	36.7	46.8
One	9,109	6,994	1,769	346	39.6	42.2	33.1	30.9
Two	5,032	3,846	990	195	21.9	23.2	18.5	17.4
Three or more	2,595	1,916	623	56	11.3	11.6	11.7	5.0

(continued)

(continued from previous page)

	number of children				percent distribution			
	total living with one or both parents	living with both parents	living with mother only	living with father only	total living with one or both parents	living with both parents	living with mother only	living with father only
Homeownership status								
Owner	13,445	11,412	1,595	438	58.4%	68.9%	29.8%	39.1%
Renter	9,580	5,144	3,753	684	41.6	31.1	70.2	61.0
Median income	38,462	48,092	12,843	23,476	–	–	–	–
Living in poverty	21.8%	10.5%	55.5%	27.8%	–	–	–	–

Note: (–) means sample is too small to make a reliable estimate or not applicable.
Source: Bureau of the Census, detailed tables for Household and Family Characteristics: March 1998, *Current Population Reports, P20-515, 1998; calculations by New Strategist*

Children by Family Characteristics, 1998: Children Aged 6 to 11

(number and percent distribution of children aged 6 to 11 by selected characteristics of family and type of family, 1998; numbers in thousands)

	number of children				percent distribution			
	total living with one or both parents	living with both parents	living with mother only	living with father only	total living with one or both parents	living with both parents	living with mother only	living with father only
Total children aged 6 to 11	23,287	16,638	5,732	916	100.0%	100.0%	100.0%	100.0%
Age of parent								
Aged 15 to 19	4	–	1	2	0.0	–	0.0	0.2
Aged 20 to 24	365	103	247	16	1.6	0.6	4.3	1.7
Aged 25 to 29	2,594	1,300	1,209	86	11.1	7.8	21.1	9.4
Aged 30 to 34	5,434	3,355	1,887	192	23.3	20.2	32.9	21.0
Aged 35 to 39	6,699	5,154	1,299	246	28.8	31.0	22.7	26.9
Aged 40 to 44	5,122	4,161	759	202	22.0	25.0	13.2	22.1
Aged 45 to 49	2,122	1,774	239	110	9.1	10.7	4.2	12.0
Aged 50 to 54	656	562	53	41	2.8	3.4	0.9	4.5
Aged 55 to 59	165	132	22	12	0.7	0.8	0.4	1.3
Aged 60 to 64	54	47	7	–	0.2	0.3	0.1	–
Aged 65 or older	71	50	10	10	0.3	0.3	0.2	1.1
Education of parent								
Not a high school graduate	3,839	2,304	1,322	213	16.5	13.8	23.1	23.3
High school graduate	7,480	4,994	2,112	373	32.1	30.0	36.8	40.7
Some college or associate's degree	6,565	4,551	1,805	209	28.2	27.4	31.5	22.8
College graduate	5,402	4,789	493	120	23.2	28.8	8.6	13.1
Number of siblings in household								
None	3,058	1,622	1,161	274	13.1	9.7	20.3	29.9
One	9,389	6,951	2,089	348	40.3	41.8	36.4	38.0
Two	6,856	5,193	1,483	180	29.4	31.2	25.9	19.7
Three or more	3,985	2,872	999	114	17.1	17.3	17.4	12.4

(continued)

(continued from previous page)

	number of children				percent distribution			
	total living with one or both parents	living with both parents	living with mother only	living with father only	total living with one or both parents	living with both parents	living with mother only	living with father only
Homeownership status								
Owner	15,437	12,819	2,094	524	66.3%	77.0%	36.5%	57.2%
Renter	7,850	3,819	3,638	392	33.7	23.0	63.5	42.8
Median income	42,128	53,087	15,671	29,753	–	–	–	–
Percent in poverty	19.8%	9.7%	49.4%	19.5%	–	–	–	–

Note: (–) means sample is too small to make a reliable estimate or not applicable.
Source: Bureau of the Census, detailed tables for Household and Family Characteristics: March 1998, Current Population Reports, P20-515, 1998; calculations by New Strategist

Children by Family Characteristics, 1998: Children Aged 12 to 17

(number and percent distribution of children aged 12 to 17 by selected characteristics of family and type of family, 1998; numbers in thousands)

| | number of children | | | | percent distribution | | | |
	total living with one or both parents	living with both parents	living with mother only	living with father only	total living with one or both parents	living with both parents	living with mother only	living with father only
Total children aged 12 to 17	**22,107**	**15,447**	**5,554**	**1,106**	**100.0%**	**100.0%**	**100.0%**	**100.0%**
Age of parent								
Aged 15 to 19	13	2	6	5	0.1	0.0	0.1	0.5
Aged 20 to 24	25	13	6	5	0.1	0.1	0.1	0.5
Aged 25 to 29	226	115	101	10	1.0	0.7	1.8	0.9
Aged 30 to 34	2,185	1,082	1,042	61	9.9	7.0	18.8	5.5
Aged 35 to 39	5,392	3,443	1,681	267	24.4	22.3	30.3	24.1
Aged 40 to 44	6,880	5,057	1,470	353	31.1	32.7	26.5	31.9
Aged 45 to 49	4,563	3,490	835	239	20.6	22.6	15.0	21.6
Aged 50 to 54	2,019	1,617	303	98	9.1	10.5	5.5	8.9
Aged 55 to 59	551	423	88	40	2.5	2.7	1.6	3.6
Aged 60 to 64	157	137	7	14	0.7	0.9	0.1	1.3
Aged 65 or older	97	70	15	12	0.4	0.5	0.3	1.1
Education of parent								
Not a high school graduate	3,776	2,275	1,311	190	17.1	14.7	23.6	17.2
High school graduate	7,294	4,830	1,986	477	33.0	31.3	35.8	43.1
Some college or associate's degree	6,032	4,186	1,562	284	27.3	27.1	28.1	25.7
College graduate	5,005	4,156	695	154	22.6	26.9	12.5	13.9
Number of siblings in household								
None	4,141	2,329	1,403	409	18.7	15.1	25.3	37.0
One	8,638	6,306	1,940	392	39.1	40.8	34.9	35.4
Two	5,764	4,287	1,275	202	26.1	27.8	23.0	18.3
Three or more	3,564	2,525	936	104	16.1	16.3	16.9	9.4

(continued)

(continued from previous page)

	number of children				percent distribution			
	total living with one or both parents	living with both parents	living with mother only	living with father only	total living with one or both parents	living with both parents	living with mother only	living with father only
Homeownership status								
Owner	15,868	12,644	2,527	697	71.8%	81.9%	45.5%	63.0%
Renter	6,239	2,804	3,027	409	28.2	18.2	54.5	37.0
Median income	46,670	57,613	20,453	34,044	–	–	–	–
Percent in poverty	15.4%	7.5%	37.8%	12.3%	–	–	–	–

Note: (–) means sample is too small to make a reliable estimate or not applicable.
Source: Bureau of the Census, detailed tables for Household and Family Characteristics: March 1998, *Current Population Reports, P20-515, 1998; calculations by New Strategist*

Most Young Adults Live at Home

Men are more likely than women to live with their parents.

Among people aged 15 to 24, 70 percent of men and 60 percent of women live with their parents. These figures include college students living in dormitories because they are considered dependents. The proportion of young adults who live with their parents falls with age, particularly for women. Half of men aged 20 to 24 still live with Mom and Dad. Women are less likely to live with their parents because they marry at a younger age.

Living with nonrelatives is the second most common type of living arrangement among young adults, and fully 19 percent of 20-to-24-year-olds do so. Living with a spouse ranks third. Among 20-to-24-year-olds, 24 percent of women live with a spouse versus only 13 percent of their male counterparts. Women are also more likely than men to head other families (such as single-parent families)—11 percent of women aged 20 to 24 head other families compared with only 4 percent of men in the age group.

♦ As more young adults puruse a college degree, the dependency of childhood has stretched well into the twenties.

Many young adults live with parents

(percent of people aged 15 to 24 who live with their parents, by age and sex, 1998)

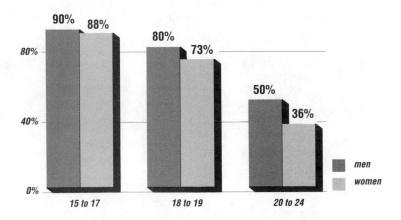

Living Arrangements of Men Aged 15 to 24, 1998

(number and percent distribution of men aged 15 to 24 by living arrangement, 1998; numbers in thousands)

| | total | aged 15 to 24 | | |
		15 to 17	18 to 19	20 to 24
Total men	**18,747**	**6,114**	**3,807**	**8,826**
Living with parents	12,917	5,518	3,030	4,369
Living with other family member(s)	1,229	376	252	601
Living with spouse	1,246	6	61	1,179
Other family householder	551	65	102	384
Living alone	722	10	63	649
Living with nonrelatives	2,081	139	298	1,644
Total men	**100.0%**	**100.0%**	**100.0%**	**100.0%**
Living with parents	68.9	90.3	79.6	49.5
Living with other family member(s)	6.6	6.1	6.6	6.8
Living with spouse	6.6	0.1	1.6	13.4
Other family householder	2.9	1.1	2.7	4.4
Living alone	3.9	0.2	1.7	7.4
Living with nonrelatives	11.1	2.3	7.8	18.6

Source: Bureau of the Census, detailed tables from Marital Status and Living Arrangements: March 1998, *Current Population Reports, P20-514, 1998, Internet site <www.census.gov/population/www/socdemo/ms-la.html>; calculations by New Strategist*

Living Arrangements of Women Aged 15 to 24, 1998

(number and percent distribution of women aged 15 to 24 by living arrangement, 1998; numbers in thousands)

	total	aged 15 to 24		
		15 to 17	*18 to 19*	*20 to 24*
Total women	**18,333**	**5,765**	**3,780**	**8,788**
Living with parents	11,055	5,081	2,767	3,207
Living with other family member(s)	966	399	229	338
Living with spouse	2,366	51	180	2,135
Other family householder	1,094	43	109	942
Living alone	528	5	60	463
Living with nonrelatives	2,324	186	435	1,703
Total women	**100.0%**	**100.0%**	**100.0%**	**100.0%**
Living with parents	60.3	88.1	73.2	36.5
Living with other family member(s)	5.3	6.9	6.1	3.8
Living with spouse	12.9	0.9	4.8	24.3
Other family householder	6.0	0.7	2.9	10.7
Living alone	2.9	0.1	1.6	5.3
Living with nonrelatives	12.7	3.2	11.5	19.4

Source: Bureau of the Census, detailed tables from Marital Status and Living Arrangements: March 1998, *Current Population Reports, P20-514, 1998, Internet site <www.census.gov/population/www/socdemo/ms-la.html>; calculations by New Strategist*

Among Young Adults, Women Are More Likely Than Men to Be Married

Most 15-to-24-year-olds are still single, however.

Among all Americans aged 15 or older, men are slightly more likely to be married than women. But among 15-to-24-year-olds, women are more likely to be married than men. In 1998, only 8 percent of men aged 15 to 24 were married compared with 15 percent of their female counterparts. In the 20-to-24 age group, marriage has claimed 27 percent of women and only 15 percent of men. Behind these differences is the fact that women marry at a younger age than men.

The proportion of young adults who are unmarried has grown enormously in the past three decades as more pursued a college degree. Among men aged 20 to 24, the never-married proportion rose from 55 percent in 1970 to 83 percent in 1998. Among women in the age group, the figure rose from 36 to 70 percent during those years.

♦ The great diversity in the living arrangements of young adults is the consequence of postponed marriages.

Many more young adults are single

(percent of people aged 20 to 24 who have never married, by sex, 1970 and 1998)

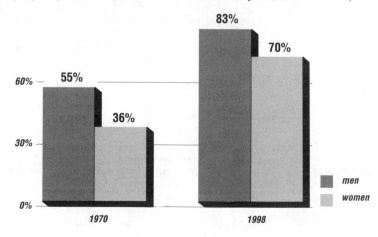

Marital Status of People Aged 15 to 24 by Sex, 1998

(number and percent distribution of people aged 15 or older and aged 15 to 24 by marital status and sex, 1998; numbers in thousands)

	total	aged 15 to 24 total	aged 15 to 24 15 to 19	aged 15 to 24 20 to 24
Total men	**101,123**	**18,747**	**9,921**	**8,826**
Never married	31,591	17,138	9,778	7,360
Married	58,633	1,453	121	1,332
Divorced	8,331	152	19	133
Widowed	2,569	3	3	–
Total women	**108,168**	**18,333**	**9,545**	**8,788**
Never married	26,713	15,413	9,235	6,178
Married	59,333	2,661	289	2,372
Divorced	11,093	242	20	222
Widowed	11,029	19	2	17
Percent distribution				
Total men	**100.0%**	**100.0%**	**100.0%**	**100.0%**
Never married	31.2	91.4	98.6	83.4
Married	58.0	7.8	1.2	15.1
Divorced	8.2	0.8	0.2	1.5
Widowed	2.5	0.0	0.0	–
Total women	**100.0**	**100.0**	**100.0**	**100.0**
Never married	24.7	84.1	96.8	70.3
Married	54.9	14.5	3.0	27.0
Divorced	10.3	1.3	0.2	2.5
Widowed	10.2	0.1	0.0	0.2

Note: (–) means sample is too small to make a reliable estimate.
Source: Bureau of the Census, detailed tables from Marital Status and Living Arrangements: March 1998, *Current Population Reports, P20-514, 1998, Internet site <www.census.gov/population/www/socdemo/ms-la.html>*

7

Population

♦ The millennial generation spanned ages 7 to 24 in 2001. Its 71 million members, many of them children of baby boomers, account for the great majority of Americans under age 25.

♦ The number of people under age 25 will increase just 4.6 percent between 2001 and 2010, less than the 7.9 percent gain projected for the U.S. population as a whole.

♦ America's children and young adults are much more diverse than its middle-aged or older people. While non-Hispanic whites account for 71 percent of all Americans, their share is a smaller 64 percent among people under age 25.

♦ More than 660,000 immigrants arrived in the U.S. in 1998, 257,000 of them under age 25. Many people immigrate as teens and young adults, looking for job opportunities.

♦ In California, only 39 percent of people under age 25 are non-Hispanic white. The 43 percent plurality are Hispanic, while an additional 12 percent are Asian.

♦ Among people under age 25, the mobility rate varies widely. Fully 33 percent of people aged 20 to 24 moved between March 1998 and March 1999 compared with only 13 to 14 percent of children aged 10 to 17.

Males Outnumber Females among the Young

Among people under age 25, there are 105 males per 100 females.

One in four Americans is a child under age 18. The nation's 71 million children are about evenly divided among preschoolers (under age 6), elementary-schoolers (6 to 11), and teens (12 to 17)—with 23 million to 24 million in each group. A slightly larger number, 27 million, are young adults aged 18 to 24. Overall, 35 percent of Americans are under age 25.

The millennial generation—those born between 1977 and 1994—spanned ages 7 to 24 in 2001. Its 71 million members, many of them children of baby boomers, account for the great majority of Americans under age 25.

Among all Americans, females outnumber males by a considerable margin. Among people under age 25, however, males outnumber females. Males are more numerous among the young because more males are born than females. But because males at all ages have a higher mortality rate, females begin to outnumber them in the thirtysomething age group.

♦ Because the large millennial generation almost completely fills the under-25 age group, the nation's children and young adults have a strong voice in our culture, a voice unheard since the baby-boom generation departed the age group.

Among people under age 25, age groups are about equal in size

(number of people under age 25 by age group, 2001; numbers in thousands)

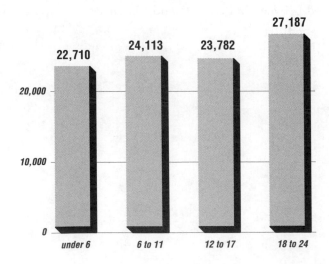

Population under Age 25 by Sex, 2001

(total number of people and number under age 25 by selected age groups, single-year-of-age, and sex; sex ratio by age, 2001; numbers in thousands)

	total	males	females	sex ratio
Total people	**277,803**	**135,795**	**142,008**	**96**
Total people under age 25	**97,793**	**50,033**	**47,760**	**105**
Under age 5	18,899	9,654	9,245	104
Aged 5 to 9	19,546	10,001	9,546	105
Aged 10 to 14	20,270	10,380	9,891	105
Aged 15 to 19	20,065	10,313	9,751	106
Aged 20 to 24	19,012	9,685	9,327	104
Under age 6	22,710	11,604	11,107	104
Aged 6 to 11	24,113	12,343	11,770	105
Aged 12 to 17	23,782	12,213	11,569	106
Aged 18 to 21	16,284	8,342	7,943	105
Aged 22 to 24	10,903	5,533	5,371	103
Under age 18	70,606	36,159	34,446	105
Aged 18 to 24	27,187	13,874	13,313	104
Aged 0	3,803	1,942	1,861	104
Aged 1	3,757	1,919	1,838	104
Aged 2	3,758	1,921	1,838	105
Aged 3	3,762	1,922	1,840	104
Aged 4	3,819	1,951	1,868	104
Aged 5	3,811	1,949	1,862	105
Aged 6	3,851	1,969	1,882	105
Aged 7	3,903	1,996	1,907	105
Aged 8	3,811	1,952	1,859	105
Aged 9	4,171	2,134	2,036	105
Aged 10	4,226	2,166	2,060	105
Aged 11	4,152	2,126	2,026	105
Aged 12	4,004	2,048	1,956	105
Aged 13	3,957	2,024	1,933	105
Aged 14	3,931	2,016	1,915	105
Aged 15	3,964	2,036	1,927	106
Aged 16	3,975	2,048	1,927	106
Aged 17	3,952	2,041	1,911	107

(continued)

(continued from previous page)

	total	males	females	sex ratio
Aged 18	3,970	2,037	1,933	105
Aged 19	4,205	2,152	2,054	105
Aged 20	4,094	2,097	1,997	105
Aged 21	4,015	2,055	1,959	105
Aged 22	3,720	1,898	1,821	104
Aged 23	3,574	1,813	1,761	103
Aged 24	3,610	1,822	1,789	102

Note: The sex ratio is the number of males per 100 females.
Source: Bureau of the Census Internet site <www.census.gov/projections/nation/summary/np-t4-a.txt>; calculations by New Strategist

Number of Children Will Grow Slowly during Next Decade

As millennials move out, the age group will stabilize.

The number of people under age 25 will increase just 4.6 percent between 2001 and 2010, less than the 7.9 percent gain projected for the U.S. population as a whole. Behind the small increase is uneven growth by age group as the Millennial generation grows up.

The number of 22-to-24-year-olds will increase the fastest between 2001 and 2010, up 12 percent, as larger cohorts of millennials enter the age group. A decline is projected for the 6-to-11 age group as smaller cohorts that follow millennials enter their elementary-school years.

♦ The substantial growth in the number of young adults during the next decade is good news for colleges looking for applicants and businesses looking for entry-level workers.

Uneven growth in number of children and young adults

(percent change in number of people under age 25 by age group, 2001–10)

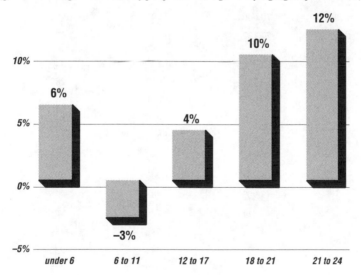

Population under Age 25, 2001 and 2010

(total number of people and number under age 25 by selected age groups and single-year-of-age, 2001 and 2010; numerical and percent change, 2001–10; numbers in thousands)

	2001	2010	change, 2001–10 numerical	change, 2001–10 percent
Total people	**277,803**	**299,862**	**22,059**	**7.9%**
Total under age 25	**97,793**	**102,263**	**4,470**	**4.6**
Under age 5	18,899	20,099	1,200	6.3
Aged 5 to 9	19,546	19,438	−109	−0.6
Aged 10 to 14	20,270	19,908	−363	−1.8
Aged 15 to 19	20,065	21,668	1,603	8.0
Aged 20 to 24	19,012	21,151	2,139	11.2
Under age 6	22,710	24,038	1,380	5.8
Aged 6 to 11	24,113	23,433	−679	−2.8
Aged 12 to 17	23,782	24,630	847	3.6
Aged 18 to 21	16,284	17,939	1,655	10.2
Aged 22 to 24	10,903	12,223	1,320	12.1
Under age 18	70,606	72,101	1,495	2.1
Aged 18 to 24	27,187	30,163	2,975	10.9
Aged 0	3,803	4,123	320	8.4
Aged 1	3,757	4,039	282	7.5
Aged 2	3,758	4,001	243	6.5
Aged 3	3,762	3,960	198	5.3
Aged 4	3,819	3,976	157	4.1
Aged 5	3,811	3,939	128	3.3
Aged 6	3,851	3,903	53	1.4
Aged 7	3,903	3,888	−15	−0.4
Aged 8	3,811	3,726	−85	−2.2
Aged 9	4,171	3,982	−189	−4.5
Aged 10	4,226	3,994	−232	−5.5
Aged 11	4,152	3,940	−211	−5.1
Aged 12	4,004	3,949	−55	−1.4
Aged 13	3,957	3,999	42	1.1
Aged 14	3,931	4,025	94	2.4
Aged 15	3,964	4,117	153	3.9
Aged 16	3,975	4,191	216	5.4

(continued)

(continued from previous page)

| | 2001 | 2010 | change, 2001–10 | |
			numerical	percent
Aged 17	3,952	4,349	398	10.1%
Aged 18	3,970	4,361	392	9.9
Aged 19	4,205	4,650	445	10.6
Aged 20	4,094	4,592	497	12.1
Aged 21	4,015	4,336	322	8.0
Aged 22	3,720	4,120	400	10.8
Aged 23	3,574	4,019	445	12.4
Aged 24	3,610	4,085	474	13.1

Source: Bureau of the Census, Internet site <www.census.gov/projections/nation/summary/np-t4-a.txt>; calculations by New Strategist

The Nation's Children Are Diverse

Hispanics outnumber non-Hispanic blacks among the under-25 population.

America's children and young adults are much more diverse than middle-aged or older people. While non-Hispanic whites account for 71 percent of all Americans, their share is a smaller 64 percent among people under age 25. Among children under age 5, non-Hispanic whites account for only 61 percent of the population.

Sixteen percent of people under age 25 are Hispanic, while 14 percent are non-Hispanic black. Among preschoolers, Hispanics outnumber non-Hispanic blacks by more than 1 million. Hispanics may be of any race and fully 91 percent are white—a figure that does not vary much by age.

♦ Racial and ethnic differences between young and old may divide the nation in the years ahead as older non-Hispanic whites attempt to lead young Hispanics and blacks.

Minorities account for a large share of children and young adults

(percent of people under age 25 by race and Hispanic origin, 2001)

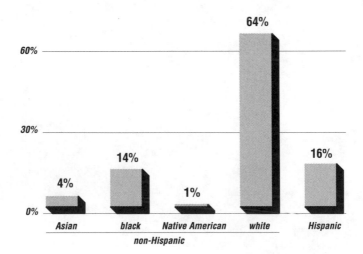

Population under Age 25 by Race and Hispanic Origin, 2001

(number and percent distribution of total people and people under age 25 by selected age groups, race, and Hispanic origin, 2001; numbers in thousands)

	total	non-Hispanic total	Asian	black	Native American	white	Hispanic
Total people	277,803	244,187	10,990	33,876	2,072	197,249	33,616
Total under age 25	97,793	81,869	4,158	14,119	924	62,669	15,924
Under age 5	18,899	15,248	886	2,607	166	11,589	3,651
Aged 5 to 9	19,546	16,137	856	2,810	174	12,298	3,409
Aged 10 to 14	20,270	17,235	836	3,071	211	13,117	3,036
Aged 15 to 19	20,065	17,148	806	2,926	200	13,216	2,916
Aged 20 to 24	19,012	16,100	774	2,705	173	12,449	2,912
Under age 6	22,710	18,374	1,060	3,123	200	13,991	4,337
Aged 6 to 11	24,113	20,087	1,027	3,552	222	15,284	4,026
Aged 12 to 17	23,782	20,335	977	3,552	252	15,554	3,447
Aged 18 to 21	16,284	13,856	645	2,357	151	10,703	2,428
Aged 22 to 24	10,903	9,218	448	1,535	99	7,136	1,685
Under age 18	70,606	58,795	3,064	10,227	674	44,830	11,810
Aged 18 to 24	27,187	23,074	1,093	3,892	249	17,839	4,114

PERCENT DISTRIBUTION BY RACE AND HISPANIC ORIGIN

	total	non-Hispanic total	Asian	black	Native American	white	Hispanic
Total people	100.0%	87.9%	4.0%	12.2%	0.7%	71.0%	12.1%
Total under age 25	100.0	83.7	4.3	14.4	0.9	64.1	16.3
Under age 5	100.0	80.7	4.7	13.8	0.9	61.3	19.3
Aged 5 to 9	100.0	82.6	4.4	14.4	0.9	62.9	17.4
Aged 10 to 14	100.0	85.0	4.1	15.2	1.0	64.7	15.0
Aged 15 to 19	100.0	85.5	4.0	14.6	1.0	65.9	14.5
Aged 20 to 24	100.0	84.7	4.1	14.2	0.9	65.5	15.3
Under age 6	100.0	80.9	4.7	13.8	0.9	61.6	19.1
Aged 6 to 11	100.0	83.3	4.3	14.7	0.9	63.4	16.7
Aged 12 to 17	100.0	85.5	4.1	14.9	1.1	65.4	14.5
Aged 18 to 21	100.0	85.1	4.0	14.5	0.9	65.7	14.9
Aged 22 to 24	100.0	84.5	4.1	14.1	0.9	65.5	15.5
Under age 18	100.0	83.3	4.3	14.5	1.0	63.5	16.7
Aged 18 to 24	100.0	84.9	4.0	14.3	0.9	65.6	15.1

Source: Bureau of the Census, Internet site <www.census.gov/projections/nation/summary/np-t4-a.txt>; calculations by New Strategist

Hispanics under Age 25 by Race, 2001

(number and percent distribution of total Hispanics and Hispanics under age 25 by selected age groups and race, 2000; numbers in thousands)

| | Hispanic | | | | |
	total	Asian	black	Native American	white
Total people	**33,616**	**675**	**1,908**	**399**	**30,635**
Total under age 25	**15,924**	**318**	**890**	**199**	**14,516**
Under age 5	3,651	66	201	40	3,344
Aged 5 to 9	3,409	68	193	36	3,111
Aged 10 to 14	3,036	67	179	43	2,747
Aged 15 to 19	2,916	61	164	42	2,650
Aged 20 to 24	2,912	56	154	38	2,664
Under age 6	4,337	80	239	48	3,970
Aged 6 to 11	4,026	82	229	45	3,670
Aged 12 to 17	3,447	77	202	52	3,117
Aged 18 to 21	2,428	47	133	32	2,216
Aged 22 to 24	1,685	32	88	22	1,543
Under age 18	11,810	239	670	145	10,757
Aged 18 to 24	4,114	79	221	54	3,759

PERCENT DISTRIBUTION BY RACE

	total	Asian	black	Native American	white
Total people	**100.0%**	**2.0%**	**5.7%**	**1.2%**	**91.1%**
Total under age 25	**100.0**	**2.0**	**5.6**	**1.2**	**91.2**
Under age 5	100.0	1.8	5.5	1.1	91.6
Aged 5 to 9	100.0	2.0	5.6	1.1	91.3
Aged 10 to 14	100.0	2.2	5.9	1.4	90.5
Aged 15 to 19	100.0	2.1	5.6	1.4	90.9
Aged 20 to 24	100.0	1.9	5.3	1.3	91.5
Under age 6	100.0	1.8	5.5	1.1	91.5
Aged 6 to 11	100.0	2.0	5.7	1.1	91.1
Aged 12 to 17	100.0	2.2	5.8	1.5	90.4
Aged 18 to 21	100.0	1.9	5.5	1.3	91.3
Aged 22 to 24	100.0	1.9	5.2	1.3	91.6
Under age 18	100.0	2.0	5.7	1.2	91.1
Aged 18 to 24	100.0	1.9	5.4	1.3	91.4

Source: Bureau of the Census, Internet site <www.census.gov/projections/nation/summary/np-t4-a.txt>; calculations by New Strategist

Few Children Are Foreign-Born

But many young adults were born in another country.

While 10 percent of all Americans are foreign born, the proportion is far lower among people under age 20. The figure climbs to an above-average 13 percent among those aged 20 to 24. A large share of 20-to-24-year-olds are foreign born because young adults migrate to the U.S. in search of job opportunities. Among the 2 million 20-to-24-year-olds who were born in a foreign country, only 15 percent are naturalized citizens.

Among the foreign born in the 20-to-24 age group, fully 49 percent were born in Central America (which includes Mexico in these statistics), while 24 percent were born in Asia. Only 8 percent were born in Europe.

♦ The foreign-born population adds to the diversity of young adults. Because most are not citizens, however, they lack political power.

Among foreign-born young adults, most are from Latin America

(percent distribution of foreign-born people aged 20 to 24 by region of birth, 2000)

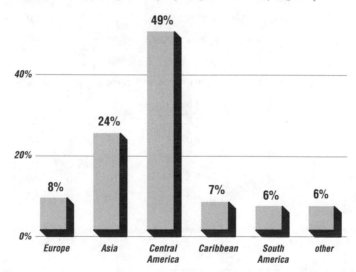

Population under age 25 by Citizenship Status, 2000

(number and percent distribution of total people and people under age 25 by citizenship status, 2000; numbers in thousands)

	total	native-born	foreign-born total	foreign-born naturalized citizen	foreign-born not a citizen
Total people	274,087	245,708	28,380	10,622	17,758
Total under age 25	98,857	92,872	5,985	834	5,151
Under age 5	19,607	19,319	289	54	235
Aged 5 to 9	20,379	19,719	659	62	597
Aged 10 to 14	20,328	19,269	1,059	142	917
Aged 15 to 19	20,102	18,490	1,612	210	1,402
Aged 20 to 24	18,441	16,075	2,366	366	2,000
Percent distribution by citizenship status					
Total people	**100.0%**	**89.6%**	**10.4%**	**3.9%**	**6.5%**
Total under age 25	100.0	93.9	6.1	0.8	5.2
Under age 5	100.0	98.5	1.5	0.3	1.2
Aged 5 to 9	100.0	96.8	3.2	0.3	2.9
Aged 10 to 14	100.0	94.8	5.2	0.7	4.5
Aged 15 to 19	100.0	92.0	8.0	1.0	7.0
Aged 20 to 24	100.0	87.2	12.8	2.0	10.8
Percent distribution by age					
Total people	**100.0%**	**100.0%**	**100.0%**	**100.0%**	**100.0%**
Total under age 25	36.1	37.8	21.1	7.9	29.0
Under age 5	7.2	7.9	1.0	0.5	1.3
Aged 5 to 9	7.4	8.0	2.3	0.6	3.4
Aged 10 to 14	7.4	7.8	3.7	1.3	5.2
Aged 15 to 19	7.3	7.5	5.7	2.0	7.9
Aged 20 to 24	6.7	6.5	8.3	3.4	11.3

Source: Bureau of the Census, Internet site <www.census.gov/population/www/socdemo/foreign.html>; calculations by New Strategist

Foreign-Born Population under Age 25, 2000

(number and percent distribution of total people and people under age 25 by foreign born status and region of birth, 2000; numbers in thousands)

		foreign born						
					Latin America			
	total	total	Europe	Asia	Central America	Caribbean	South America	other
Total people	**274,087**	**28,380**	**4,355**	**7,246**	**9,789**	**2,813**	**1,876**	**2,301**
Total under age 25	98,857	5,985	531	1,418	2,697	468	417	454
Under age 5	19,607	289	24	71	118	14	25	37
Aged 5 to 9	20,379	659	74	120	293	44	46	82
Aged 10 to 14	20,328	1,059	76	271	420	123	89	80
Aged 15 to 19	20,102	1,612	156	388	711	129	118	110
Aged 20 to 24	18,441	2,366	201	568	1,155	158	139	145

Percent distribution of foreign-born by region of birth

Total people	–	**100.0%**	**15.3%**	**25.5%**	**34.5%**	**9.9%**	**6.6%**	**8.1%**
Total under age 25	–	100.0	8.9	23.7	45.1	7.8	7.0	7.6
Under age 5		100.0	8.3	24.6	40.8	4.8	8.7	12.8
Aged 5 to 9	–	100.0	11.2	18.2	44.5	6.7	7.0	12.4
Aged 10 to 14	–	100.0	7.2	25.6	39.7	11.6	8.4	7.6
Aged 15 to 19	–	100.0	9.7	24.1	44.1	8.0	7.3	6.8
Aged 20 to 24	–	100.0	8.5	24.0	48.8	6.7	5.9	6.1

Percent distribution by age

Total people	**100.0%**	**100.0%**	**100.0%**	**100.0%**	**100.0%**	**100.0%**	**100.0%**	**100.0%**
Total under age 25	36.1	21.1	12.2	19.6	27.6	16.6	22.2	19.7
Under age 5	7.2	1.0	0.6	1.0	1.2	0.5	1.3	1.6
Aged 5 to 9	7.4	2.3	1.7	1.7	3.0	1.6	2.5	3.6
Aged 10 to 14	7.4	3.7	1.7	3.7	4.3	4.4	4.7	3.5
Aged 15 to 19	7.3	5.7	3.6	5.4	7.3	4.6	6.3	4.8
Aged 20 to 24	6.7	8.3	4.6	7.8	11.8	5.6	7.4	6.3

Note: Central America includes Mexico in these statistics; (–) means not applicable.
Source: Bureau of the Census, Internet site <www.census.gov/population/www/socdemo/foreign.html>; calculations by New Strategist

Among Immigrants, the Young Count

More than one-third of immigrants are under age 25.

Of the more than 660,000 immigrants admitted to the U.S. in 1998, 257,000 were under age 25. Many people immigrate as teens and young adults, looking for job opportunities.

The most common country of origin for U.S. immigrants in 1998 was Mexico. Overall, one in five immigrants is from Mexico. Among people under age 25, a larger 24 percent are from Mexico.

♦ Because most immigrants are children or young adults, immigration has a much greater impact on the diversity of young Americans than on older populations.

Total and Mexican Immigrants under Age 25, 1998

(number and percent distribution of total immigrants and immigrants from Mexico by age for ages under 25, and percent of immigrants from Mexico, 1998)

	total immigrants		immigrants from Mexico		
	number	percent distribution	number	percent distribution	percent of total
Total immigrants	660,477	100.0%	131,575	100.0%	19.9%
Total under age 25	257,219	38.9	61,002	46.4	23.7
Under age 5	33,797	5.1	4,069	3.1	12.0
Aged 5 to 9	39,035	5.9	8,425	6.4	21.6
Aged 10 to 14	56,459	8.5	16,039	12.2	28.4
Aged 15 to 19	68,319	10.3	17,285	13.1	25.3
Aged 20 to 24	59,609	9.0	15,184	11.5	25.5

Source: Immigration and Naturalization Service, 1998 Statistical Yearbook of the Immigration and Naturalization Service, 2000; calculations by New Strategist

In Some States, Minorities Are the Majority of Millennials

In the nation's two most populous states, the majority of people under age 25 are Asian, black, Native American, or Hispanic.

In the Pacific states, non-Hispanic whites account for only 46 percent of the population under age 25. In the West South Central states, non-Hispanic whites account for only 52 percent of people under age 25. Behind these numbers are the rapidly changing demographics of the nation's two most-populous states—California and Texas.

In California, just 48 percent of residents are non-Hispanic white. Among Californian's under age 25, however, non-Hispanic whites are an even smaller minority, accounting for just 39 percent of the total. The 43 percent plurality of Californians under age 25 are Hispanic, while an additional 12 percent are Asian. In Texas, the second-most populous state, just 45 percent of residents under age 25 are non-Hispanic white while 40 percent are Hispanic.

In most states, children and young adults are far more diverse than middle-aged and older people. As the millennial generation grows up, the diversity of the nation will increase dramatically.

♦ Young adults are much less likely to vote than middle-aged and older Americans, greatly reducing the political clout of minorities.

Population under Age 25 by Region, Race, and Hispanic Origin, 2001

(number and percent distribution of total people and people under age 25 by region, division, race, and Hispanic origin, 2061; numbers in thousands)

		non-Hispanic					non-Hispanic				
	total	Asian	black	Native American	white	Hispanic	Asian	black	Native American	white	Hispanic
UNITED STATES, TOTAL	277,803	10,990	33,876	2,072	197,249	33,616	4.0%	12.2%	0.7%	71.0%	12.1%
Total, under age 25	97,793	4,158	14,119	924	62,669	15,924	4.3	14.4	0.9	64.1	16.3
Under age 5	18,899	886	2,607	166	11,589	3,651	4.7	13.8	0.9	61.3	19.3
Aged 5 to 9	19,546	856	2,810	174	12,298	3,409	4.4	14.4	0.9	62.9	17.4
Aged 10 to 14	20,270	836	3,071	211	13,117	3,036	4.1	15.2	1.0	64.7	15.0
Aged 15 to 19	20,065	806	2,926	200	13,216	2,916	4.0	14.6	1.0	65.9	14.5
Aged 20 to 24	19,012	774	2,705	173	12,449	2,912	4.1	14.2	0.9	65.5	15.3
NORTHEAST, TOTAL	52,282	2,176	5,626	114	39,274	5,092	4.2	10.8	0.2	75.1	9.7
Total, under age 25	17,340	823	2,240	42	11,948	2,288	4.7	12.9	0.2	68.9	13.2
Under age 5	3,322	186	418	7	2,180	531	5.6	12.6	0.2	65.6	16.0
Aged 5 to 9	3,413	181	450	7	2,284	491	5.3	13.2	0.2	66.9	14.4
Aged 10 to 14	3,686	161	496	9	2,576	444	4.4	13.5	0.3	69.9	12.0
Aged 15 to 19	3,655	152	470	10	2,601	423	4.2	12.8	0.3	71.2	11.6
Aged 20 to 24	3,264	144	406	8	2,307	399	4.4	12.4	0.2	70.7	12.2

(continued)

(continued from previous page)

	non-Hispanic						non-Hispanic				
	total	Asian	black	Native American	white	Hispanic	Asian	black	Native American	white	Hispanic
New England, total	**13,642**	**402**	**701**	**31**	**11,663**	**844**	**2.9%**	**5.1%**	**0.2%**	**85.5%**	**6.2%**
Total, under age 25	**4,483**	**172**	**308**	**12**	**3,570**	**420**	**3.8**	**6.9**	**0.3**	**79.6**	**9.4**
Under age 5	844	39	59	2	646	98	4.7	6.9	0.3	76.5	11.6
Aged 5 to 9	870	39	66	3	670	93	4.5	7.5	0.3	77.0	10.6
Aged 10 to 14	948	36	71	3	758	81	3.8	7.5	0.3	79.9	8.5
Aged 15 to 19	979	29	62	3	806	79	3.0	6.3	0.3	82.3	8.1
Aged 20 to 24	842	29	51	2	690	70	3.4	6.1	0.3	82.0	8.3
Middle Atlantic, total	**38,641**	**1,774**	**4,926**	**83**	**27,611**	**4,247**	**4.6**	**12.7**	**0.2**	**71.5**	**11.0**
Total, under age 25	**12,857**	**651**	**1,932**	**29**	**8,378**	**1,867**	**5.1**	**15.0**	**0.2**	**65.2**	**14.5**
Under age 5	2,478	146	359	5	1,534	434	5.9	14.5	0.2	61.9	17.5
Aged 5 to 9	2,542	141	385	5	1,614	398	5.6	15.1	0.2	63.5	15.7
Aged 10 to 14	2,738	125	425	7	1,818	364	4.6	15.5	0.2	66.4	13.3
Aged 15 to 19	2,677	123	408	7	1,795	343	4.6	15.2	0.3	67.1	12.8
Aged 20 to 24	2,422	116	355	6	1,617	329	4.8	14.6	0.2	66.8	13.6

(continued)

(continued from previous page)

	total	non-Hispanic					non-Hispanic				
		Asian	black	Native American	white	Hispanic	Asian	black	Native American	white	Hispanic
MIDWEST, TOTAL	**63,341**	**1,218**	**6,347**	**364**	**52,715**	**2,698**	**1.9%**	**10.0%**	**0.6%**	**83.2%**	**4.3%**
Total, under age 25	**22,274**	**515**	**2,760**	**173**	**17,481**	**1,345**	**2.3**	**12.4**	**0.8**	**78.5**	**6.0**
Under age 5	4,137	111	508	31	3,175	312	2.7	12.3	0.7	76.8	7.5
Aged 5 to 9	4,363	110	556	33	3,369	295	2.5	12.7	0.7	77.2	6.8
Aged 10 to 14	4,588	101	624	39	3,576	249	2.2	13.6	0.9	77.9	5.4
Aged 15 to 19	4,710	100	565	38	3,759	248	2.1	12.0	0.8	79.8	5.3
Aged 20 to 24	4,476	94	506	32	3,602	241	2.1	11.3	0.7	80.5	5.4
East North Central, total	**44,414**	**885**	**5,289**	**149**	**35,923**	**2,169**	**2.0**	**11.9**	**0.3**	**80.9**	**4.9**
Total, under age 25	**15,572**	**358**	**2,288**	**60**	**11,792**	**1,075**	**2.3**	**14.7**	**0.4**	**75.7**	**6.9**
Under age 5	2,919	77	422	10	2,159	250	2.7	14.4	0.4	74.0	8.6
Aged 5 to 9	3,071	76	462	10	2,287	236	2.5	15.0	0.3	74.4	7.7
Aged 10 to 14	3,238	69	521	13	2,436	199	2.1	16.1	0.4	75.2	6.1
Aged 15 to 19	3,266	69	467	14	2,519	198	2.1	14.3	0.4	77.1	6.1
Aged 20 to 24	3,078	66	417	12	2,391	191	2.2	13.5	0.4	77.7	6.2

(continued)

(continued from previous page)

	total	non-Hispanic					non-Hispanic				
		Asian	black	Native American	white	Hispanic	Asian	black	Native American	white	Hispanic
West North Central, total	**18,927**	**333**	**1,058**	**215**	**16,792**	**529**	**1.8%**	**5.6%**	**1.1%**	**88.7%**	**2.8%**
Total, under age 25	**6,702**	**157**	**471**	**113**	**5,690**	**271**	**2.3**	**7.0**	**1.7**	**84.9**	**4.0**
Under age 5	1,217	33	86	20	1,016	62	2.7	7.1	1.7	83.4	5.1
Aged 5 to 9	1,291	34	94	22	1,083	59	2.6	7.3	1.7	83.8	4.5
Aged 10 to 14	1,351	32	103	26	1,140	50	2.3	7.6	2.0	84.4	3.7
Aged 15 to 19	1,444	31	99	24	1,240	51	2.1	6.8	1.7	85.9	3.5
Aged 20 to 24	1,399	28	90	20	1,212	50	2.0	6.4	1.4	86.6	3.6
SOUTH, TOTAL	**99,226**	**1,978**	**18,900**	**591**	**67,129**	**10,627**	**2.0**	**19.0**	**0.6**	**67.7**	**10.7**
Total, under age 25	**34,990**	**761**	**7,963**	**244**	**21,100**	**4,921**	**2.2**	**22.8**	**0.7**	**60.3**	**14.1**
Under age 5	6,816	167	1,478	45	3,995	1,130	2.5	21.7	0.7	58.6	16.6
Aged 5 to 9	7,108	162	1,591	46	4,256	1,053	2.3	22.4	0.7	59.9	14.8
Aged 10 to 14	7,163	148	1,700	52	4,362	901	2.1	23.7	0.7	60.9	12.6
Aged 15 to 19	7,081	144	1,635	52	4,342	907	2.0	23.1	0.7	61.3	12.8
Aged 20 to 24	6,822	139	1,560	48	4,145	929	2.0	22.9	0.7	60.8	13.6

(continued)

(continued from previous page)

	total	non-Hispanic				Hispanic	non-Hispanic				Hispanic
		Asian	black	Native American	white		Asian	black	Native American	white	
South Atlantic, total	**51,044**	**1,145**	**10,986**	**205**	**35,128**	**3,581**	**2.2%**	**21.5%**	**0.4%**	**68.8%**	**7.0%**
Total, under age 25	**17,280**	**434**	**4,553**	**81**	**10,764**	**1,447**	**2.5**	**26.4**	**0.5**	**62.3**	**8.4**
Under age 5	3,340	96	848	15	2,052	329	2.9	25.4	0.4	61.4	9.9
Aged 5 to 9	3,502	92	916	15	2,183	296	2.6	26.1	0.4	62.3	8.4
Aged 10 to 14	3,608	85	985	18	2,255	265	2.4	27.3	0.5	62.5	7.3
Aged 15 to 19	3,543	82	940	17	2,227	276	2.3	26.5	0.5	62.9	7.8
Aged 20 to 24	3,286	78	864	15	2,047	281	2.4	26.3	0.5	62.3	8.6
East South Central, total	**16,839**	**138**	**3,396**	**40**	**13,080**	**185**	**0.8**	**20.2**	**0.2**	**77.7**	**1.1**
Total, under age 25	**5,781**	**55**	**1,465**	**15**	**4,159**	**87**	**1.0**	**25.3**	**0.3**	**71.9**	**1.5**
Under age 5	1,105	13	275	3	795	20	1.1	24.9	0.2	71.9	1.9
Aged 5 to 9	1,170	12	295	3	841	19	1.1	25.2	0.2	71.9	1.6
Aged 10 to 14	1,180	10	308	3	844	15	0.9	26.1	0.2	71.5	1.3
Aged 15 to 19	1,158	10	291	3	839	15	0.9	25.1	0.3	72.4	1.3
Aged 20 to 24	1,167	10	297	3	840	16	0.9	25.4	0.3	72.0	1.4

(continued)

(continued from previous page)

		non-Hispanic						non-Hispanic			
	total	Asian	black	Native American	white	Hispanic	Asian	black	Native American	white	Hispanic
West South Central, total	**31,343**	**696**	**4,519**	**346**	**18,921**	**6,861**	**2.2%**	**14.4%**	**1.1%**	**60.4%**	**21.9%**
Total, under age 25	**11,929**	**272**	**1,945**	**148**	**6,177**	**3,387**	**2.3**	**16.3**	**1.2**	**51.8**	**28.4**
Under age 5	2,370	59	355	27	1,149	780	2.5	15.0	1.2	48.5	32.9
Aged 5 to 9	2,436	58	381	28	1,232	738	2.4	15.6	1.2	50.6	30.3
Aged 10 to 14	2,375	53	407	31	1,262	621	2.2	17.1	1.3	53.2	26.2
Aged 15 to 19	2,380	52	404	32	1,276	615	2.2	17.0	1.3	53.6	25.9
Aged 20 to 24	2,369	50	399	30	1,258	632	2.1	16.8	1.3	53.1	26.7
WEST, TOTAL	**62,953**	**5,618**	**3,002**	**1,003**	**38,131**	**15,200**	**8.9**	**4.8**	**1.6**	**60.6**	**24.1**
Total, under age 25	**23,189**	**2,058**	**1,157**	**465**	**12,139**	**7,370**	**8.9**	**5.0**	**2.0**	**52.3**	**31.8**
Under age 5	4,625	422	204	83	2,238	1,678	9.1	4.4	1.8	48.4	36.3
Aged 5 to 9	4,663	403	212	88	2,389	1,570	8.6	4.6	1.9	51.2	33.7
Aged 10 to 14	4,832	426	251	110	2,604	1,441	8.8	5.2	2.3	53.9	29.8
Aged 15 to 19	4,619	410	257	100	2,513	1,338	8.9	5.6	2.2	54.4	29.0
Aged 20 to 24	4,451	397	233	84	2,395	1,343	8.9	5.2	1.9	53.8	30.2

(continued)

(continued from previous page)

| | non-Hispanic | | | | | | non-Hispanic | | | |
	total	Asian	black	Native American	white	Hispanic	Asian	black	Native American	white	Hispanic
Mountain, total	**18,245**	**406**	**523**	**581**	**13,399**	**3,337**	**2.2%**	**2.9%**	**3.2%**	**73.4%**	**18.3%**
Total, under age 25	**6,939**	**168**	**215**	**289**	**4,584**	**1,684**	**2.4**	**3.1**	**4.2**	**66.1**	**24.3**
Under age 5	1,355	37	37	52	846	384	2.7	2.7	3.8	62.4	28.3
Aged 5 to 9	1,417	36	40	56	917	369	2.6	2.8	3.9	64.7	26.0
Aged 10 to 14	1,386	33	46	70	930	307	2.4	3.3	5.1	67.1	22.1
Aged 15 to 19	1,406	32	48	61	951	314	2.3	3.4	4.3	67.6	22.3
Aged 20 to 24	1,374	30	44	50	941	310	2.2	3.2	3.6	68.5	22.5
Pacific, total	**44,708**	**5,212**	**2,480**	**421**	**24,732**	**11,863**	**11.7**	**5.5**	**0.9**	**55.3**	**26.5**
Total, under age 25	**16,250**	**1,890**	**942**	**177**	**7,555**	**5,686**	**11.6**	**5.8**	**1.1**	**46.5**	**35.0**
Under age 5	3,270	385	167	31	1,393	1,294	11.8	5.1	1.0	42.6	39.6
Aged 5 to 9	3,246	367	173	32	1,472	1,201	11.3	5.3	1.0	45.4	37.0
Aged 10 to 14	3,446	393	205	40	1,674	1,134	11.4	5.9	1.1	48.6	32.9
Aged 15 to 19	3,213	378	209	39	1,563	1,024	11.8	6.5	1.2	48.6	31.9
Aged 20 to 24	3,076	367	189	34	1,454	1,053	11.9	6.1	1.1	47.3	33.6

Source: Projections by New Strategist

Population under Age 25 by State, Race, and Hispanic Origin, 2001

(number and percent distribution of total people and people under age 25 by state, race, and Hispanic origin, 2001)

	total	non-Hispanic					non-Hispanic				
		Asian	black	Native American	white	Hispanic	Asian	black	Native American	white	Hispanic
Alabama, total	4,384,221	29,645	1,138,711	13,504	3,154,028	48,333	0.7%	26.0%	0.3%	71.9%	1.1%
Total, under age 25	1,486,926	11,752	476,734	4,478	971,016	22,946	0.8	32.1	0.3	65.3	1.5
Under age 5	286,592	2,671	89,850	753	187,879	5,439	0.9	31.4	0.3	65.6	1.9
Aged 5 to 9	302,239	2,631	95,361	639	198,457	5,152	0.9	31.6	0.2	65.7	1.7
Aged 10 to 14	303,697	2,267	99,345	751	197,142	4,191	0.7	32.7	0.2	64.9	1.4
Aged 15 to 19	294,328	2,014	93,661	1,024	193,691	3,937	0.7	31.8	0.3	65.8	1.3
Aged 20 to 24	300,070	2,169	98,517	1,310	193,847	4,227	0.7	32.8	0.4	64.6	1.4
Alaska, total	632,279	30,855	22,887	102,856	448,805	26,876	4.9	3.6	16.3	71.0	4.3
Total, under age 25	263,065	13,483	9,947	59,503	166,826	13,305	5.1	3.8	22.6	63.4	5.1
Under age 5	46,547	2,459	1,835	10,687	28,434	3,133	5.3	3.9	23.0	61.1	6.7
Aged 5 to 9	50,433	2,524	1,940	12,098	30,845	3,026	5.0	3.8	24.0	61.2	6.0
Aged 10 to 14	57,521	2,898	2,005	14,882	35,384	2,352	5.0	3.5	25.9	61.5	4.1
Aged 15 to 19	56,872	2,809	2,168	12,312	37,181	2,402	4.9	3.8	21.6	65.4	4.2
Aged 20 to 24	51,691	2,793	1,998	9,525	34,981	2,393	5.4	3.9	18.4	67.7	4.6

(continued)

(continued from previous page)

| | non-Hispanic | | | | | | non-Hispanic | | | | |
	total	Asian	black	Native American	white	Hispanic	Asian	black	Native American	white	Hispanic
Arizona, total	**5,142,570**	**101,287**	**156,590**	**249,620**	**3,398,853**	**1,236,220**	**2.0%**	**3.0%**	**4.9%**	**66.1%**	**24.0%**
Total, under age 25	**1,956,476**	**40,945**	**64,363**	**127,853**	**1,074,755**	**648,560**	**2.1**	**3.3**	**6.5**	**54.9**	**33.1**
Under age 5	396,656	8,532	10,986	22,829	203,020	151,289	2.2	2.8	5.8	51.2	38.1
Aged 5 to 9	412,013	8,316	11,638	24,651	220,090	147,318	2.0	2.8	6.0	53.4	35.8
Aged 10 to 14	400,497	8,244	13,808	31,998	227,084	119,363	2.1	3.4	8.0	56.7	29.8
Aged 15 to 19	387,396	8,394	14,581	27,111	219,674	117,635	2.2	3.8	7.0	56.7	30.4
Aged 20 to 24	359,914	7,460	13,350	21,263	204,887	112,955	2.1	3.7	5.9	56.9	31.4
Arkansas, total	**2,639,837**	**19,681**	**424,342**	**13,436**	**2,122,641**	**59,736**	**0.7**	**16.1**	**0.5**	**80.4**	**2.3**
Total, under age 25	**938,315**	**8,248**	**195,911**	**5,580**	**697,694**	**30,883**	**0.9**	**20.9**	**0.6**	**74.4**	**3.3**
Under age 5	176,728	1,886	36,059	1,213	130,682	6,888	1.1	20.4	0.7	73.9	3.9
Aged 5 to 9	189,499	1,867	39,216	1,303	140,654	6,459	1.0	20.7	0.7	74.2	3.4
Aged 10 to 14	189,559	1,481	40,307	1,033	140,901	5,838	0.8	21.3	0.5	74.3	3.1
Aged 15 to 19	193,131	1,514	40,047	1,052	144,655	5,864	0.8	20.7	0.5	74.9	3.0
Aged 20 to 24	189,399	1,500	40,282	980	140,803	5,835	0.8	21.3	0.5	74.3	3.1
California, total	**33,631,107**	**3,984,000**	**2,177,927**	**180,270**	**16,199,492**	**11,089,413**	**11.8**	**6.5**	**0.5**	**48.2**	**33.0**
Total, under age 25	**12,363,871**	**1,430,900**	**819,821**	**58,307**	**4,766,168**	**5,288,675**	**11.6**	**6.6**	**0.5**	**38.5**	**42.8**
Under age 5	2,539,246	290,978	144,820	10,016	889,558	1,203,874	11.5	5.7	0.4	35.0	47.4
Aged 5 to 9	2,484,847	273,617	149,798	9,188	936,579	1,115,665	11.0	6.0	0.4	37.7	44.9
Aged 10 to 14	2,649,766	297,198	180,192	11,963	1,099,617	1,060,797	11.2	6.8	0.5	41.5	40.0
Aged 15 to 19	2,399,034	290,146	181,595	14,072	963,472	949,750	12.1	7.6	0.6	40.2	39.6
Aged 20 to 24	2,290,978	278,962	163,417	13,068	876,941	958,539	12.2	7.1	0.6	38.3	41.8

(continued)

*continued from previous page)

| | | non-Hispanic | | | | | | non-Hispanic | | | |
	total	Asian	black	Native American	white	Hispanic	Asian	black	Native American	white	Hispanic
Colorado, total	**4,294,082**	**103,800**	**166,265**	**27,558**	**3,330,641**	**665,818**	**2.4%**	**3.9%**	**0.6%**	**77.6%**	**15.5%**
Total, under age 25	**1,534,899**	**42,405**	**67,122**	**10,769**	**1,081,656**	**332,947**	**2.8**	**4.4**	**0.7**	**70.5**	**21.7**
Under age 5	294,823	9,342	11,537	1,998	196,786	75,160	3.2	3.9	0.7	66.7	25.5
Aged 5 to 9	305,478	9,229	12,264	2,011	209,658	72,317	3.0	4.0	0.7	68.6	23.7
Aged 10 to 14	304,113	7,843	14,226	2,234	219,607	60,203	2.6	4.7	0.7	72.2	19.8
Aged 15 to 19	319,895	8,186	15,022	2,403	231,173	63,111	2.6	4.7	0.8	72.3	19.7
Aged 20 to 24	310,590	7,806	14,073	2,123	224,432	62,157	2.5	4.5	0.7	72.3	20.0
Connecticut, total	**3,322,822**	**89,375**	**291,787**	**6,130**	**2,631,480**	**304,050**	**2.7**	**8.8**	**0.2**	**79.2**	**9.2**
Total, under age 25	**1,130,433**	**35,906**	**121,524**	**2,296**	**820,348**	**150,359**	**3.2**	**10.8**	**0.2**	**72.6**	**13.3**
Under age 5	214,846	8,027	21,972	462	149,344	35,041	3.7	10.2	0.2	69.5	16.3
Aged 5 to 9	224,806	7,814	23,766	477	159,548	33,199	3.5	10.6	0.2	71.0	14.8
Aged 10 to 14	242,672	7,100	26,742	510	179,890	28,429	2.9	11.0	0.2	74.1	11.7
Aged 15 to 19	247,568	6,784	27,145	451	184,154	29,033	2.7	11.0	0.2	74.4	11.7
Aged 20 to 24	200,542	6,180	21,899	395	147,411	24,656	3.1	10.9	0.2	73.5	12.3
Delaware, total	**775,832**	**16,920**	**151,956**	**2,107**	**574,331**	**30,518**	**2.2**	**19.6**	**0.3**	**74.0**	**3.9**
Total, under age 25	**258,700**	**6,199**	**61,420**	**652**	**175,770**	**14,659**	**2.4**	**23.7**	**0.3**	**67.9**	**5.7**
Under age 5	50,612	1,376	11,678	102	34,015	3,441	2.7	23.1	0.2	67.2	6.8
Aged 5 to 9	52,918	1,305	12,471	84	35,826	3,231	2.5	23.6	0.2	67.7	6.1
Aged 10 to 14	53,700	1,201	13,286	150	36,331	2,732	2.2	24.7	0.3	67.7	5.1
Aged 15 to 19	52,084	1,199	12,410	159	35,664	2,652	2.3	23.8	0.3	68.5	5.1
Aged 20 to 24	49,386	1,118	11,575	157	33,935	2,603	2.3	23.4	0.3	68.7	5.3

(continued)

(continued from previous page)

		non-Hispanic					non-Hispanic				
	total	Asian	black	Native American	white	Hispanic	Asian	black	Native American	white	Hispanic
District of Columbia, total	**544,362**	**16,919**	**322,614**	**1,295**	**160,923**	**42,610**	**3.1%**	**59.3%**	**0.2%**	**29.6%**	**7.8%**
Total, under age 25	**146,635**	**4,315**	**101,417**	**229**	**26,140**	**14,534**	**2.9**	**69.2**	**0.2**	**17.8**	**9.9**
Under age 5	31,629	961	20,329	53	6,484	3,802	3.0	64.3	0.2	20.5	12.0
Aged 5 to 9	30,529	662	22,183	26	4,416	3,242	2.2	72.7	0.1	14.5	10.6
Aged 10 to 14	33,950	1,233	26,067	49	3,772	2,830	3.6	76.8	0.1	11.1	8.3
Aged 15 to 19	25,220	604	18,703	57	3,531	2,325	2.4	74.2	0.2	14.0	9.2
Aged 20 to 24	25,307	855	14,135	44	7,937	2,336	3.4	55.9	0.2	31.4	9.2
Florida, total	**15,532,043**	**283,693**	**2,342,519**	**44,951**	**10,386,051**	**2,474,829**	**1.8**	**15.1**	**0.3**	**66.9**	**15.9**
Total, under age 25	**5,116,888**	**106,005**	**1,062,000**	**16,157**	**2,992,767**	**939,958**	**2.1**	**20.8**	**0.3**	**58.5**	**18.4**
Under age 5	985,133	23,024	192,777	2,904	557,573	208,855	2.3	19.6	0.3	56.6	21.2
Aged 5 to 9	1,022,563	22,147	212,540	2,927	600,856	184,094	2.2	20.8	0.3	58.8	18.0
Aged 10 to 14	1,072,339	20,591	231,743	3,384	643,943	172,678	1.9	21.6	0.3	60.1	16.1
Aged 15 to 19	1,071,642	20,835	224,241	3,710	636,910	185,946	1.9	20.9	0.3	59.4	17.4
Aged 20 to 24	965,210	19,408	200,700	3,233	553,484	188,385	2.0	20.8	0.3	57.3	19.5
Georgia, total	**8,230,273**	**173,994**	**2,352,884**	**15,972**	**5,420,960**	**266,463**	**2.1**	**28.6**	**0.2**	**65.9**	**3.2**
Total, under age 25	**2,961,331**	**67,275**	**999,301**	**5,405**	**1,760,484**	**128,866**	**2.3**	**33.7**	**0.2**	**59.4**	**4.4**
Under age 5	585,303	15,053	190,382	1,001	348,361	30,506	2.6	32.5	0.2	59.5	5.2
Aged 5 to 9	623,169	14,464	205,703	959	373,247	28,796	2.3	33.0	0.2	59.9	4.6
Aged 10 to 14	607,417	13,114	213,305	1,017	357,291	22,691	2.2	35.1	0.2	58.8	3.7
Aged 15 to 19	587,130	12,598	200,269	1,228	350,172	22,862	2.1	34.1	0.2	59.6	3.9
Aged 20 to 24	558,313	12,046	189,643	1,200	331,413	24,011	2.2	34.0	0.2	59.4	4.3

(continued)

(continued from previous page)

	non-Hispanic					non-Hispanic				
	total	Asian	black	Native American	white	Hispanic	Asian	black	Native American	white	Hispanic
Hawaii, total	**1,192,110**	**721,181**	**30,354**	**4,697**	**336,790**	**99,089**	**60.5%**	**2.5%**	**0.4%**	**28.3%**	**8.3%**
Total, under age 25	**406,534**	**254,928**	**10,456**	**1,814**	**92,826**	**46,510**	**62.7**	**2.6**	**0.4**	**22.8**	**11.4**
Under age 5	81,012	51,367	2,016	390	16,923	10,316	63.4	2.5	0.5	20.9	12.7
Aged 5 to 9	80,466	51,397	1,916	422	17,097	9,634	63.9	2.4	0.5	21.2	12.0
Aged 10 to 14	86,596	56,457	2,052	431	18,716	8,941	65.2	2.4	0.5	21.6	10.3
Aged 15 to 19	78,167	47,478	2,158	294	19,554	8,683	60.7	2.8	0.4	25.0	11.1
Aged 20 to 24	80,292	48,229	2,315	277	20,537	8,935	60.1	2.9	0.3	25.6	11.1
Idaho, total	**1,302,182**	**14,399**	**5,235**	**14,610**	**1,163,698**	**104,240**	**1.1**	**0.4**	**1.1**	**89.4**	**8.0**
Total, under age 25	**497,055**	**5,873**	**2,029**	**6,171**	**426,889**	**56,093**	**1.2**	**0.4**	**1.2**	**85.9**	**11.3**
Under age 5	91,392	1,271	373	1,119	75,972	12,656	1.4	0.4	1.2	83.1	13.8
Aged 5 to 9	97,242	1,219	373	1,129	82,338	12,183	1.3	0.4	1.2	84.7	12.5
Aged 10 to 14	97,071	1,094	351	1,363	84,276	9,989	1.1	0.4	1.4	86.8	10.3
Aged 15 to 19	102,033	1,126	436	1,344	88,791	10,336	1.1	0.4	1.3	87.0	10.1
Aged 20 to 24	109,317	1,164	496	1,216	95,513	10,928	1.1	0.5	1.1	87.4	10.0
Illinois, total	**12,236,810**	**419,996**	**1,826,510**	**17,816**	**8,603,296**	**1,369,192**	**3.4**	**14.9**	**0.1**	**70.3**	**11.2**
Total, under age 25	**4,374,281**	**158,301**	**796,927**	**5,615**	**2,737,689**	**675,750**	**3.6**	**18.2**	**0.1**	**62.6**	**15.4**
Under age 5	855,589	34,359	149,288	976	512,729	158,238	4.0	17.4	0.1	59.9	18.5
Aged 5 to 9	894,373	33,222	165,509	899	544,954	149,789	3.7	18.5	0.1	60.9	16.7
Aged 10 to 14	922,810	30,782	184,276	1,081	580,345	126,326	3.3	20.0	0.1	62.9	13.7
Aged 15 to 19	877,027	30,103	156,206	1,402	566,926	122,390	3.4	17.8	0.2	64.6	14.0
Aged 20 to 24	824,482	29,834	141,648	1,258	532,735	119,007	3.6	17.2	0.2	64.6	14.4

(continued)

(continued from previous page)

		non-Hispanic					non-Hispanic				
	total	Asian	black	Native American	white	Hispanic	Asian	black	Native American	white	Hispanic
Indiana, total	**6,021,673**	**61,191**	**496,582**	**12,799**	**5,286,550**	**164,551**	**1.0%**	**8.2%**	**0.2%**	**87.8%**	**2.7%**
Total, under age 25	**2,110,792**	**24,036**	**212,382**	**4,194**	**1,790,633**	**79,542**	**1.1**	**10.1**	**0.2**	**84.8**	**3.8**
Under age 5	400,540	5,484	39,367	683	336,802	18,205	1.4	9.8	0.2	84.1	4.5
Aged 5 to 9	426,015	5,313	42,666	602	360,476	16,959	1.2	10.0	0.1	84.6	4.0
Aged 10 to 14	432,600	4,492	45,430	850	367,381	14,448	1.0	10.5	0.2	84.9	3.3
Aged 15 to 19	432,227	4,232	44,011	1,014	363,130	14,840	1.0	10.2	0.2	85.2	3.4
Aged 20 to 24	419,409	4,516	40,908	1,047	357,848	15,091	1.1	9.8	0.2	85.3	3.6
Iowa, total	**2,851,879**	**40,172**	**56,547**	**7,663**	**2,681,004**	**66,493**	**1.4**	**2.0**	**0.3**	**94.0**	**2.3**
Total, under age 25	**982,712**	**18,295**	**25,422**	**3,612**	**901,414**	**33,970**	**1.9**	**2.6**	**0.4**	**91.7**	**3.5**
Under age 5	176,569	4,070	4,518	716	159,559	7,706	2.3	2.6	0.4	90.4	4.4
Aged 5 to 9	186,662	4,084	4,946	761	169,649	7,224	2.2	2.6	0.4	90.9	3.9
Aged 10 to 14	196,355	3,428	5,127	747	180,859	6,194	1.7	2.6	0.4	92.1	3.2
Aged 15 to 19	210,817	3,322	5,443	731	194,862	6,459	1.6	2.6	0.3	92.4	3.1
Aged 20 to 24	212,309	3,392	5,387	658	196,485	6,387	1.6	2.5	0.3	92.5	3.0
Kansas, total	**2,648,632**	**48,859**	**150,801**	**19,931**	**2,269,128**	**159,913**	**1.8**	**5.7**	**0.8**	**85.7**	**6.0**
Total, under age 25	**953,040**	**20,779**	**64,830**	**7,764**	**776,913**	**82,754**	**2.2**	**6.8**	**0.8**	**81.5**	**8.7**
Under age 5	176,538	4,510	11,686	1,364	140,121	18,858	2.6	6.6	0.8	79.4	10.7
Aged 5 to 9	186,623	4,398	12,663	1,294	150,253	18,015	2.4	6.8	0.7	80.5	9.7
Aged 10 to 14	188,250	4,130	13,479	1,561	154,216	14,853	2.2	7.2	0.8	81.9	7.9
Aged 15 to 19	201,499	3,823	13,783	1,725	166,624	15,544	1.9	6.8	0.9	82.7	7.7
Aged 20 to 24	200,131	3,918	13,219	1,819	165,699	15,474	2.0	6.6	0.9	82.8	7.7

(continued)

(continued from previous page)

		non-Hispanic					non-Hispanic				
	total	Asian	black	Native American	white	Hispanic	Asian	black	Native American	white	Hispanic
Kentucky, total	**3,991,661**	**28,831**	**285,738**	**5,247**	**3,633,831**	**38,013**	**0.7%**	**7.2%**	**0.1%**	**91.0%**	**1.0%**
Total, under age 25	**1,340,408**	**11,097**	**116,454**	**1,685**	**1,193,588**	**17,584**	**0.8**	**8.7**	**0.1**	**89.0**	**1.3**
Under age 5	253,095	2,469	21,352	339	224,707	4,229	1.0	8.4	0.1	88.8	1.7
Aged 5 to 9	266,737	2,379	22,543	329	237,484	4,001	0.9	8.5	0.1	89.0	1.5
Aged 10 to 14	270,792	2,089	23,836	321	241,534	3,012	0.8	8.8	0.1	89.2	1.1
Aged 15 to 19	271,881	2,102	23,778	340	242,698	2,962	0.8	8.7	0.1	89.3	1.1
Aged 20 to 24	277,903	2,057	24,945	356	247,166	3,379	0.7	9.0	0.1	88.9	1.2
Louisiana, total	**4,406,460**	**56,147**	**1,426,667**	**17,619**	**2,782,565**	**123,462**	**1.3**	**32.4**	**0.4**	**63.1**	**2.8**
Total, under age 25	**1,644,082**	**24,114**	**647,268**	**7,261**	**914,954**	**50,486**	**1.5**	**39.4**	**0.4**	**55.7**	**3.1**
Under age 5	306,583	4,892	119,783	1,310	169,203	11,395	1.6	39.1	0.4	55.2	3.7
Aged 5 to 9	325,824	4,901	130,496	1,316	178,906	10,205	1.5	40.1	0.4	54.9	3.1
Aged 10 to 14	331,546	4,783	133,962	1,425	182,332	9,044	1.4	40.4	0.4	55.0	2.7
Aged 15 to 19	334,426	4,623	130,136	1,588	188,720	9,359	1.4	38.9	0.5	56.4	2.8
Aged 20 to 24	345,702	4,914	132,891	1,623	195,792	10,482	1.4	38.4	0.5	56.6	3.0
Maine, total	**1,241,038**	**10,099**	**5,812**	**5,613**	**1,209,665**	**9,849**	**0.8**	**0.5**	**0.5**	**97.5**	**0.8**
Total, under age 25	**390,490**	**4,225**	**2,096**	**2,407**	**377,483**	**4,280**	**1.1**	**0.5**	**0.6**	**96.7**	**1.1**
Under age 5	67,238	958	385	479	64,353	1,064	1.4	0.6	0.7	95.7	1.6
Aged 5 to 9	68,683	940	357	499	65,923	963	1.4	0.5	0.7	96.0	1.4
Aged 10 to 14	79,119	787	366	424	76,777	765	1.0	0.5	0.5	97.0	1.0
Aged 15 to 19	90,677	771	509	518	88,136	744	0.9	0.6	0.6	97.2	0.8
Aged 20 to 24	84,773	770	478	487	82,293	745	0.9	0.6	0.6	97.1	0.9

(continued)

(continued from previous page)

		non-Hispanic					non-Hispanic				
	total	Asian	black	Native American	white	Hispanic	Asian	black	Native American	white	Hispanic
Maryland, total	**5,225,461**	**217,519**	**1,464,230**	**13,343**	**3,318,656**	**211,713**	**4.2%**	**28.0%**	**0.3%**	**63.5%**	**4.1%**
Total, under age 25	**1,792,547**	**82,061**	**573,347**	**4,854**	**1,042,209**	**90,077**	**4.6**	**32.0**	**0.3**	**58.1**	**5.0**
Under age 5	341,876	17,247	111,051	924	192,045	20,609	5.0	32.5	0.3	56.2	6.0
Aged 5 to 9	360,085	16,689	120,654	945	203,400	18,398	4.6	33.5	0.3	56.5	5.1
Aged 10 to 14	383,867	16,862	121,558	982	227,310	17,155	4.4	31.7	0.3	59.2	4.5
Aged 15 to 19	377,311	16,469	116,576	1,052	226,259	16,955	4.4	30.9	0.3	60.0	4.5
Aged 20 to 24	329,408	14,794	103,509	952	193,194	16,960	4.5	31.4	0.3	58.6	5.1
Massachusetts, total	**6,230,757**	**255,901**	**350,793**	**11,452**	**5,185,448**	**427,163**	**4.1**	**5.6**	**0.2**	**83.2**	**6.9**
Total, under age 25	**2,020,138**	**112,563**	**162,419**	**4,322**	**1,525,324**	**215,509**	**5.6**	**8.0**	**0.2**	**75.5**	**10.7**
Under age 5	391,979	26,502	32,338	851	282,155	50,132	6.8	8.3	0.2	72.0	12.8
Aged 5 to 9	401,733	26,738	37,543	856	289,008	47,589	6.7	9.3	0.2	71.9	11.8
Aged 10 to 14	427,673	23,783	39,406	967	322,042	41,475	5.5	9.2	0.2	75.3	9.7
Aged 15 to 19	428,026	17,785	29,008	889	340,189	40,156	4.2	6.8	0.2	79.5	9.4
Aged 20 to 24	370,728	17,755	24,125	760	291,931	36,158	4.8	6.5	0.2	78.7	9.8
Michigan, total	**9,754,892**	**173,910**	**1,382,026**	**53,265**	**7,855,358**	**290,332**	**1.8**	**14.2**	**0.5**	**80.5**	**3.0**
Total, under age 25	**3,423,218**	**70,948**	**582,120**	**21,658**	**2,602,424**	**146,069**	**2.1**	**17.0**	**0.6**	**76.0**	**4.3**
Under age 5	628,585	15,599	105,250	3,702	469,788	34,246	2.5	16.7	0.6	74.7	5.4
Aged 5 to 9	660,708	15,286	112,722	3,638	496,540	32,522	2.3	17.1	0.6	75.2	4.9
Aged 10 to 14	720,005	12,613	135,367	4,553	540,751	26,721	1.8	18.8	0.6	75.1	3.7
Aged 15 to 19	737,527	14,361	122,917	5,099	568,051	27,059	1.9	16.7	0.7	77.0	3.7
Aged 20 to 24	676,394	13,089	105,864	4,666	527,294	25,481	1.9	15.7	0.7	78.0	3.8

(continued)

(*continued from previous page*)

		non-Hispanic					non-Hispanic				
	total	Asian	black	Native American	white	Hispanic	Asian	black	Native American	white	Hispanic
Minnesota, total	**4,866,164**	**145,120**	**154,660**	**58,314**	**4,405,511**	**102,559**	**3.0%**	**3.2%**	**1.2%**	**90.5%**	**2.1%**
Total, under age 25	**1,742,076**	**76,003**	**74,968**	**30,328**	**1,506,286**	**54,492**	**4.4**	**4.3**	**1.7**	**86.5**	**3.1**
Under age 5	313,378	15,260	14,119	5,096	266,237	12,666	4.9	4.5	1.6	85.0	4.0
Aged 5 to 9	332,653	15,647	16,018	5,466	283,209	12,313	4.7	4.8	1.6	85.1	3.7
Aged 10 to 14	352,708	15,694	16,226	7,534	303,061	10,193	4.4	4.6	2.1	85.9	2.9
Aged 15 to 19	385,818	16,127	15,661	6,844	337,153	10,033	4.2	4.1	1.8	87.4	2.6
Aged 20 to 24	357,519	13,275	12,943	5,388	316,625	9,287	3.7	3.6	1.5	88.6	2.6
Mississippi, total	**2,815,653**	**20,902**	**1,031,240**	**10,132**	**1,727,748**	**25,630**	**0.7**	**36.6**	**0.4**	**61.4**	**0.9**
Total, under age 25	**1,051,845**	**8,959**	**468,736**	**4,903**	**557,660**	**11,586**	**0.9**	**44.6**	**0.5**	**53.0**	**1.1**
Under age 5	199,017	1,920	87,951	927	105,454	2,766	1.0	44.2	0.5	53.0	1.4
Aged 5 to 9	212,697	1,903	94,990	985	112,261	2,559	0.9	44.7	0.5	52.8	1.2
Aged 10 to 14	214,358	1,752	97,289	1,078	112,219	2,020	0.8	45.4	0.5	52.4	0.9
Aged 15 to 19	209,310	1,691	92,134	1,004	112,508	1,972	0.8	44.0	0.5	53.8	0.9
Aged 20 to 24	216,463	1,694	96,372	908	115,220	2,270	0.8	44.5	0.4	53.2	1.0
Missouri, total	**5,508,337**	**64,449**	**620,633**	**18,496**	**4,706,327**	**98,432**	**1.2**	**11.3**	**0.3**	**85.4**	**1.8**
Total, under age 25	**1,921,011**	**25,972**	**272,005**	**6,615**	**1,569,588**	**46,831**	**1.4**	**14.2**	**0.3**	**81.7**	**2.4**
Under age 5	353,086	5,942	49,295	1,167	285,735	10,947	1.7	14.0	0.3	80.9	3.1
Aged 5 to 9	375,426	5,804	53,686	1,135	304,609	10,192	1.5	14.3	0.3	81.1	2.7
Aged 10 to 14	394,443	4,989	61,327	1,290	318,436	8,400	1.3	15.5	0.3	80.7	2.1
Aged 15 to 19	408,023	4,483	56,508	1,541	337,015	8,475	1.1	13.8	0.4	82.6	2.1
Aged 20 to 24	390,033	4,754	51,189	1,481	323,793	8,816	1.2	13.1	0.4	83.0	2.3

(*continued*)

(continued from previous page)

	total	non-Hispanic				Hispanic	non-Hispanic				Hispanic
		Asian	black	Native American	white		Asian	black	Native American	white	
Montana, total	**882,820**	**5,741**	**2,697**	**58,246**	**798,514**	**17,621**	**0.7%**	**0.3%**	**6.6%**	**90.5%**	**2.0%**
Total, under age 25	**306,806**	**2,662**	**1,038**	**31,081**	**263,095**	**8,930**	**0.9**	**0.3**	**10.1**	**85.8**	**2.9**
Under age 5	52,070	533	162	5,602	43,699	2,074	1.0	0.3	10.8	83.9	4.0
Aged 5 to 9	55,120	526	145	6,130	46,290	2,029	1.0	0.3	11.1	84.0	3.7
Aged 10 to 14	61,008	525	204	7,167	51,570	1,541	0.9	0.3	11.7	84.5	2.5
Aged 15 to 19	68,421	591	264	6,609	59,406	1,550	0.9	0.4	9.7	86.8	2.3
Aged 20 to 24	70,188	488	262	5,572	62,131	1,736	0.7	0.4	7.9	88.5	2.5
Nebraska, total	**1,684,819**	**23,665**	**66,897**	**14,444**	**1,496,600**	**83,213**	**1.4**	**4.0**	**0.9**	**88.8**	**4.9**
Total, under age 25	**611,541**	**11,061**	**30,340**	**7,880**	**519,213**	**43,049**	**1.8**	**5.0**	**1.3**	**84.9**	**7.0**
Under age 5	111,502	2,411	5,463	1,537	92,657	9,433	2.2	4.9	1.4	83.1	8.5
Aged 5 to 9	118,240	2,460	5,956	1,718	99,301	8,805	2.1	5.0	1.5	84.0	7.4
Aged 10 to 14	121,096	2,251	6,212	1,795	102,665	8,172	1.9	5.1	1.5	84.8	6.7
Aged 15 to 19	131,178	2,067	6,644	1,525	112,489	8,454	1.6	5.1	1.2	85.8	6.4
Aged 20 to 24	129,525	1,871	6,064	1,305	112,101	8,184	1.4	4.7	1.0	86.5	6.3
Nevada, total	**2,023,150**	**94,375**	**140,237**	**28,871**	**1,399,984**	**359,683**	**4.7**	**6.9**	**1.4**	**69.2**	**17.8**
Total, under age 25	**741,581**	**36,272**	**60,087**	**11,780**	**454,020**	**179,421**	**4.9**	**8.1**	**1.6**	**61.2**	**24.2**
Under age 5	150,323	8,124	10,526	2,019	88,079	41,576	5.4	7.0	1.3	58.6	27.7
Aged 5 to 9	159,255	8,037	11,690	2,065	97,542	39,921	5.0	7.3	1.3	61.2	25.1
Aged 10 to 14	152,542	7,164	13,621	2,719	95,439	33,559	4.7	8.9	1.8	62.6	22.0
Aged 15 to 19	149,264	6,895	13,215	2,748	92,949	33,457	4.6	8.9	1.8	62.3	22.4
Aged 20 to 24	130,196	6,053	11,034	2,230	80,012	30,868	4.5	8.5	1.7	63.5	23.7

(continued)

		non-Hispanic						non-Hispanic			
	total	Asian	black	Native American	white	Hispanic	Asian	black	Native American	white	Hispanic
New Hampshire, total	**1,227,695**	**16,211**	**7,814**	**2,463**	**1,180,038**	**21,170**	**1.3%**	**0.6%**	**0.2%**	**96.1%**	**1.7%**
Total, under age 25	**413,232**	**6,085**	**2,748**	**961**	**393,463**	**9,976**	**1.5**	**0.7**	**0.2**	**95.2**	**2.4**
Under age 5	73,654	1,290	467	169	69,475	2,253	1.8	0.6	0.2	94.3	3.1
Aged 5 to 9	76,705	1,191	455	165	72,837	2,057	1.6	0.6	0.2	95.0	2.7
Aged 10 to 14	86,725	1,103	498	204	83,027	1,893	1.3	0.6	0.2	95.7	2.2
Aged 15 to 19	95,592	1,305	648	222	91,403	2,015	1.4	0.7	0.2	95.6	2.1
Aged 20 to 24	80,557	1,195	681	202	76,721	1,758	1.5	0.8	0.3	95.2	2.2
New Jersey, total	**8,233,712**	**494,767**	**1,106,547**	**14,165**	**5,538,618**	**1,079,614**	**6.0**	**13.4**	**0.2**	**67.3**	**13.1**
Total, under age 25	**2,770,912**	**185,433**	**443,006**	**4,990**	**1,682,387**	**455,096**	**6.7**	**16.0**	**0.2**	**60.7**	**16.4**
Under age 5	541,936	42,140	84,402	886	310,889	103,619	7.8	15.6	0.2	57.4	19.1
Aged 5 to 9	559,831	41,395	92,267	871	332,433	92,864	7.4	16.5	0.2	59.4	16.6
Aged 10 to 14	594,137	33,016	96,545	1,285	376,306	86,985	5.6	16.2	0.2	63.3	14.6
Aged 15 to 19	574,649	35,990	89,979	1,072	360,311	87,296	6.3	15.7	0.2	62.7	15.2
Aged 20 to 24	500,360	32,891	79,813	877	302,448	84,332	6.6	16.0	0.2	60.4	16.9
New Mexico, total	**1,804,261**	**22,325**	**31,983**	**163,333**	**835,261**	**751,358**	**1.2**	**1.8**	**9.1**	**46.3**	**41.6**
Total, under age 25	**702,885**	**8,859**	**11,728**	**81,045**	**250,288**	**350,965**	**1.3**	**1.7**	**11.5**	**35.6**	**49.9**
Under age 5	137,107	1,854	1,931	14,678	42,650	75,994	1.4	1.4	10.7	31.1	55.4
Aged 5 to 9	134,982	1,775	1,931	15,676	44,827	70,774	1.3	1.4	11.6	33.2	52.4
Aged 10 to 14	140,103	1,736	2,315	20,181	52,086	63,784	1.2	1.7	14.4	37.2	45.5
Aged 15 to 19	145,853	1,785	2,766	16,637	55,408	69,256	1.2	1.9	11.4	38.0	47.5
Aged 20 to 24	144,840	1,709	2,784	13,873	55,316	71,158	1.2	1.9	9.6	38.2	49.1

(continued)

(continued from previous page)

	non-Hispanic						non-Hispanic				
	total	Asian	black	Native American	white	Hispanic	Asian	black	Native American	white	Hispanic
New York, total	**18,506,065**	**1,066,459**	**2,685,962**	**54,345**	**11,881,393**	**2,817,905**	**5.8%**	**14.5%**	**0.3%**	**64.2%**	**15.2%**
Total, under age 25	**6,212,857**	**380,193**	**1,020,507**	**18,729**	**3,552,561**	**1,240,868**	**6.1**	**16.4**	**0.3**	**57.2**	**20.0**
Under age 5	1,234,714	85,936	189,698	3,024	664,621	291,434	7.0	15.4	0.2	53.8	23.6
Aged 5 to 9	1,250,577	82,230	199,430	2,751	696,964	269,203	6.6	15.9	0.2	55.7	21.5
Aged 10 to 14	1,329,708	75,237	221,290	4,337	785,135	243,709	5.7	16.6	0.3	59.0	18.3
Aged 15 to 19	1,253,005	70,492	218,644	4,721	736,117	223,032	5.6	17.4	0.4	58.7	17.8
Aged 20 to 24	1,144,852	66,298	191,445	3,895	669,724	213,490	5.8	16.7	0.3	58.5	18.6
North Carolina, total	**8,006,174**	**115,792**	**1,741,574**	**100,761**	**5,850,794**	**197,253**	**1.4**	**21.8**	**1.3**	**73.1**	**2.5**
Total, under age 25	**2,771,773**	**49,229**	**721,562**	**44,607**	**1,854,462**	**101,913**	**1.8**	**26.0**	**1.6**	**66.9**	**3.7**
Under age 5	537,226	11,440	131,923	8,324	361,002	24,538	2.1	24.6	1.5	67.2	4.6
Aged 5 to 9	573,692	11,412	142,209	8,766	387,391	23,915	2.0	24.8	1.5	67.5	4.2
Aged 10 to 14	583,518	9,559	159,001	10,600	386,101	18,256	1.6	27.2	1.8	56.2	3.1
Aged 15 to 19	566,491	8,753	152,354	9,223	378,313	17,848	1.5	26.9	1.6	56.8	3.2
Aged 20 to 24	510,846	8,065	136,075	7,694	341,656	17,356	1.6	26.6	1.5	66.9	3.4
North Dakota, total	**625,354**	**5,555**	**3,955**	**31,983**	**575,780**	**8,080**	**0.9**	**0.6**	**5.1**	**92.1**	**1.3**
Total, under age 25	**217,547**	**2,603**	**1,798**	**18,140**	**190,782**	**4,224**	**1.2**	**0.8**	**8.3**	**87.7**	**1.9**
Under age 5	38,050	580	374	3,429	32,635	1,032	1.5	1.0	9.0	85.8	2.7
Aged 5 to 9	39,991	589	416	3,834	34,177	975	1.5	1.0	9.6	85.5	2.4
Aged 10 to 14	42,471	556	336	4,356	36,459	764	1.3	0.8	10.3	85.8	1.8
Aged 15 to 19	47,605	448	337	3,629	42,435	757	0.9	0.7	7.6	89.1	1.6
Aged 20 to 24	49,430	431	334	2,892	45,076	696	0.9	0.7	5.9	91.2	1.4

(continued)

(continued from previous page)

		non-Hispanic					non-Hispanic				
	total	Asian	black	Native American	white	Hispanic	Asian	black	Native American	white	Hispanic
Ohio, total	**11,133,387**	**138,613**	**1,285,748**	**20,324**	**9,494,770**	**193,933**	**1.2%**	**11.5%**	**0.2%**	**85.3%**	**1.7%**
Total, under age 25	**3,830,456**	**56,047**	**552,731**	**7,324**	**3,119,763**	**94,591**	**1.5**	**14.4**	**0.2**	**81.4**	**2.5**
Under age 5	709,318	12,413	102,214	1,398	571,520	21,773	1.7	14.4	0.2	80.6	3.1
Aged 5 to 9	749,648	12,285	112,547	1,422	602,918	20,477	1.6	15.0	0.2	80.4	2.7
Aged 10 to 14	791,616	11,013	123,922	1,501	637,959	17,220	1.4	15.7	0.2	80.6	2.2
Aged 15 to 19	811,849	10,183	112,551	1,560	669,814	17,740	1.3	13.9	0.2	82.5	2.2
Aged 20 to 24	768,026	10,154	101,496	1,442	637,553	17,381	1.3	13.2	0.2	83.0	2.3
Oklahoma, total	**3,393,941**	**46,101**	**261,693**	**255,494**	**2,681,500**	**149,153**	**1.4**	**7.7**	**7.5**	**79.0**	**4.4**
Total, under age 25	**1,220,626**	**18,893**	**116,577**	**116,957**	**889,733**	**78,466**	**1.5**	**9.6**	**9.6**	**72.9**	**6.4**
Under age 5	226,702	4,206	20,952	21,573	161,997	17,974	1.9	9.2	9.5	71.5	7.9
Aged 5 to 9	240,760	4,184	22,845	22,850	173,660	17,221	1.7	9.5	9.5	72.1	7.2
Aged 10 to 14	245,722	3,683	24,229	25,176	178,664	13,969	1.5	9.9	10.2	72.7	5.7
Aged 15 to 19	253,888	3,381	24,317	24,572	187,121	14,497	1.3	9.6	9.7	73.7	5.7
Aged 20 to 24	253,554	3,439	24,234	22,785	188,291	14,805	1.4	9.6	9.0	74.3	5.8
Oregon, total	**3,383,144**	**116,429**	**56,341**	**40,239**	**2,935,130**	**235,005**	**3.4**	**1.7**	**1.2**	**86.8**	**6.9**
Total, under age 25	**1,158,532**	**46,984**	**23,270**	**16,400**	**949,275**	**122,603**	**4.1**	**2.0**	**1.4**	**81.9**	**10.6**
Under age 5	217,434	10,336	4,049	2,921	172,416	27,712	4.8	1.9	1.3	79.3	12.7
Aged 5 to 9	228,486	10,014	4,276	2,959	184,601	26,636	4.4	1.9	1.3	80.8	11.7
Aged 10 to 14	230,945	9,076	4,756	3,465	191,291	22,357	3.9	2.1	1.5	82.8	9.7
Aged 15 to 19	244,704	8,697	5,297	3,758	203,942	23,010	3.6	2.2	1.5	83.3	9.4
Aged 20 to 24	236,963	8,861	4,893	3,297	197,025	22,887	3.7	2.1	1.4	83.1	9.7

(continued)

(continued from previous page)

		non-Hispanic						non-Hispanic			
	total	Asian	black	Native American	white	Hispanic	Asian	black	Native American	white	Hispanic
Pennsylvania, total	**11,900,815**	**212,698**	**1,133,085**	**14,443**	**10,190,796**	**349,794**	**1.8%**	**9.5%**	**0.1%**	**85.6%**	**2.9%**
Total, under age 25	**3,873,075**	**85,028**	**468,070**	**5,311**	**3,143,146**	**171,520**	**2.2**	**12.1**	**0.1**	**81.2**	**4.4**
Under age 5	701,238	18,116	85,033	997	558,495	38,597	2.6	12.1	0.1	79.6	5.5
Aged 5 to 9	731,774	17,581	92,935	1,015	584,181	36,062	2.4	12.7	0.1	79.8	4.9
Aged 10 to 14	814,587	16,675	107,254	1,079	656,710	32,868	2.0	13.2	0.1	80.6	4.0
Aged 15 to 19	849,062	16,314	99,371	1,184	699,044	33,149	1.9	11.7	0.1	82.3	3.9
Aged 20 to 24	776,414	16,341	83,478	1,036	644,717	30,842	2.1	10.8	0.1	83.0	4.0
Rhode Island, total	**1,022,464**	**24,793**	**41,553**	**4,474**	**874,816**	**76,827**	**2.4**	**4.1**	**0.4**	**85.6**	**7.5**
Total, under age 25	**338,732**	**11,368**	**18,272**	**2,155**	**268,997**	**37,939**	**3.4**	**5.4**	**0.6**	**79.4**	**11.2**
Under age 5	63,633	2,272	3,203	473	48,894	8,791	3.6	5.0	0.7	76.8	13.8
Aged 5 to 9	65,269	2,272	3,441	529	50,701	8,325	3.5	5.3	0.8	77.7	12.8
Aged 10 to 14	73,097	2,464	4,123	508	58,366	7,637	3.4	5.6	0.7	79.8	10.4
Aged 15 to 19	72,972	2,180	4,009	365	59,296	7,122	3.0	5.5	0.5	81.3	9.8
Aged 20 to 24	63,762	2,181	3,497	280	51,740	6,064	3.4	5.5	0.4	81.1	9.5
South Carolina, total	**3,959,112**	**37,136**	**1,168,538**	**8,931**	**2,685,792**	**58,714**	**0.9**	**29.5**	**0.2**	**67.8**	**1.5**
Total, under age 25	**1,345,535**	**14,264**	**477,565**	**3,250**	**823,262**	**27,194**	**1.1**	**35.5**	**0.2**	**61.2**	**2.0**
Under age 5	255,591	3,189	86,928	596	158,384	6,495	1.2	34.0	0.2	62.0	2.5
Aged 5 to 9	267,288	3,038	91,167	564	166,539	5,981	1.1	34.1	0.2	62.3	2.2
Aged 10 to 14	279,187	2,753	101,820	644	169,166	4,805	1.0	36.5	0.2	50.6	1.7
Aged 15 to 19	273,069	2,577	99,827	702	165,315	4,649	0.9	36.6	0.3	50.5	1.7
Aged 20 to 24	270,399	2,708	97,823	745	163,860	5,254	1.0	36.2	0.3	60.6	1.9

(continued)

(continued from previous page)

		non-Hispanic						non-Hispanic			
	total	Asian	black	Native American	white	Hispanic	Asian	black	Native American	white	Hispanic
South Dakota, total	**741,566**	**5,317**	**4,967**	**64,053**	**657,305**	**9,924**	**0.7%**	**0.7%**	**8.6%**	**88.6%**	**1.3%**
Total, under age 25	**273,862**	**2,648**	**2,015**	**38,382**	**225,591**	**5,226**	**1.0**	**0.7**	**14.0**	**82.4**	**1.9**
Under age 5	48,347	590	411	7,111	39,002	1,233	1.2	0.9	14.7	80.7	2.6
Aged 5 to 9	51,724	614	445	7,956	41,528	1,182	1.2	0.9	15.4	80.3	2.3
Aged 10 to 14	55,248	548	384	9,192	44,170	953	1.0	0.7	16.6	79.9	1.7
Aged 15 to 19	58,740	474	381	7,828	49,131	925	0.8	0.6	13.3	83.6	1.6
Aged 20 to 24	59,804	421	394	6,296	51,760	933	0.7	0.7	10.5	86.6	1.6
Tennessee, total	**5,647,268**	**58,368**	**939,824**	**11,069**	**4,564,647**	**73,359**	**1.0**	**16.6**	**0.2**	**80.8**	**1.3**
Total, under age 25	**1,901,465**	**23,682**	**403,129**	**3,844**	**1,436,352**	**34,458**	**1.2**	**21.2**	**0.2**	**75.5**	**1.8**
Under age 5	366,163	5,445	75,456	681	276,539	8,042	1.5	20.6	0.2	75.5	2.2
Aged 5 to 9	388,605	5,409	81,930	656	293,119	7,491	1.4	21.1	0.2	75.4	1.9
Aged 10 to 14	391,533	4,265	87,200	792	293,081	6,195	1.1	22.3	0.2	74.9	1.6
Aged 15 to 19	382,492	4,243	81,473	858	289,805	6,112	1.1	21.3	0.2	75.8	1.6
Aged 20 to 24	372,672	4,321	77,070	856	283,808	6,618	1.2	20.7	0.2	76.2	1.8
Texas, total	**20,902,754**	**573,589**	**2,406,664**	**59,250**	**11,334,734**	**6,528,517**	**2.7**	**11.5**	**0.3**	**54.2**	**31.2**
Total, under age 25	**8,126,425**	**220,791**	**985,143**	**18,556**	**3,674,880**	**3,227,055**	**2.7**	**12.1**	**0.2**	**45.2**	**39.7**
Under age 5	1,660,191	48,065	177,831	3,174	686,885	744,236	2.9	10.7	0.2	41.4	44.8
Aged 5 to 9	1,680,150	46,782	188,089	2,930	738,565	703,784	2.8	11.2	0.2	44.0	41.9
Aged 10 to 14	1,607,851	43,089	208,007	3,710	760,479	592,567	2.7	12.9	0.2	47.3	36.9
Aged 15 to 19	1,598,155	42,341	209,649	4,464	755,922	585,779	2.6	13.1	0.3	47.3	36.7
Aged 20 to 24	1,580,078	40,515	201,566	4,278	733,030	600,688	2.6	12.8	0.3	46.4	38.0

(continued)

(continued from previous page)

	total	non-Hispanic				Hispanic	Asian	non-Hispanic			Hispanic
		Asian	black	Native American	white			black	Native American	white	
Utah, total	**2,308,066**	**60,284**	**16,097**	**28,482**	**2,032,956**	**170,248**	**2.6%**	**0.7%**	**1.2%**	**88.1%**	**7.4%**
Total, under age 25	**1,022,726**	**28,750**	**6,930**	**14,706**	**881,110**	**91,230**	**2.8**	**0.7**	**1.4**	**86.2**	**8.9**
Under age 5	202,832	6,610	1,226	2,740	170,564	21,692	3.3	0.6	1.4	84.1	10.7
Aged 5 to 9	221,151	6,740	1,311	2,920	189,203	20,977	3.0	0.6	1.3	85.6	9.5
Aged 10 to 14	196,942	5,657	1,319	3,419	170,658	15,888	2.9	0.7	1.7	86.7	8.1
Aged 15 to 19	194,692	4,931	1,449	3,051	169,263	15,999	2.5	0.7	1.6	86.9	8.2
Aged 20 to 24	207,110	4,812	1,624	2,577	181,422	16,675	2.3	0.8	1.2	87.6	8.1
Vermont, total	**597,053**	**5,389**	**3,002**	**1,330**	**581,891**	**5,441**	**0.9**	**0.5**	**0.2**	**97.5**	**0.9**
Total, under age 25	**189,948**	**2,176**	**1,036**	**349**	**184,227**	**2,159**	**1.1**	**0.5**	**0.2**	**97.0**	**1.1**
Under age 5	32,545	447	151	49	31,432	466	1.4	0.5	0.2	96.6	1.4
Aged 5 to 9	33,140	404	122	27	32,206	380	1.2	0.4	0.1	97.2	1.1
Aged 10 to 14	38,774	404	196	69	37,728	377	1.0	0.5	0.2	97.3	1.0
Aged 15 to 19	43,842	426	273	97	42,671	376	1.0	0.6	0.2	97.3	0.9
Aged 20 to 24	41,646	495	294	108	40,190	560	1.2	0.7	0.3	96.5	1.3
Virginia, total	**7,018,920**	**274,299**	**1,389,102**	**15,712**	**5,051,800**	**288,006**	**3.9**	**19.8**	**0.2**	**72.0**	**4.1**
Total, under age 25	**2,340,514**	**101,402**	**538,110**	**4,827**	**1,570,505**	**125,670**	**4.3**	**23.0**	**0.2**	**67.1**	**5.4**
Under age 5	454,702	23,013	100,499	952	300,228	30,011	5.1	22.1	0.2	66.0	6.6
Aged 5 to 9	470,168	21,983	106,048	884	314,058	27,196	4.7	22.6	0.2	66.8	5.8
Aged 10 to 14	483,934	19,130	114,620	870	326,630	22,684	4.0	23.7	0.2	67.5	4.7
Aged 15 to 19	475,293	18,747	110,789	1,079	322,251	22,427	3.9	23.3	0.2	67.8	4.7
Aged 20 to 24	456,416	18,530	106,154	1,043	307,338	23,352	4.1	23.3	0.2	67.3	5.1

(continued)

continued from previous page

		non-Hispanic					non-Hispanic				
	total	Asian	black	Native American	white	Hispanic	Asian	black	Native American	white	Hispanic
Washington, total	**5,869,110**	**359,064**	**192,157**	**93,375**	**4,811,861**	**412,653**	**6.1%**	**3.3%**	**1.6%**	**82.0%**	**7.0%**
Total, under age 25	**2,058,310**	**144,161**	**78,541**	**40,503**	**1,579,781**	**215,324**	**7.0**	**3.8**	**2.0**	**76.8**	**10.5**
Under age 5	385,710	30,269	14,089	7,316	285,182	48,854	7.8	3.7	1.9	73.9	12.7
Aged 5 to 9	401,481	29,413	14,902	7,581	303,101	46,484	7.3	3.7	1.9	75.5	11.6
Aged 10 to 14	421,010	27,846	15,882	8,796	328,515	39,971	6.6	3.8	2.1	78.0	9.5
Aged 15 to 19	433,825	28,839	17,419	8,956	338,641	39,970	6.6	4.0	2.1	78.1	9.2
Aged 20 to 24	416,284	27,794	16,249	7,853	324,343	40,045	6.7	3.9	1.9	77.9	9.6
West Virginia, total	**1,751,951**	**8,751**	**52,115**	**2,094**	**1,678,399**	**10,592**	**0.5**	**3.0**	**0.1**	**95.8**	**0.6**
Total, under age 25	**545,710**	**3,129**	**18,775**	**544**	**518,894**	**4,368**	**0.6**	**3.4**	**0.1**	**95.1**	**0.8**
Under age 5	98,358	561	2,888	77	93,833	999	0.6	2.9	0.1	95.4	1.0
Aged 5 to 9	101,456	511	2,744	52	97,239	910	0.5	2.7	0.1	95.8	0.9
Aged 10 to 14	110,491	625	4,060	108	104,906	792	0.6	3.7	0.1	94.9	0.7
Aged 15 to 19	114,693	647	4,355	155	108,749	787	0.6	3.8	0.1	94.8	0.7
Aged 20 to 24	120,712	785	4,729	152	114,167	880	0.6	3.9	0.1	94.6	0.7
Wisconsin, total	**5,267,492**	**90,966**	**297,975**	**44,610**	**4,682,908**	**151,032**	**1.7**	**5.7**	**0.8**	**88.9**	**2.9**
Total, under age 25	**1,833,572**	**48,401**	**143,998**	**21,334**	**1,541,094**	**78,745**	**2.6**	**7.9**	**1.2**	**84.0**	**4.3**
Under age 5	325,147	9,628	25,654	3,692	268,599	17,573	3.0	7.9	1.1	82.6	5.4
Aged 5 to 9	340,650	9,942	28,395	3,841	281,758	16,715	2.9	8.3	1.1	82.7	4.9
Aged 10 to 14	370,850	10,140	32,080	4,947	309,284	14,399	2.7	8.7	1.3	83.4	3.9
Aged 15 to 19	407,549	10,034	30,908	4,823	346,243	15,541	2.5	7.6	1.2	85.0	3.8
Aged 20 to 24	389,376	8,656	26,962	4,031	335,210	14,518	2.2	6.9	1.0	86.1	3.7

(continued)

(continued from previous page)

		non-Hispanic					non-Hispanic				
	total	Asian	black	Native American	white	Hispanic	Asian	black	Native American	white	Hispanic
Wyoming, total	**488,358**	**4,112**	**3,561**	**10,604**	**438,687**	**31,394**	**0.8%**	**0.7%**	**2.2%**	**89.8%**	**6.4%**
Total, under age 25	**176,616**	**1,790**	**1,403**	**5,420**	**152,291**	**15,712**	**1.0**	**0.8**	**3.1**	**86.2**	**8.9**
Under age 5	30,235	326	264	960	25,195	3,490	1.1	0.9	3.2	83.3	11.5
Aged 5 to 9	31,654	302	273	1,033	26,723	3,324	1.0	0.9	3.3	84.4	10.5
Aged 10 to 14	33,872	360	247	1,233	29,398	2,634	1.1	0.7	3.6	86.8	7.8
Aged 15 to 19	38,710	403	274	1,140	33,949	2,945	1.0	0.7	2.9	87.7	7.6
Aged 20 to 24	42,145	400	345	1,055	37,026	3,319	0.9	0.8	2.5	87.9	7.9

Source: Projections by New Strategist

Mobility Rate Is below Average for Teens

Few parents want to uproot their children during their teen years.

One in five people under age 25 moved between March 1998 and March 1999. This share was higher than the 16 percent of all Americans aged 1 or older who moved during the year. Within the under-25 age group, however, the mobility rate varies widely. Twenty-four percent of children aged 1 to 4 moved between March 1998 and March 1999, compared with only 13 to 14 percent of children aged 10 to 17. Among young adults aged 20 to 24, fully 33 percent moved as they graduated from college or left military service, seeking job opportunities elsewhere. Most movers stay within the same county.

One reason for the lower mobility of teens is that parents are reluctant to uproot their children from well-established school routines and friendships. While 28 percent of families with preschoolers moved between March 1998 and March 1999, the proportion stood at just 13 percent among families with children aged 6 to 17.

♦ Another reason why parents with teens are less likely to move is that many are homeowners, and homeowners are much less likely to move than renters.

Geographical Mobility of People under Age 25, 1998 to 1999

(total number and percent distribution of people aged 1 or older and under age 25 by mobility status between March 1998 and March 1999; numbers in thousands)

	total	nonmovers	total	same county	different county, same state	different state, same division	different division, same region	different region	movers from abroad
						movers			
Total, aged 1 or older	267,933	225,297	42,636	25,268	8,423	3,250	988	3,278	1,429
Total under age 25	94,180	74,652	19,527	12,049	3,586	1,388	410	1,442	652
Aged 1 to 4	15,792	12,039	3,752	2,448	515	217	75	296	101
Aged 5 to 9	20,557	16,681	3,876	2,572	580	298	64	255	107
Aged 10 to 14	19,909	17,187	2,723	1,691	488	197	48	232	67
Aged 15 to 17	11,955	10,380	1,575	985	275	100	20	108	87
Aged 18 to 19	7,909	6,300	1,609	893	346	127	47	123	73
Aged 20 to 24	18,058	12,065	5,992	3,460	1,282	449	156	428	217
PERCENT DISTRIBUTION BY MOBILITY STATUS									
Total, aged 1 or older	100.0%	84.1%	15.9%	9.4%	3.1%	1.2%	0.4%	1.2%	0.5%
Total under age 25	100.0	79.3	20.7	12.8	3.8	1.5	0.4	1.5	0.7
Aged 1 to 4	100.0	76.2	23.8	15.5	3.9	1.4	0.5	1.9	0.6
Aged 5 to 9	100.0	81.1	18.9	12.5	2.8	1.4	0.3	1.2	0.5
Aged 10 to 14	100.0	86.3	13.7	8.5	2.5	1.0	0.2	1.2	0.3
Aged 15 to 17	100.0	86.8	13.2	8.2	2.3	0.8	0.2	0.9	0.7
Aged 18 to 19	100.0	79.7	20.3	11.3	4.4	1.6	0.6	1.6	0.9
Aged 20 to 24	100.0	66.8	33.2	19.2	7.1	2.5	0.9	2.4	1.2

(continued)

(continued from previous page)

PERCENT DISTRIBUTION OF MOVERS BY TYPE OF MOVE

	total	nonmovers	total	same county	different county, same state	different state, same division	different division, same region	different region	movers from abroad
							movers		
Total, aged 1 or older	–	–	**100.0%**	**59.3%**	**19.8%**	**7.6%**	**2.3%**	**7.7%**	**3.4%**
Total under age 25	–	–	**100.0**	**61.7**	**18.4**	**7.1**	**2.1**	**7.4**	**3.3**
Aged 1 to 4	–	–	100.0	65.2	16.4	5.8	2.0	7.9	2.7
Aged 5 to 9	–	–	100.0	66.4	15.0	7.7	1.7	6.6	2.8
Aged 10 to 14	–	–	100.0	62.1	17.9	7.2	1.8	8.5	2.5
Aged 15 to 17	–	–	100.0	62.5	17.5	6.3	1.3	6.9	5.5
Aged 18 to 19	–	–	100.0	55.5	21.5	7.9	2.9	7.6	4.5
Aged 20 to 24	–	–	100.0	57.7	21.4	7.5	2.6	7.1	3.6

Note: (–) means not applicable.
Source: Bureau of the Census, Geographical Mobility: March 1998 to March 1999 (Update), detailed tables for Current Population Report P20-531, 2000; Internet site <www.census.gov/population/www/socdemo/migrate.html#cps>; calculations by New Strategist

Mobility of Families with Children, 1998 to 1999

(total number and percent distribution of householders under age 55 by presence of own children under age 18 at home and mobility status between March 1998 and March 1999; numbers in thousands)

	total	nonmovers	movers						
			total	same county	different county, same state	different state, same division	different division, same region	different region	movers from abroad
Total householders	**68,730**	**54,516**	**14,213**	**8,463**	**2,925**	**1,100**	**320**	**1,013**	**392**
No children under 18	35,125	26,864	8,262	4,625	1,911	676	198	588	264
With children under 18	33,605	27,652	5,952	3,838	1,014	425	122	425	128
Under age 6 only	8,095	5,789	2,306	1,460	415	154	62	164	51
Under age 6 and 6 to 17	7,026	5,748	1,278	897	166	95	12	73	35
Aged 6 to 17 only	18,484	16,115	2,368	1,481	433	176	48	188	42
PERCENT DISTRIBUTION BY MOBILITY STATUS									
Total householders	**100.0%**	**79.3%**	**20.7%**	**12.3%**	**4.3%**	**1.6%**	**0.5%**	**1.5%**	**0.6%**
No children under 18	100.0	76.5	23.5	13.2	5.4	1.9	0.6	1.7	0.8
With children under 18	100.0	82.3	17.7	11.4	3.0	1.3	0.4	1.3	0.4
Under age 6 only	100.0	71.5	28.5	18.0	5.1	1.9	0.8	2.0	0.6
Under age 6 and 6 to 17	100.0	81.8	18.2	12.8	2.4	1.4	0.2	1.0	0.5
Aged 6 to 17 only	100.0	87.2	12.8	8.0	2.3	1.0	0.3	1.0	0.2

(continued)

(continued from previous page)

PERCENT DISTRIBUTION OF MOVERS BY TYPE OF MOVE

	total	nonmovers		movers						
			total	same county	different county, same state	different state, same division	different division, same region	different region	movers from abroad
Total householders	–	–	**100.0%**	**59.5%**	**20.6%**	**7.7%**	**2.3%**	**7.1%**	**2.8%**
No children under 18	–	–	100.0	56.0	23.1	8.2	2.4	7.1	3.2
With children under 18	–	–	100.0	64.5	17.0	7.1	2.0	7.1	2.2
Under age 6 only	–	–	100.0	63.3	18.0	6.7	2.7	7.1	2.2
Under age 6 and 6 to 17	–	–	100.0	70.2	13.0	7.4	0.9	5.7	2.7
Aged 6 to 17 only	–	–	100.0	62.5	18.3	7.4	2.0	7.9	1.8

Note: (–) means not applicable.
Source: Bureau of the Census, Geographical Mobility: March 1998 to March 1999 (Update), detailed tables for Current Population Report P20-531, 2000; Internet site <www.census.gov/population/www/socdemo/migrate.html#cps>; calculations by New Strategist

8

Spending

♦ Households headed by people under age 25 spent 3 percent more in 1999 than in 1990, after adjusting for inflation. In many categories, however, millennials cut their spending.

♦ The incomes of married couples with preschoolers rose 12 percent between 1990 and 1999, while their spending increased just 3 percent. Apparently, the recession of the early 1990s left its mark, making these families cautious spenders despite the more recent economic boom.

♦ Married couples with school-aged children rank among the most affluent households in the nation. Their affluence grew substantially during the 1990s because they kept their spending in check. While their income rose 12 percent, after adjusting for inflation, their spending rose just 4 percent.

♦ Married couples with children aged 18 or older at home are the most affluent household type. Despite their lofty incomes, their spending has been downright stingy. In 1999, they spent 0.6 percent less than they did in 1990—despite a 6 percent gain in income.

♦ The economic boom of the 1990s benefited single-parent families, and their spending reveals pent-up demand for many products and services. Single parents spent 14 percent more in 1999 than in 1990, after adjusting for inflation.

Millennials Are Spending More

Spending by householders under age 25 outpaced income during the 1990s.

The average household boosted its spending by 2 percent between 1990 and 1999, after adjusting for inflation. Households headed by people under age 25 spent 3 percent more in 1999 than in 1990. In many categories, however, millennials cut their spending—sometimes substantially.

Householders under age 25 spent 19 percent less on food away from home in 1999 than in 1990. They spent 9 percent less on alcoholic beverages. They also reduced their spending on housekeeping supplies but spent more on furnishings and equipment. As homeownership rates rose during the decade, millennials spent fully 50 percent more on owned dwellings in 1999 than in 1990. They also spent more on transportation, health care, and entertainment. They spent considerably more on children's clothes in 1999 than in 1990, and their spending on footwear nearly doubled during those years.

Many householders under age 25 are in college, and their spending on education rose 23 percent between 1990 and 1999 thanks to rising tuition. Despite their education, young adults are not the readers that older generations are. Their spending on reading material fell 27 percent between 1990 and 1999—a troubling trend for the print media.

♦ Householders under age 25 are a diverse mix of single parents, people living alone, and friends living together. Their spending patterns reflect this diversity.

Average Spending of Householders under Age 25, 1990 and 1999

(average annual spending of total consumer units and consumer units headed by people under age 25, 1990 and 1999; percent change, 1990–99; in 1999 dollars)

	total consumer units			under age 25		
	1990	*1999*	*percent change 1990–99*	*1990*	*1999*	*percent change 1990–99*
Number of consumer units (in 000s)	**96,968**	**108,465**	**11.9%**	**7,581**	**8,164**	**7.7%**
Average before-tax income	**$40,648**	**$43,951**	**8.1**	**$17,959**	**$18,276**	**1.8**
Average annual spending	**36,176**	**37,027**	**2.4**	**21,064**	**21,725**	**3.1**
FOOD	**$5,476**	**$5,031**	**–8.1%**	**$3,519**	**$3,354**	**–4.7%**
Food at home	**3,168**	**2,915**	**–8.0**	**1,638**	**1,828**	**11.6**
Cereals and bakery products	469	448	–4.5	233	271	16.3
Cereals and cereal products	164	160	–2.4	92	102	10.9
Bakery products	306	288	–5.9	141	169	19.9
Meats, poultry, fish, and eggs	851	749	–12.0	377	469	24.4
Beef	278	220	–20.9	124	155	25.0
Pork	168	157	–6.5	75	93	24.0
Other meats	126	97	–23.0	61	61	0.0
Poultry	138	136	–1.4	50	82	64.0
Fish and seafood	105	106	1.0	45	59	31.1
Eggs	38	32	–15.8	22	19	–13.6
Dairy products	376	322	–14.4	199	195	–2.0
Fresh milk and cream	178	122	–31.5	103	78	–24.3
Other dairy products	198	200	1.0	96	117	21.9
Fruits and vegetables	520	500	–3.8	240	283	17.9
Fresh fruits	162	152	–6.2	59	77	30.5
Fresh vegetables	150	149	–0.7	73	79	8.2
Processed fruits	119	113	–5.0	61	77	26.2
Processed vegetables	89	86	–3.4	47	49	4.3
Other food at home	951	896	–5.8	589	610	3.6
Sugar and other sweets	120	112	–6.7	61	71	16.4
Fats and oils	87	84	–3.4	40	54	35.0
Miscellaneous foods	428	420	–1.9	307	300	–2.3
Nonalcoholic beverages	272	242	–11.0	162	167	3.1
Food prepared by household on trips	45	39	–13.3	19	19	0.0

(continued)

(continued from previous page)

	total consumer units			under age 25		
	1990	*1999*	*percent change 1990–99*	*1990*	*1999*	*percent change 1990–99*
Food away from home	$2,308	$2,116	–8.3%	$1,881	$1,526	–18.9%
ALCOHOLIC BEVERAGES	373	318	–14.7	405	369	–8.9
HOUSING	11,093	12,057	8.7	6,176	6,585	6.6
Shelter	6,164	7,016	13.8	3,842	4,140	7.8
Owned dwellings	3,764	4,525	20.2	396	596	50.5
Mortgage interest and charges	2,316	2,547	10.0	297	311	4.7
Property taxes	761	1,123	47.6	34	168	394.1
Maintenance, repairs, insurance, other expenses	688	855	24.3	65	117	80.0
Rented dwellings	1,954	2,027	3.7	3,192	3,296	3.3
Other lodging	445	464	4.3	255	248	–2.7
Utilities, fuels, public services	2,409	2,377	–1.3	1,155	1,166	1.0
Natural gas	314	270	–14.0	120	92	–23.3
Electricity	966	899	–6.9	404	426	5.4
Fuel oil and other fuels	127	74	–41.7	22	14	–36.4
Telephone services	755	849	12.5	548	562	2.6
Water and other public services	246	285	15.9	61	72	18.0
Household services	569	666	17.0	186	181	–2.7
Personal services	279	323	15.8	127	121	–4.7
Other household services	289	343	18.7	59	60	1.7
Housekeeping supplies	518	498	–3.9	227	221	–2.6
Laundry and cleaning supplies	144	121	–16.0	60	64	6.7
Other household products	218	250	14.7	75	86	14.7
Postage and stationery	156	127	–18.6	92	71	–22.8
Household furnishings, equipment	1,434	1,499	4.5	766	877	14.5
Household textiles	126	114	–9.5	50	41	–18.0
Furniture	395	365	–7.6	324	283	–12.7
Floor coverings	117	44	–62.4	11	11	0.0
Major appliances	187	183	–2.1	83	91	9.6
Small appliances, misc. housewares	96	102	6.3	51	47	–7.8
Miscellaneous household equipment	512	692	35.2	247	405	64.0

(continued)

(continued from previous page)

	total consumer units			under age 25		
	1990	1999	percent change 1990–99	1990	1999	percent change 1990–99
APPAREL AND SERVICES	$2,062	$1,743	–15.5%	$1,318	$1,192	–9.6%
Men and boys	501	421	–16.0	402	238	–40.8
Men, aged 16 or older	413	328	–20.6	386	209	–45.9
Boys, aged 2 to 15	89	93	4.5	17	29	70.6
Women and girls	858	655	–23.7	402	422	5.0
Women, aged 16 or older	747	548	–26.6	370	377	1.9
Girls, aged 2 to 15	111	107	–3.6	33	45	36.4
Children under age 2	89	67	–24.7	107	99	–7.5
Footwear	287	303	5.6	120	234	95.0
Other apparel products and services	329	297	–9.7	288	199	–30.9
TRANSPORTATION	6,526	7,011	7.4	4,454	5,037	13.1
Vehicle purchases	2,714	3,305	21.8	2,028	2,859	41.0
Cars and trucks, new	1,477	1,628	10.2	936	857	–8.4
Cars and trucks, used	1,208	1,641	35.8	1,064	1,974	85.5
Other vehicles	28	36	28.6	29	28	–3.4
Gasoline and motor oil	1,335	1,055	–21.0	920	708	–23.0
Other vehicle expenses	2,093	2,254	7.7	1,277	1,253	–1.9
Vehicle finance charges	382	320	–16.2	247	209	–15.4
Maintenance and repairs	751	664	–11.6	496	402	–19.0
Vehicle insurance	718	756	5.3	412	408	–1.0
Vehicle rental, leases, licenses, other charges	242	513	112.0	124	234	88.7
Public transportation	385	397	3.1	228	217	–4.8
HEALTH CARE	1,887	1,959	3.8	514	551	7.2
Health insurance	741	923	24.6	135	233	72.6
Medical services	716	558	–22.1	242	184	–24.0
Drugs	321	370	15.3	83	97	16.9
Medical supplies	108	109	0.9	52	36	–30.8
ENTERTAINMENT	1,813	1,891	4.3	1,062	1,149	8.2
Fees and admissions	473	459	–3.0	278	262	–5.8
Television, radio, sound equipment	579	608	5.0	438	485	10.7
Pets, toys, and playground equipment	352	346	–1.7	149	185	24.2
Other entertainment supplies, services	409	478	16.9	198	217	9.6

(continued)

(continued from previous page)

	total consumer units			under age 25		
	1990	1999	percent change 1990–99	1990	1999	percent change 1990–99
PERSONAL CARE PRODUCTS AND SERVICES	$464	$408	–12.1%	$270	$254	–5.9%
READING	195	159	–18.5	96	70	–27.1
EDUCATION	518	635	22.6	1,041	1,277	22.7
TOBACCO PRODUCTS AND SMOKING SUPPLIES	349	300	–14.0	275	220	–20.0
MISCELLANEOUS	1,073	889	–17.1	509	370	–27.3
CASH CONTRIBUTIONS	1,040	1,190	14.4	186	186	0.0
PERSONAL INSURANCE AND PENSIONS	3,304	3,436	4.0	1,239	1,110	–10.4
Life and other personal insurance	440	394	–10.5	62	61	–1.6
Pensions and Social Security	2,865	3,042	6.2	1,175	1,049	–10.7
PERSONAL TAXES	3,763	3,588	–4.7	1,075	845	–21.4
Federal income taxes	2,956	2,802	–5.2	818	630	–23.0
State and local income taxes	711	616	–13.4	245	208	–15.1
Other taxes	96	170	77.1	13	7	–46.2
GIFTS	1,161	1,083	–6.7	535	515	–3.7
Food	121	83	–31.4	32	19	–40.6
Housing	296	292	–1.4	120	139	15.8
Housekeeping supplies	45	41	–8.9	24	14	–41.7
Household textiles	18	17	–5.6	6	3	–50.0
Appliances and misc. housewares	34	32	–5.9	11	5	–54.5
Major appliances	9	9	0.0	–	2	–
Small appliances, misc. housewares	25	24	–4.0	10	2	–80.0
Miscellaneous household equipment	64	66	3.1	37	42	13.5
Other housing	136	136	0.0	42	75	78.6
Apparel and services	301	210	–30.2	157	118	–24.8
Males, aged 2 or older	78	54	–30.8	23	24	4.3
Females, aged 2 or older	121	71	–41.3	48	35	–27.1
Children under age 2	40	33	–17.5	27	23	–14.8
Other apparel products and services	61	52	–14.8	59	36	–39.0
Jewelry and watches	32	27	–15.6	47	22	–53.2
All other apparel products, services	29	25	–13.8	11	14	27.3

(continued)

(continued from previous page)

	total consumer units			under age 25		
	1990	**1999**	**percent change 1990–99**	**1990**	**1999**	**percent change 1990–99**
Transportation	$68	$63	–7.4%	$23	$65	182.6%
Health care	57	40	–29.8	6	5	–16.7
Entertainment	84	98	16.7	41	63	53.7
Toys, games, hobbies, and tricycles	32	32	0.0	11	10	–9.1
Other entertainment	52	66	26.9	29	53	82.8
Education	122	166	36.1	29	42	44.8
All other gifts	112	131	17.0	127	65	–48.8

Note: The Bureau of Labor Statistics uses consumer units rather than households as the sampling unit in the Consumer Expenditure Survey. For the definition of consumer unit, see the glossary. Spending on gifts is included in the preceding product and service categories
Source: Bureau of Labor Statistics, 1990 and 1999 Consumer Expenditure Surveys, Internet site <www.bls.gov/csxhome.htm>; calculations by New Strategist

Young Adults Spend Less on Most Things

Householders under age 25 spend just 59 percent as much as the average household.

The incomes of young adults are well below average, and so is their spending. On some things, however, millennials spend more. They spend 16 percent more than the average household on alcoholic beverages and 63 percent more on rent. Because many young householders are single parents, they spend 48 percent more than the average household on clothes for children under age 2. They spend 20 percent more on used cars and trucks. millennial householders spend twice as much as the average household on education. Many are students paying for college tuition at least partly out of their own pocket.

On most items, millennials spend far less than the average household. They spend only 13 percent as much as the average household on owned dwellings, for example, because most are renters. They spend only 28 percent of the average on health care since most are in good health and have few medical needs. Their spending on reading material is just 44 percent of the average.

♦ As millennial householders complete their education and embark on careers, their spending will rise with their income.

Average and Indexed Spending of Householders under Age 25, 1999

(average annual spending of total consumer units and average annual and indexed spending of consumer units headed by people under age 25, 1999)

	total consumer units	consumer units headed by people under age 25	
		average spending	indexed spending*
Number of consumer units (in 000s)	108,465	$8,164	–
Average before-tax Income	$43,951	18,276	42
Average annual spending	37,027	21,725	59
FOOD	**$5,031**	**$3,354**	67
Food at home	**2,915**	**1,828**	63
Cereals and bakery products	448	271	60
Cereals and cereal products	160	102	64
Bakery products	288	169	59
Meats, poultry, fish, and eggs	749	469	63
Beef	220	155	70
Pork	157	93	59
Other meats	97	61	63
Poultry	136	82	60
Fish and seafood	106	59	56
Eggs	32	19	59
Dairy products	322	195	61
Fresh milk and cream	122	78	64
Other dairy products	200	117	59
Fruits and vegetables	500	283	57
Fresh fruits	152	77	51
Fresh vegetables	149	79	53
Processed fruits	113	77	68
Processed vegetables	86	49	57
Other food at home	896	610	68
Sugar and other sweets	112	71	63
Fats and oils	84	54	64
Miscellaneous foods	420	300	71
Nonalcoholic beverages	242	167	69
Food prepared by household on trips	39	19	49

(continued)

(continued from previous page)

	total consumer units	consumer units headed by people under age 25	
		average spending	indexed spending*
Food away from home	**$2,116**	**$1,526**	**72**
ALCOHOLIC BEVERAGES	**318**	**369**	**116**
HOUSING	**12,057**	**6,585**	**55**
Shelter	**7,016**	**4,140**	**59**
Owned dwellings	4,525	596	13
Mortgage interest and charges	2,547	311	12
Property taxes	1,123	168	15
Maintenance, repairs, insurance, other expenses	855	117	14
Rented dwellings	2,027	3,296	163
Other lodging	464	248	53
Utilities, fuels, public services	**2,377**	**1,166**	**49**
Natural gas	270	92	34
Electricity	899	426	47
Fuel oil and other fuels	74	14	19
Telephone services	849	562	66
Water and other public services	285	72	25
Household services	**666**	**181**	**27**
Personal services	323	121	37
Other household services	343	60	17
Housekeeping supplies	**498**	**221**	**44**
Laundry and cleaning supplies	121	64	53
Other household products	250	86	34
Postage and stationery	127	71	56
Household furnishings and equipment	**1,499**	**877**	**59**
Household textiles	114	41	36
Furniture	365	283	78
Floor coverings	44	11	25
Major appliances	183	91	50
Small appliances, miscellaneous housewares	102	47	46
Miscellaneous household equipment	692	405	59

(continued)

(continued from previous page)

	total consumer units	consumer units headed by people under age 25	
		average spending	indexed spendingl
APPAREL AND SERVICES	**$1,743**	**$1,192**	**68**
Men and boys	**421**	**238**	**57**
Men, aged 16 or older	328	209	64
Boys, aged 2 to 15	93	29	31
Women and girls	**655**	**422**	**64**
Women, aged 16 or older	548	377	69
Girls, aged 2 to 15	107	45	42
Children under age 2	**67**	**99**	**148**
Footwear	**303**	**234**	**77**
Other apparel products and services	**297**	**199**	**67**
TRANSPORTATION	**7,011**	**5,037**	**72**
Vehicle purchases	**3,305**	**2,859**	**87**
Cars and trucks, new	1,628	857	53
Cars and trucks, used	1,641	1,974	120
Other vehicles	36	28	78
Gasoline and motor oil	**1,055**	**708**	**67**
Other vehicle expenses	**2,254**	**1,253**	**56**
Vehicle finance charges	320	209	65
Maintenance and repairs	664	402	61
Vehicle insurance	756	408	54
Vehicle rental, leases, licenses, other charges	513	234	46
Public transportation	**397**	**217**	**55**
HEALTH CARE	**1,959**	**551**	**28**
Health insurance	923	233	25
Medical services	558	184	33
Drugs	370	97	26
Medical supplies	109	36	33
ENTERTAINMENT	**1,891**	**1,149**	**61**
Fees and admissions	459	262	57
Television, radio, sound equipment	608	485	80
Pets, toys, and playground equipment	346	185	53
Other entertainment supplies, services	478	217	45

(continued)

(continued from previous page)

	total consumer units	consumer units headed by people under age 25	
		average spending	indexed spending*
PERSONAL CARE PRODUCTS AND SERVICES	$408	$254	62
READING	159	70	44
EDUCATION	635	1,277	201
TOBACCO PRODUCTS AND SMOKING SUPPLIES	300	220	73
MISCELLANEOUS	889	370	42
CASH CONTRIBUTIONS	1,190	186	16
PERSONAL INSURANCE AND PENSIONS	3,436	1,110	32
Life and other personal insurance	394	61	15
Pensions and Social Security	3,042	1,049	34
PERSONAL TAXES	3,588	845	24
Federal income taxes	2,802	630	22
State and local income taxes	616	208	34
Other taxes	170	7	4
GIFTS	1,083	515	48
Food	83	19	23
Housing	292	139	48
Housekeeping supplies	41	14	34
Household textiles	17	3	18
Appliances and miscellaneous housewares	32	5	16
Major appliances	9	2	22
Small appliances and miscellaneous housewares	24	2	8
Miscellaneous household equipment	66	42	64
Other housing	136	75	55
Apparel and services	210	118	56
Males, aged 2 or older	54	24	44
Females, aged 2 or older	71	35	49
Children under age 2	33	23	70
Other apparel products and services	52	36	69
Jewelry and watches	27	22	81
All other apparel products and services	25	14	56

(continued)

(continued from previous page)

	total consumer units	consumer units headed by people under age 25	
		average spending	indexed spending*
TRANSPORTATION	$63	$65	103
HEALTH CARE	40	5	13
ENTERTAINMENT	98	63	64
Toys, games, hobbies, and tricycles	32	10	31
Other entertainment	66	53	80
EDUCATION	166	42	25
ALL OTHER GIFTS	131	65	50

* The index compares the spending of consumer units headed by people under age 25 with the spending of the average consumer unit by dividing the spending of people under age 25 by average spending in each category and multiplying by 100. An index of 100 means the spending of people under age 25 equals average spending. An index of 130 means the spending of people under age 25 is 30 percent above average, while an index of 70 means it is 30 percent below average.

Note: The Bureau of Labor Statistics uses consumer units rather than households as the sampling unit in the Consumer Expenditure Survey. For the definition of consumer unit, see the glossary. Spending on gifts is included in the preceding product and service categories.

Source: Bureau of Labor Statistics, 1990 and 1999 Consumer Expenditure Surveys, Internet site <www.bls.gov/ csxhome.htm>; calculations by New Strategist

Parents of Preschoolers Spend Cautiously

The incomes of married couples with preschoolers rose much more than their spending between 1990 and 1999.

The incomes of married couples with children under age 6 rose 12 percent between 1990 and 1999, after adjusting for inflation. Their spending increased just 3 percent. Apparently, the recession of the early 1990s left its mark, making these families cautious spenders despite the more recent economic boom.

Couples with preschoolers cut their spending on both discretionary and nondiscretionary items. They spent 11 percent less on groceries (food at home) in 1999 than in 1990, while they cut their food-away-from-home spending by a smaller 6 percent. They spent 23 percent less on alcoholic beverages. As homeownership rates rose, they spent more on owned dwellings and less on rent. Household personal service spending (mostly day care) grew 6 percent. They spent less on apparel overall, but 13 percent more on footwear. Spending on new cars and trucks fell, but spending on used and leased vehicles rose sharply. Health insurance spending rose 22 percent. While couples with preschoolers spent 3 percent more on entertainment, they spent 2 percent less on pets, toys, and playground equipment.

♦ The spending pattern of couples with preschoolers reveals an underlying economic insecurity which their rising incomes have not quelled. Already cautious spenders, these householders should be able to weather an economic downturn.

Average Spending of Married Couples with Children under Age 6, 1990 and 1999

(average annual spending of married-couple consumer units with children under age 6, 1990 and 1999; percent change, 1990–99; in 1999 dollars)

	1990	1999	percent change 1990–99
Number of consumer units (in 000s)	6,403	5,304	–17.2%
Average before-tax income	$51,862	$57,922	11.7
Average annual spending	44,638	46,091	3.3
FOOD	**$5,940**	**$5,379**	**–9.4%**
Food at home	3,788	3,360	–11.3
Cereals and bakery products	540	503	–6.9
Cereals and cereal products	206	185	–10.2
Bakery products	334	318	–4.8
Meats, poultry, fish, and eggs	957	769	–19.6
Beef	307	230	–25.1
Pork	191	144	–24.6
Other meats	134	97	–27.6
Poultry	147	160	8.8
Fish and seafood	134	106	–20.9
Eggs	43	32	–25.6
Dairy products	496	407	–17.9
Fresh milk and cream	247	170	–31.2
Other dairy products	249	237	–4.8
Fruits and vegetables	585	560	–4.3
Fresh fruits	164	162	–1.2
Fresh vegetables	164	169	3.0
Processed fruits	159	139	–12.6
Processed vegetables	98	90	–8.2
Other food at home	1,211	1,120	–7.5
Sugar and other sweets	121	115	–5.0
Fats and oils	97	78	–19.6
Miscellaneous foods	622	620	–0.3
Nonalcoholic beverages	315	265	–15.9
Food prepared by household on trips	56	44	–21.4

(continued)

	1990	1999	percent change 1990–99
Food away from home	**$2,150**	**$2,020**	**–6.0%**
ALCOHOLIC BEVERAGES	**339**	**261**	**–23.0**
HOUSING	**15,882**	**17,170**	**8.1**
Shelter	**8,649**	**10,076**	**16.5**
Owned dwellings	5,769	7,565	31.1
Mortgage interest and charges	4,366	5,132	17.5
Property taxes	800	1,370	71.3
Maintenance, repairs, insurance, other expenses	603	1,063	76.3
Rented dwellings	2,557	2,244	–12.2
Other lodging	321	267	–16.8
Utilities, fuels, public services	**2,591**	**2,570**	**–0.8**
Natural gas	326	293	–10.1
Electricity	1,048	903	–13.8
Fuel oil and other fuels	122	74	–39.3
Telephone services	830	989	19.2
Water and other public services	264	312	18.2
Household services	**2,009**	**2,142**	**6.6**
Personal services	1,689	1,784	5.6
Other household services	319	359	12.5
Housekeeping supplies	**599**	**535**	**–10.7**
Laundry and cleaning supplies	172	122	–29.1
Other household products	241	262	8.7
Postage and stationery	186	152	–18.3
Household furnishings and equipment	**2,036**	**1,848**	**–9.2**
Household textiles	172	117	–32.0
Furniture	563	588	4.4
Floor coverings	306	65	–78.8
Major appliances	232	210	–9.5
Small appliances, miscellaneous housewares	99	90	–9.1
Miscellaneous household equipment	663	778	17.3

(continued)

(continued from previous page)

	1990	1999	percent change 1990–99
APPAREL AND SERVICES	**$2,399**	**$2,078**	**−13.4%**
Men and boys	**516**	**413**	**−20.0**
Men, aged 16 or older	404	297	−26.5
Boys, aged 2 to 15	112	115	2.7
Women and girls	**772**	**636**	**−17.6**
Women, aged 16 or older	622	501	−19.5
Girls, aged 2 to 15	150	135	−10.0
Children under age 2	**472**	**412**	**−12.7**
Footwear	**266**	**301**	**13.2**
Other apparel products and services	**371**	**316**	**−14.8**
TRANSPORTATION	**7,935**	**9,368**	**18.1**
Vehicle purchases	**3,527**	**4,855**	**37.7**
Cars and trucks, new	1,978	1,765	−10.8
Cars and trucks, used	1,517	3,043	100.6
Other vehicles	32	46	43.8
Gasoline and motor oil	**1,517**	**1,281**	**−15.6**
Other vehicle expenses	**2,553**	**2,904**	**13.7**
Vehicle finance charges	608	487	−19.9
Maintenance and repairs	806	674	−16.4
Vehicle insurance	806	858	6.5
Vehicle rental, leases, licenses, other charges	335	885	164.2
Public transportation	**338**	**328**	**−3.0**
HEALTH CARE	**1,977**	**1,705**	**−13.8**
Health insurance	737	905	22.8
Medical services	915	517	−43.5
Drugs	251	199	−20.7
Medical supplies	74	84	13.5
ENTERTAINMENT	**2,056**	**2,111**	**2.7**
Fees and admissions	446	426	−4.5
Television, radio, sound equipment	636	683	7.4
Pets, toys, and playground equipment	519	508	−2.1
Other entertainment supplies, services	455	494	8.6

(continued)

(continued from previous page)

	1990	1999	percent change 1990–99
PERSONAL CARE PRODUCTS AND SERVICES	$472	$450	−4.7%
READING	235	160	−31.9
EDUCATION	325	317	−2.5
TOBACCO PRODUCTS AND SMOKING SUPPLIES	317	239	−24.6
MISCELLANEOUS	1,242	1,094	−11.9
CASH CONTRIBUTIONS	682	808	18.5
PERSONAL INSURANCE AND PENSIONS	4,837	4,951	2.4
Life and other personal insurance	481	398	−17.3
Pensions and Social Security	4,356	4,553	4.5
PERSONAL TAXES	4,633	4,057	−12.4
Federal income taxes	3,602	2,975	−17.4
State and local income taxes	950	882	−7.2
Other taxes	82	199	142.7
GIFTS	905	767	−15.2
Food	47	40	−14.9
Housing	322	317	−1.6
Housekeeping supplies	40	46	15.0
Household textiles	19	8	−57.9
Appliances and miscellaneous housewares	17	17	0.0
Major appliances	3	2	−33.3
Small appliances and miscellaneous housewares	14	15	7.1
Miscellaneous household equipment	84	39	−53.6
Other housing	163	207	27.0
Apparel and services	289	199	−31.1
Males, aged 2 or older	74	35	−52.7
Females, aged 2 or older	94	53	−43.6
Children under age 2	76	91	19.7
Other apparel products and services	45	21	−53.3
Jewelry and watches	11	9	−18.2
All other apparel products and services	32	12	−62.5

(continued)

(continued from previous page)

	1990	1999	percent change 1990–99
Transportation	**$24**	**$11**	**−54.2%**
Health care	**15**	**9**	**−40.0**
Entertainment	**99**	**69**	**−30.3**
Toys, games, hobbies, and tricycles	32	29	−9.4
Other entertainment	68	40	−41.2
Education	**41**	**49**	**19.5**
All other gifts	**66**	**73**	**10.6**

Note: The Bureau of Labor Statistics uses consumer units rather than households as the sampling unit in the Consumer Expenditure Survey. For the definition of consumer unit, see the glossary. Spending on gifts is included in the preceding product and service categories.
Source: Bureau of Labor Statistics, 1990 and 1999 Consumer Expenditure Surveys, Internet site <www.bls.gov/ csxhome.htm>; calculations by New Strategist

Many Spending Cuts for Couples with School-Aged Children

A few discretionary categories saw spending gains during the 1990s.

Married couples with school-aged children rank among the most affluent households in the nation. Their affluence grew substantially during the 1990s because they kept their spending in check. While their income rose 12 percent, after adjusting for inflation, their spending rose just 4 percent.

The recession of the early 1990s greatly affected the baby-boom generation, making them cautious spenders. Many boomers now number among the nation's married couples with school-aged children. Their caution can be seen in the spending trends for this household type, which show declines in many discretionary categories. Couples with school-aged children cut their spending on food away from home by 4 percent, for example, and they spent 13 percent less on alcoholic beverages. While they spent more on owned dwellings because of rising homeownership rates, their spending on household furnishings and equipment fell 3 percent. They spent less on new vehicles but more on used and leased vehicles.

Couples with school-aged children spent 24 percent more on public transportation in 1999 than in 1990—a category that includes airline fares. They spent 11 percent more on entertainment—including a 67 percent increase in spending on "other entertainment," a category that includes sports equipment. They spent more on gifts of entertainment, but less on gifts overall.

♦ With gains in income outstripping those in spending, married couples with children are in better shape financially than they were a decade ago.

Average Spending of Married Couples with Children Aged 6 to 17, 1990 and 1999

(average annual spending of married-couple consumer units with children aged 6 to 17, 1990 and 1999; percent change, 1990–99; in 1999 dollars)

	1990	1999	percent change 1990–99
Number of consumer units (in 000s)	13,701	15,378	12.2%
Average before-tax income	$56,886	$63,558	11.7
Average annual spending	49,460	51,493	4.1
FOOD	**$7,886**	**$7,472**	**–5.2%**
Food at home	**4,665**	**4,381**	**–6.1**
Cereals and bakery products	733	713	–2.7
Cereals and cereal products	266	267	0.4
Bakery products	467	445	–4.7
Meats, poultry, fish, and eggs	1,179	1,078	–8.6
Beef	385	336	–12.7
Pork	231	220	–4.8
Other meats	177	147	–16.9
Poultry	194	191	–1.5
Fish and seafood	140	139	–0.7
Eggs	52	45	–13.5
Dairy products	579	521	–10.0
Fresh milk and cream	275	202	–26.5
Other dairy products	303	319	5.3
Fruits and vegetables	701	716	2.1
Fresh fruits	218	215	–1.4
Fresh vegetables	199	201	1.0
Processed fruits	154	169	9.7
Processed vegetables	129	131	1.6
Other food at home	1,474	1,353	–8.2
Sugar and other sweets	199	174	–12.6
Fats and oils	127	117	–7.9
Miscellaneous foods	677	646	–4.6
Nonalcoholic beverages	405	354	–12.6
Food prepared by household on trips	64	61	–4.7

(continued)

(continued from previous page)

	1990	*1999*	*percent change 1990–99*
FOOD AWAY FROM HOME	$3,221	$3,090	–4.1%
ALCOHOLIC BEVERAGES	368	322	–12.5
HOUSING	14,572	16,408	12.6
Shelter	7,788	9,470	21.6
Owned dwellings	5,886	7,567	28.6
Mortgage interest and charges	4,261	5,063	18.8
Property taxes	915	1,565	71.0
Maintenance, repairs, insurance, other expenses	710	938	32.1
Rented dwellings	1,373	1,418	3.3
Other lodging	529	485	–8.3
Utilities, fuels, public services	3,017	3,009	–0.3
Natural gas	394	342	–13.2
Electricity	1,258	1,159	–7.9
Fuel oil and other fuels	182	89	–51.1
Telephone services	829	1,016	22.6
Water and other public services	356	403	13.2
Household services	853	1,066	25.0
Personal services	539	603	11.9
Other household services	314	463	47.5
Housekeeping supplies	757	770	1.7
Laundry and cleaning supplies	223	176	–21.1
Other household products	345	414	20.0
Postage and stationery	187	181	–3.2
Household furnishings and equipment	2,158	2,093	–3.0
Household textiles	181	144	–20.4
Furniture	585	588	0.5
Floor coverings	252	59	–76.6
Major appliances	255	220	–13.7
Small appliances, miscellaneous housewares	120	101	–15.8
Miscellaneous household equipment	765	980	28.1

(continued)

(continued from previous page)

	1990	1999	percent change 1990–99
APPAREL AND SERVICES	$3,027	$2,696	−10.9%
Men and boys	846	765	−9.6
Men, aged 16 or older	547	462	−15.5
Boys, aged 2 to 15	300	303	1.0
Women and girls	1,235	985	−20.2
Women, aged 16 or older	855	643	−24.8
Girls, aged 2 to 15	380	342	−10.0
Children under age 2	96	92	−4.2
Footwear	423	504	19.1
Other apparel products and services	427	350	−18.0
TRANSPORTATION	9,124	9,585	5.1
Vehicle purchases	4,348	4,727	8.7
Cars and trucks, new	2,335	2,277	−2.5
Cars and trucks, used	1,974	2,376	20.4
Other vehicles	38	74	94.7
Gasoline and motor oil	1,853	1,454	−21.5
Other vehicle expenses	2,589	2,988	15.4
Vehicle finance charges	556	509	−8.5
Maintenance and repairs	897	884	−1.4
Vehicle insurance	834	927	11.2
Vehicle rental, leases, licenses, other charges	301	668	121.9
Public transportation	335	417	24.5
HEALTH CARE	2,036	2,154	5.8
Health insurance	732	993	35.7
Medical services	899	741	−17.6
Drugs	282	291	3.2
Medical supplies	124	129	4.0
ENTERTAINMENT	2,825	3,141	11.2
Fees and admissions	778	705	−9.4
Television, radio, sound equipment	872	845	−3.1
Pets, toys, and playground equipment	572	583	1.9
Other entertainment supplies, services	603	1,007	67.0

(continued)

(continued from previous page)

	1990	1999	percent change 1990–99
PERSONAL CARE PRODUCTS AND SERVICES	$636	$552	–13.2%
READING	246	201	–18.3
EDUCATION	707	1,030	45.7
TOBACCO PRODUCTS AND SMOKING SUPPLIES	413	344	–16.7
MISCELLANEOUS	1,400	1,001	–28.5
CASH CONTRIBUTIONS	1,106	1,206	9.0
PERSONAL INSURANCE AND PENSIONS	5,113	5,382	5.3
Life and other personal insurance	727	703	–3.3
Pensions and Social Security	4,385	4,679	6.7
PERSONAL TAXES	5,292	4,709	–11.0
Federal income taxes	4,175	3,629	–13.1
State and local income taxes	998	894	–10.4
Other taxes	120	186	55.0
GIFTS	1,203	1,127	–6.3
Food	168	81	–51.8
Housing	377	342	–9.3
Housekeeping supplies	56	60	7.1
Household textiles	18	9	–50.0
Appliances and miscellaneous housewares	33	25	–24.2
Major appliances	5	4	–20.0
Small appliances and miscellaneous housewares	28	21	–25.0
Miscellaneous household equipment	79	64	–19.0
Other housing	191	183	–4.2
Apparel and services	306	193	–36.9
Males, aged 2 or older	83	49	–41.0
Females, aged 2 or older	127	64	–49.6
Children under age 2	48	53	10.4
Other apparel products and services	47	28	–40.4
Jewelry and watches	19	7	–63.2
All other apparel products and services	28	20	–28.6

(continued)

(continued from previous page)

	1990	1999	percent change 1990–99
Transportation	$36	$68	88.9%
Health care	14	15	7.1
Entertainment	70	93	32.9
Toys, games, hobbies, and tricycles	23	28	21.7
Other entertainment	47	65	38.3
Education	98	239	143.9
All other gifts	135	96	–28.9

Note: The Bureau of Labor Statistics uses consumer units rather than households as the sampling unit in the Consumer Expenditure Survey. For the definition of consumer unit, see the glossary. Spending on gifts is included in the preceding product and service categories.
Source: Bureau of Labor Statistics, 1990 and 1999 Consumer Expenditure Surveys, Internet site <www.bls.gov/csxhome.htm>; calculations by New Strategist

Couples with Adult Children at Home Are Spending Less

The spending cut was small, and hurt some categories more than others.

Married couples with grown children (aged 18 or older) at home are the most affluent household type. That's because these households have twice as many earners—2.6 versus 1.3 earners in the average household. Despite their lofty incomes, the spending of these crowded nests has been downright stingy. In 1999, couples with children aged 18 or older at home spent 0.6 percent less than they did in 1990—despite a 6 percent gain in income.

Married couples with adult children at home spent much less on many discretionary categories. They spent 14 percent less on food-away-from-home in 1999 than in 1990. They spent 37 percent less on alcoholic beverages. While spending on owned homes increased as homeownership rates rose, spending on furniture fell 17 percent. Spending on "other lodging" rose 12 percent, but most of this increase may have been nondiscretionary since the category includes housing while at school. Apparel spending fell, although spending on clothes for children aged 2 to 15 increased. Some couples live with grandchildren as well as children.

Spending on new vehicles rose among couples with grown children at home. So did spending on public transportation—although much of the increase could have been the expense of sending college-aged children to and from school. Spending on entertainment rose only 0.4 percent for this household type, while spending on education climbed 15 percent and personal taxes were up a substantial 90 percent.

♦ The rise in nondiscretionary expenses has greatly curtailed impulse spending by the nation's most affluent households. This may be why the economy has seen so little inflation despite the economic boom of the late 1990s.

Average Spending of Married Couples with Children Aged 18 or Older at Home, 1990 and 1999

(average annual spending of married-couple consumer units with children aged 18 or older at home, 1990 and 1999; percent change, 1990–99; in 1999 dollars)

	1990	1999	percent change 1990–99
Number of consumer units (in 000s)	7,886	7,853	–0.4%
Average before-tax income	$63,988	$68,094	6.4
Average annual spending	54,571	54,248	–0.6
FOOD	**$8,779**	**$7,415**	**–15.5%**
Food at home	**5,142**	**4,287**	**–16.6**
Cereals and bakery products	778	646	–17.0
Cereals and cereal products	257	223	–13.2
Bakery products	520	423	–18.7
Meats, poultry, fish, and eggs	1,475	1,152	–21.9
Beef	493	369	–25.2
Pork	291	229	–21.3
Other meats	236	145	–38.6
Poultry	227	212	–6.6
Fish and seafood	167	150	–10.2
Eggs	60	47	–21.7
Dairy products	604	465	–23.0
Fresh milk and cream	294	173	–41.2
Other dairy products	310	292	–5.8
Fruits and vegetables	779	702	–9.9
Fresh fruits	233	213	–8.6
Fresh vegetables	232	208	–10.3
Processed fruits	185	159	–14.1
Processed vegetables	129	122	–5.4
Other food at home	1,507	1,322	–12.3
Sugar and other sweets	194	150	–22.7
Fats and oils	143	121	–15.4
Miscellaneous foods	659	611	–7.3
Nonalcoholic beverages	455	374	–17.8
Food prepared by household on trips	56	65	16.1

(continued)

(continued from previous page)

	1990	*1999*	*percent change 1990–99*
Food away from home	**$3,637**	**$3,129**	**−14.0%**
ALCOHOLIC BEVERAGES	**435**	**276**	**−36.6**
HOUSING	**14,048**	**15,739**	**12.0**
Shelter	**7,338**	**8,861**	**20.8**
Owned dwellings	5,482	6,890	25.7
Mortgage interest and charges	3,236	3,971	22.7
Property taxes	1,331	1,774	33.3
Maintenance, repairs, insurance, other expenses	914	1,145	25.3
Rented dwellings	1,001	1,012	1.1
Other lodging	855	959	12.2
Utilities, fuels, public services	**3,537**	**3,326**	**−6.0**
Natural gas	491	359	−26.9
Electricity	1,434	1,271	−11.4
Fuel oil and other fuels	206	111	−46.1
Telephone services	1,032	1,148	11.2
Water and other public services	373	438	17.4
Household services	**352**	**559**	**58.8**
Personal services	50	110	120.0
Other household services	303	449	48.2
Housekeeping supplies	**792**	**793**	**0.1**
Laundry and cleaning supplies	242	191	−21.1
Other household products	343	456	32.9
Postage and stationery	208	145	−30.3
Household furnishings and equipment	**2,028**	**2,201**	**8.5**
Household textiles	270	201	−25.6
Furniture	435	360	−17.2
Floor coverings	127	56	−55.9
Major appliances	257	300	16.7
Small appliances, miscellaneous housewares	162	159	−1.9
Miscellaneous household equipment	778	1,125	44.6

(continued)

(continued from previous page)

	1990	1999	percent change 1990–99
APPAREL AND SERVICES	**$3,128**	**$2,496**	**−20.2%**
Men and boys	**830**	**653**	**−21.3**
Men, aged 16 or older	775	579	−25.3
Boys, aged 2 to 15	56	74	32.1
Women and girls	**1,380**	**947**	**−31.4**
Women, aged 16 or older	1,270	825	−35.0
Girls, aged 2 to 15	111	121	9.0
Children under age 2	**89**	**57**	**−36.0**
Footwear	**373**	**436**	**16.9**
Other apparel products and services	**454**	**404**	**−11.0**
TRANSPORTATION	**11,459**	**12,029**	**5.0**
Vehicle purchases	**4,980**	**5,435**	**9.1**
Cars and trucks, new	2,656	2,717	2.3
Cars and trucks, used	2,277	2,672	17.3
Other vehicles	47	46	−2.1
Gasoline and motor oil	**2,291**	**1,819**	**−20.6**
Other vehicle expenses	**3,670**	**4,153**	**13.2**
Vehicle finance charges	714	602	−15.7
Maintenance and repairs	1,234	1,222	−1.0
Vehicle insurance	1,344	1,468	9.2
Vehicle rental, leases, licenses, other charges	379	861	127.2
Public transportation	**519**	**621**	**19.7**
HEALTH CARE	**2,510**	**2,630**	**4.8**
Health insurance	1,027	1,255	22.2
Medical services	911	811	−11.0
Drugs	421	402	−4.5
Medical supplies	152	162	6.6
ENTERTAINMENT	**2,539**	**2,549**	**0.4**
Fees and admissions	672	723	7.6
Television, radio, sound equipment	790	849	7.5
Pets, toys, and playground equipment	427	392	−8.2
Other entertainment supplies, services	651	585	−10.1

(continued)

(continued from previous page)

	1990	1999	percent change 1990–99
PERSONAL CARE PRODUCTS AND SERVICES	$790	$597	−24.4%
READING	255	214	−16.1
EDUCATION	1,590	1,822	14.6
TOBACCO PRODUCTS AND SMOKING SUPPLIES	562	406	−27.8
MISCELLANEOUS	1,338	1,236	−7.6
CASH CONTRIBUTIONS	1,751	1,458	−16.7
PERSONAL INSURANCE AND PENSIONS	5,387	5,380	−0.1
Life and other personal insurance	811	693	−14.5
Pensions and Social Security	4,576	4,687	2.4
PERSONAL TAXES	5,292	10,067	90.2
Federal income taxes	4,224	8,919	111.2
State and local income taxes	976	889	−8.9
Other taxes	92	258	180.4
GIFTS	2,195	1,508	−31.3
Food	303	114	−62.4
Housing	532	386	−27.4
Housekeeping supplies	59	42	−28.8
Household textiles	22	40	81.8
Appliances and miscellaneous housewares	61	45	−26.2
Major appliances	14	10	−28.6
Small appliances and miscellaneous housewares	47	35	−25.5
Miscellaneous household equipment	140	89	−36.4
Other housing	250	170	−32.0
Apparel and services	422	300	−28.9
Males, aged 2 or older	119	98	−17.6
Females, aged 2 or older	159	81	−49.1
Children under age 2	83	54	−34.9
Other apparel products and services	62	67	8.1
Jewelry and watches	32	29	−9.4
All other apparel products and services	31	38	22.6

(continued)

(continued from previous page)

	1990	1999	percent change 1990–99
Transportation	$163	$100	−38.7%
Health care	87	44	−49.4
Entertainment	107	118	10.3
Toys, games, hobbies, and tricycles	48	33	−31.3
Other entertainment	59	85	44.1
Education	447	293	−34.5
All other gifts	133	152	14.3

Note: The Bureau of Labor Statistics uses consumer units rather than households as the sampling unit in the Consumer Expenditure Survey. For the definition of consumer unit, see the glossary. Spending on gifts is included in the preceding product and service categories.
Source: Bureau of Labor Statistics, 1990 and 1999 Consumer Expenditure Surveys, Internet site <www.bls.gov/ csxhome.htm>; calculations by New Strategist

Spending of Single Parents Rises Sharply

Single parents still spend only half as much as married couples with children, however.

Single parents with children under age 18 at home spent 14 percent more in 1999 than in 1990, after adjusting for inflation. Their incomes rose even more during those years—although their spending continues to outpace their income.

Spending trends for single-parent families are quite different from those for married couples, showing gains in many categories. Single parents spent more on food-away-from-home in 1999 than in 1990 while couples with children spent less. Like most other household types, single parents spent more on owned dwellings as homeownership rates increased. They spent 32 percent more on household furnishings and equipment and even boosted their apparel spending by 2 percent. Single parents spent 151 percent more on new vehicles and 22 percent more on entertainment in 1999 than in 1990.

Single parents cut their spending in some categories. Spending on food-at-home fell 4 percent, while spending on alcoholic beverages fell a substantial 31 percent. Spending on household services (a category that includes day care) fell 4 percent. Furniture spending was also down 4 percent. Single parents spent 8 percent less on gifts in 1999 than in 1990.

♦ The economic boom of the 1990s benefited single-parent families, and their spending reveals pent-up demand for many products and services. An economic downturn could hurt these families by forcing them to live on less.

Average Spending of Single Parents with Children under Age 18 at Home, 1990 and 1999

(average annual spending of single-parent consumer units with children under age 18 at home, 1990 and 1999; percent change, 1990–99; in 1999 dollars)

	1990	1999	percent change 1990–99
Number of consumer units (in 000s)	6,074	6,571	8.2%
Average before–tax income	$22,198	$25,685	15.7
Average annual spending	24,523	27,918	13.8
FOOD	**$4,511**	**$4,526**	**0.3%**
Food at home	3,055	2,942	−3.7
Cereals and bakery products	458	509	11.1
Cereals and cereal products	180	204	13.3
Bakery products	279	305	9.3
Meats, poultry, fish, and eggs	883	770	−12.8
Beef	314	207	34.1
Pork	176	167	−5.1
Other meats	127	109	−14.2
Poultry	135	143	5.9
Fish and seafood	89	110	23.6
Eggs	41	34	−17.1
Dairy products	368	301	−18.2
Fresh milk and cream	190	123	−35.3
Other dairy products	178	178	0.0
Fruits and vegetables	461	457	−0.9
Fresh fruits	126	134	6.3
Fresh vegetables	129	128	−0.8
Processed fruits	117	111	−5.1
Processed vegetables	89	84	−5.6
Other food at home	883	904	2.4
Sugar and other sweets	115	115	0.0
Fats and oils	82	90	9.8
Miscellaneous foods	421	439	4.3
Nonalcoholic beverages	246	243	−1.2
Food prepared by household on trips	20	18	−10.0

(continued)

(continued from previous page)

	1990	1999	percent change 1990–99
Food away from hom	$1,456	$1,584	8.8%
ALCOHOLIC BEVERAGES	209	144	−31.1
HOUSING	8,826	10,103	14.5
Shelter	4,958	5,873	18.5
Owned dwellings	1,982	2,646	33.5
Mortgage interest and charges	1,271	1,590	25.1
Property taxes	326	539	65.3
Maintenance, repairs, insurance, other expenses	384	516	34.4
Rented dwellings	2,834	3,088	9.0
Other lodging	144	139	−3.5
Utilities, fuels, public services	2,037	2,194	7.7
Natural gas	279	248	−11.1
Electricity	806	852	5.7
Fuel oil and other fuels	61	40	−34.4
Telephone services	701	833	18.8
Water and other public services	191	221	15.7
Household services	738	696	−5.7
Personal services	551	529	−4.0
Other household services	187	167	−10.7
Housekeeping supplies	345	356	3.2
Laundry and cleaning supplies	125	136	8.8
Other household products	133	139	4.5
Postage and stationery	89	81	−9.0
Household furnishings and equipment	746	984	31.9
Household textiles	43	101	134.9
Furniture	265	255	−3.8
Floor coverings	37	29	−21.6
Major appliances	143	111	−22.4
Small appliances, miscellaneous housewares	41	38	−7.3
Miscellaneous household equipment	217	452	108.3

(continued)

(continued from previous page)

	1990	1999	percent change 1990–99
APPAREL AND SERVICES	**$1,916**	**$1,946**	**1.6%**
Men and boys	**371**	**369**	**–0.5**
Men, aged 16 or older	106	145	36.8
Boys, aged 2 to 15	265	224	–15.5
Women and girls	**835**	**913**	**9.3**
Women, aged 16 or older	616	649	5.4
Girls, aged 2 to 15	219	265	21.0
Children under age 2	**85**	**75**	**–11.8**
Footwear	**338**	**396**	**17.2**
Other apparel products and services	**286**	**193**	**–32.5**
TRANSPORTATION	**3,452**	**4,694**	**36.0**
Vehicle purchases	**1,310**	**2,260**	**72.5**
Cars and trucks, new	222	556	150.5
Cars and trucks, used	1,049	1,678	60.0
Other vehicles	40	25	–37.5
Gasoline and motor oil	**784**	**720**	**–8.2**
Other vehicle expenses	**1,177**	**1,484**	**26.1**
Vehicle finance charges	175	236	34.9
Maintenance and repairs	444	422	–5.0
Vehicle insurance	391	510	30.4
Vehicle rental, leases, licenses, other charges	167	316	89.2
Public transportation	**181**	**230**	**27.1**
HEALTH CARE	**802**	**1,003**	**25.1**
Health insurance	292	481	64.7
Medical services	347	306	–11.8
Drugs	107	165	54.2
Medical supplies	56	51	–8.9
ENTERTAINMENT	**1,122**	**1,367**	**21.8**
Fees and admissions	279	284	1.8
Television, radio, sound equipment	506	537	6.1
Pets, toys, and playground equipment	212	297	40.1
Other entertainment supplies, services	124	249	100.8

(continued)

(continued from previous page)

	1990	1999	percent change 1990–99
PERSONAL CARE PRODUCTS AND SERVICES	$344	$362	5.2%
READING	101	71	−29.7
EDUCATION	333	426	27.9
TOBACCO PRODUCTS AND SMOKING SUPPLIES	265	239	−9.8
MISCELLANEOUS	720	843	17.1
CASH CONTRIBUTIONS	447	368	−17.7
PERSONAL INSURANCE AND PENSIONS	1,475	1,827	23.9
Life and other personal insurance	175	170	−2.9
Pensions and Social Security	1,300	1,657	27.5
PERSONAL TAXES	1,315	909	−30.9
Federal income taxes	956	592	−38.1
State and local income taxes	310	258	−16.8
Other taxes	50	59	18.0
GIFTS	640	589	−8.0
Food	56	28	−50.0
Housing	176	187	6.3
Housekeeping supplies	27	22	−18.5
Household textiles	6	6	0.0
Appliances and miscellaneous housewares	10	12	20.0
Major appliances	3	2	−33.3
Small appliances and miscellaneous housewares	6	10	66.7
Miscellaneous household equipment	38	46	21.1
Other housing	94	101	7.4
Apparel and services	222	163	−26.6
Males, aged 2 or older	34	28	−17.6
Females, aged 2 or older	97	63	−35.1
Children under age 2	31	30	−3.2
Other apparel products and services	60	41	−31.7
Jewelry and watches	33	14	−57.6
All other apparel products and services	27	27	0.0

(continued)

(continued from previous page)

	1990	1999	percent change 1990–99
Transportation	$20	$13	−35.0%
Health care	9	13	44.4
Entertainment	41	39	−4.9
Toys, games, hobbies, and tricycles	15	12	−20.0
Other entertainment	25	28	12.0
Education	74	50	−32.4
All other gifts	45	95	111.1

Note: The Bureau of Labor Statistics uses consumer units rather than households as the sampling unit in the Consumer Expenditure Survey. For the definition of consumer unit, see the glossary. Spending on gifts is included in the preceding product and service categories.
Source: Bureau of Labor Statistics, 1990 and 1999 Consumer Expenditure Surveys, Internet site <www.bls.gov/ csxhome.htm>; calculations by New Strategist

Couples with Children Spend More Than Average

Single parents spend much less than the average household on most products and services.

Because married couples have higher than average incomes, their spending is also above average. Overall, couples with preschoolers spent 24 percent more than the average household in 1999. Couples with school-aged children spent 39 percent more, while those with grown children at home spent 47 percent more. In contrast, single-parent families spent 25 percent less than the average household in 1999.

Couples with preschoolers spend much more than average on items needed by young children—such as household personal services (including day care) and clothes for children under age 2. On most other products and services, however, they spend close to or even less than the average household.

Couples with school-aged or older children at home spend much more than average on most products and services. Those with adult children at home spend substantially more on items needed by workers (their households have twice as many workers as the average household) and by college students (many have children in college). They spend more than twice the average on "other lodging," education, and personal taxes, for example.

Single parents spend less than average in all but a few categories. They are above average spenders on some foods, rent, personal services (mostly day care), laundry and cleaning supplies, and children's clothes.

♦ On average, today's parents are cautious spenders. Married couples with children spend more than the average household, but their spending levels are well within their means. Single parents live closer to the edge.

Indexed Spending of Households with Children, 1999

(indexed spending of total consumer units, married-couple and single-parent consumer units by age of children at home, 1999)

	total consumer units	married couples with children under age 6	married couples with children aged 6 to 17	married couples with children 18 or older	single parents with children under age 18
Average before-tax income	100	132	145	155	58
Average annual spending	100	124	139	147	75
FOOD	**100**	**107**	**149**	**147**	**90**
Food at home	**100**	**115**	**150**	**147**	**101**
Cereals and bakery products	100	112	159	144	114
Cereals and cereal products	100	116	167	139	128
Bakery products	100	110	155	147	106
Meats, poultry, fish, and eggs	100	103	144	154	103
Beef	100	105	153	168	94
Pork	100	92	140	146	106
Other meats	100	100	152	149	112
Poultry	100	118	140	156	105
Fish and seafood	100	100	131	142	104
Eggs	100	100	141	147	106
Dairy products	100	126	162	144	93
Fresh milk and cream	100	139	166	142	101
Other dairy products	100	119	160	146	89
Fruits and vegetables	100	112	143	140	91
Fresh fruits	100	107	141	140	88
Fresh vegetables	100	113	135	140	86
Processed fruits	100	123	150	141	98
Processed vegetables	100	105	152	142	98
Other food at home	100	125	151	148	101
Sugar and other sweets	100	103	155	134	103
Fats and oils	100	93	139	144	107
Miscellaneous foods	100	148	154	145	105
Nonalcoholic beverages	100	110	146	155	100
Food prepared by household on trips	100	113	156	167	46

(continued)

	total consumer units	married couples			single parents:
		with children under age 6	with children aged 6 to 17	with children 18 or older	with children under age 18
Food away from home	100	95	146	148	75
ALCOHOLIC BEVERAGES	100	82	101	87	45
HOUSING	100	142	136	131	84
Shelter	100	144	135	126	84
Owned dwellings	100	167	167	152	58
Mortgage interest and charges	100	201	199	156	62
Property taxes	100	122	139	158	48
Maintenance, repairs, insurance, other expenses	100	124	110	134	60
Rented dwellings	100	111	70	50	152
Other lodging	100	58	105	207	30
Utilities, fuels, public services	100	108	127	140	92
Natural gas	100	109	127	133	92
Electricity	100	100	129	141	95
Fuel oil and other fuels	100	100	120	150	54
Telephone services	100	116	120	135	98
Water and other public services	100	109	141	154	78
Household services	100	322	160	84	105
Personal services	100	552	187	34	164
Other household services	100	105	135	131	49
Housekeeping supplies	100	107	155	159	71
Laundry and cleaning supplies	100	101	145	158	112
Other household products	100	105	166	182	56
Postage and stationery	100	120	143	114	64
Household furnishings and equipment	100	123	140	147	66
Household textiles	100	103	126	176	89
Furniture	100	161	161	99	70
Floor coverings	100	148	134	127	66
Major appliances	100	115	120	164	61
Small appliances, miscellaneous housewares	100	88	99	156	37
Miscellaneous household equipment	100	112	142	163	65

(continued)

(continued from previous page)

	total consumer units	married couples			single parents: with children under age 18
		with children under age 6	with children aged 6 to 17	with children 18 or older	
APPAREL AND SERVICES	**100**	**119**	**155**	**143**	**112**
Men and boys	**100**	**98**	**182**	**155**	**88**
Men, aged 16 or older	100	91	141	177	44
Boys, aged 2 to 15	100	124	326	80	241
Women and girls	**100**	**97**	**150**	**145**	**139**
Women, aged 16 or older	100	91	117	151	118
Girls, aged 2 to 15	100	126	320	113	248
Children under age 2	**100**	**615**	**137**	**85**	**112**
Footwear	**100**	**99**	**166**	**144**	**131**
Other apparel products and services	**100**	**106**	**118**	**136**	**65**
TRANSPORTATION	**100**	**134**	**137**	**172**	**67**
Vehicle purchases	**100**	**147**	**143**	**164**	**68**
Cars and trucks, new	100	108	140	167	34
Cars and trucks, used	100	185	145	163	102
Other vehicles	100	128	206	128	69
Gasoline and motor oil	**100**	**121**	**138**	**172**	**68**
Other vehicle expenses	**100**	**129**	**133**	**184**	**66**
Vehicle finance charges	100	152	159	188	74
Maintenance and repairs	100	102	133	184	64
Vehicle insurance	100	113	123	194	67
Vehicle rental, leases, licenses, other charges	100	173	130	168	62
Public transportation	**100**	**83**	**105**	**156**	**58**
HEALTH CARE	**100**	**87**	**110**	**134**	**51**
Health insurance	100	98	108	136	52
Medical services	100	93	133	145	55
Drugs	100	54	79	109	45
Medical supplies	100	77	118	149	47
ENTERTAINMENT	**100**	**112**	**166**	**135**	**72**
Fees and admissions	100	93	154	158	62
Television, radio, sound equipment	100	112	139	140	88
Pets, toys, and playground equipment	100	147	168	113	86
Other entertainment supplies, services	100	103	211	122	52

(continued)

(continued from previous page)

	total consumer units	married couples with children under age 6	married couples with children aged 6 to 17	married couples with children 18 or older	single parents: with children under age 18
PERSONAL CARE PRODUCTS AND SERVICES	100	110	135	146	89
READING	100	101	126	135	45
EDUCATION	100	50	162	287	67
TOBACCO PRODUCTS AND SMOKING SUPPLIES	100	80	115	135	80
MISCELLANEOUS	100	123	113	139	95
CASH CONTRIBUTIONS	100	68	101	123	31
PERSONAL INSURANCE AND PENSIONS	100	144	157	157	53
Life and other personal insurance	100	101	178	176	43
Pensions and Social Security	100	150	154	154	54
PERSONAL TAXES	100	113	131	281	25
Federal income taxes	100	106	130	318	21
State and local income taxes	100	143	145	144	42
Other taxes	100	117	109	152	35
GIFTS	100	71	104	139	54
Food	100	48	98	137	34
Housing	100	109	117	132	64
Housekeeping supplies	100	112	146	102	54
Household textiles	100	47	53	235	35
Appliances and miscellaneous housewares	100	53	78	141	38
Major appliances	100	22	44	111	22
Small appliances and misc. housewares	100	63	88	146	42
Miscellaneous household equipment	100	59	97	135	70
Other housing	100	152	135	125	74
Apparel and services	100	95	92	143	78
Males, aged 2 or older	100	65	91	181	52
Females, aged 2 or older	100	75	90	114	89
Children under age 2	100	276	161	164	91
Other apparel products and services	100	40	54	129	79
Jewelry and watches	100	33	26	107	52
All other apparel products and services	100	48	80	152	108

(continued)

(continued from previous page)

	total consumer units	married couples with children under age 6	married couples with children aged 6 to 17	married couples with children 18 or older	single parents: with children under age 18
TRANSPORTATION	100	17	108	159	21
HEALTH CARE	100	23	38	110	33
ENTERTAINMENT	100	70	95	120	40
Toys, games, hobbies, and tricycles	100	91	88	103	38
Other entertainment	100	61	98	129	42
EDUCATION	100	30	144	177	30
ALL OTHER GIFTS	100	56	73	116	73

Note: The index compares the spending of consumer units with children with the spending of the average consumer unit by dividing the spending of consumer units with children by average spending in each category and multiplying by 100. An index of 100 means the spending of consumer units with children equals average spending. An index of 130 means the spending of consumer units with children is 30 percent above average, while an index of 70 means it is 30 percent below average. The Bureau of Labor Statistics uses consumer units rather than households as the sampling unit in the Consumer Expenditure Survey. For the definition of consumer unit, see the glossary.
Source: Bureau of Labor Statistics, 1990 and 1999 Consumer Expenditure Surveys, Internet site <www.bls.gov/ csxhome.htm>; calculations by New Strategist

A Note on 2000 Census Data

The Millennials: Americans under Age 25 does not include 2000 census data, which have only begun to be released—a process that will take at least three years to complete. Consequently, most of the population and household data in *The Millennials: Americans under Age 25* are based on the Census Bureau's Current Population Survey, which is benchmarked each decade to census numbers. The benchmarking of the CPS follows the census by two or three years.

Because the 2000 census found more people in the U.S. than the Census Bureau had estimated, the CPS estimates and projections of populations and households are too low. The bureau estimated there were 275 million people in the U.S. in 2000, for example, while the 2000 census counted 281 million. Rather than growing a projected 10 percent during the 1990s, the U.S. population grew a considerably larger 13 percent.

Such a gap between estimates and reality has occurred before. The 1980 census found millions more people than had been estimated by the bureau. It took the agency until 1983 to benchmark the CPS to match census figures. This is the situation again today, and researchers will have to wait a few years before CPS and census are once more in alignment.

Users of demographic statistics should keep in mind that the figures in this and other demographic reference books now being published are somewhat below the actual numbers. The trends described in *The Millennials: Americans under Age 25*, however, are not affected by the census count. And it is the trends—not the exact numbers—that are most important in demographic research. Trends reveal opportunities, numbers tell you their size. Just bear in mind that the many opportunities described in *The Millennials: Americans under Age 25* are even bigger than the numbers suggest.

For more information about 2000 census data, including the release schedule, see Internet site <www.census.gov/dmd/www/2khome.htm>.

For More Information

The federal government is a rich source of data on almost every aspect of American life. Below are the Internet addresses of agencies collecting the data analyzed in this book. Also shown are the phone numbers of subject specialists, organized alphabetically by topic. A list of State Data Centers and Small Business Development Centers is also below to help you track down demographic and economic information for your state or local area. E-mail addresses are shown when available.

Internet addresses

Bureau of the Census .... <www.census.gov>
Bureau of Justice Statistics .... <www.ojp.usdoj.gov/bjs>
Bureau of Labor Statistics .... <www.bls.gov>
Centers for Disease Control and Prevention ....<www.cdc.gov>
Consumer Expenditure Survey ....<www.bls.gov/csxhome>
Consumer Healthcare Products Association .... <www.chpa-info.org>
Current Population Survey .... <www.bls.census.gov/cps>
Department of Agriculture, Food Surveys Research Group ....
....<www.barc.usda.gov/bhnrc/foodsurvey/home.htm>
Families and Work Institute .... <www.familiesandwork.org>
Higher Education Research Institute .... <www.gseis.ucla.edu/heri/heri.html>
Immigration and Naturalization Service ....
.... <www.ins.usdoj.gov/graphics/aboutins/statistics/index.htm>
Monitoring the Future Study ....<http://monitoringthefuture.org>
National Center For Education Statistics .... <http://nces.ed.gov/>
National Center For Health Statistics .... <www.cdc.gov/nchs>
National Opinion Research Center .... <www.norc.uchicago.edu>
National Telecommunications and Information Administration .... <www.ntia.doc.gov>
Sporting Goods Manufacturers Association .... <www.sgma.com>
U.S. Substance Abuse and Mental Health Services Administration .... <www.samhsa.gov>

Subject Specialists

Absences from work, Staff 202-691-6378
Aging population, Staff 301-457-2422
Ancestry, Staff 301-457-2403
Apportionment, Ed Byerly 301-457-2381
Bureau of Justice Statistics .... 202-307-0765; askbjs@ojp.usdoj.gov
Business expenditures, Sheldon Ziman 301-457-3315
Business investment, Charles Funk 301-457-3324
Census Bureau customer service, Staff 301-457-4100
Census 2000:
• Address list, Joel Sobel 301-457-1106
• Aging population, Staff 301-457-2378

- American Community Survey, Larry McGinn 301-457-8050
- Am. Indian and Alaska Native Program, Sydnee Chattin-Reynolds 301-457-2032
- Annexations/boundary changes, Joe Marinucci 301-457-1099
- Apportionment/redistricting, Edwin Byerly 301-457-2381
- Armed forces, Staff 301-457-2422
- Census history, Dave Pemberton 301-457-1167
- Census in schools, Kim Crews 301-457-3626
- Census operations, Mike Stump 301-457-3577
- Citizenship, Diane Schmidley 301-457-2403
- Commuting and place of work, Gloria Swieczkowski 301-457-2454
- Confidentiality and privacy, Jerry Gates 301-457-2515
- Count review, Paul Campbell 301-457-2390
- Data dissemination, Customer Services 301-457-4100
- Disability, Jack McNeil 301-457-8520
- Education, Staff 301-457-2464
- Emigration, Staff 301-457-2438
- Employment projections, demographic, Howard Fullerton 202-691-5711
- Employment/unemployment, Staff 301-457-3242
- Foreign born, Dianne Schmidley 301-457-2403
- Geographic entities, Staff 301-457-1099
- Group quarters population, Denise Smith 301-457-2378
- Hispanic origin, ethnicity, ancestry, Kevin Deardorff/Roberto Ramirez 301-457-2403
- Homeless, Edison Gore 301-457-3998
- Housing, Staff 301-457-3242
- Immigration, Dianne Schmidley 301-457-2403
- Income, Kirby Posey 301-457-3243
- Labor force status/work experience, Thomas Palumbo 301-457-3220
- Language spoken in home, Wendy Bruno 301-457-2464
- Living arrangements, Staff 301-457-2465
- Metropolitan areas, concepts and standards, Michael Ratcliffe 301-457-2419
- Microdata files, Amanda Shields 301-457-1326
- Migration, Kris Hansen/Carol Faber 301-457-2454
- Occupation/industry, Staff 301-457-3210
- Outlying areas, Idabelle Hovland 301-457-8443
- Persons without conventional housing, Edison Gore 301-457-3998
- Population (general information), Staff 301-457-2422
- Questionnaire content, Louisa Miller 301-457-2073
- Race, Staff 301-457-2402
- Residence rules, Karen Mills 301-457-2390
- Response rates, Staff 301-457-3691
- Sampling, Rajendra Singh 301-457-4199
- Service based enumeration, Annetta Clark Smith 301-457-2378
- Special places/group quarters, Denise Smith 301-457-2378
- Special populations, Staff 301-457-2378
- Special tabulations, Marie Pees 301-457-2447
- Undercount, Rajendra Singh 301-457-4199
  - Demographic, Greg Robinson 301-457-2103

- Employment, Ellen Thompson 301-457-1531
- Federal expenditure data, Gerard Keffer 301-457-1522
- Finance, Donna Hirsch 301-457-1486
- Government information, Staff 301-457-1580
- Governmental organization, Robert McArthur 301-457-1582
Group quarters population, Denise Smith 301-457-2378
Health insurance statistics, Staff 301-457-3242
Health surveys, Adrienne Oneto 301-457-3879
Higher Education Research Institute .... 310-825-1925; heri@ucla.edu
Hispanic statistics, Staff 301-457-2403
Home-based work, Staff 202-691-6378
Homeless, Edison Gore 301-457-3998
Households and families, Staff 301-457-2465
Household wealth, Staff 301-457-3242
Housing:
- American Housing Survey, Jane Kneessi/Barbara Williams 301-457-3235
- Census, Staff 301-457-3237
- Homeownership, vacancy data, Linda Cavanaugh/Robert Callis 301-457-3199
- Housing affordability, Peter Fronczek/Howard Savage 301-457-3199
- Market absorption, Alan Friedman 301-457-3199
- New York City Housing and Vacancy Survey, Peter Fronczek 301-457-3199
- Residential finance, Howard Savage 301-457-3199
Illegal immigration, Staff 301-457-3428
Immigration, general information, Staff 301-457-2422
Income statistics, Staff 301-457-3242
Industry and commodity classification, James Kristoff 301-457-4631
Industry Employment Projections:
- Aggregate economy, GDP, Betty Su 202-691-5729
- Demographics, Howard Fullerton 202-691-5711
- Employment impact studies, Norman Saunders 202-691-5701
- Employment requirements table, Art Andreassen 202-691-5689
- Personal consumption expenditures, Mitra Toossi 202-691-5721
- Foreign trade, Mirko Novakovic 202-691-5008
- Investment, government, Jay Berman 202-691-5692
- Industry classification issues (NAICS), Norman Saunders 202-691-5701
- Industry output and employment, Jay Berman 202-691-5733
- Industry projections coordination, James Franklin 202-691-5709
- Input-output tables, Art Andreassen 202-691-5689
- Input-output theory and practice, Charles Bowman 202-691-5702
- Labor force, Howard Fullerton 202-691-5711
- National income and product accounts, Norman Saunders 202-691-5701
- Population, Howard Fullerton 202-691-5711
- Productivity, James Franklin 202-691-5709
- Value added, Charles Bowman 202-691-5702
International Statistics:
- Africa, Asia, Latin Am., North Am., and Oceania, Patricia Rowe 301-457-1358
- Aging population, Victoria Velkoff 301-457-1371

Special censuses, Josephine Ruffin 301-457-1429
Special surveys, Ron Dopkowski 301-457-3801
Special tabulations, Marie Pees 301-457-2447
Sporting Goods Manufacturers Association .... 561-842-4100; info@sgma.com
State populations and projections, Staff 301-457-2422
Statistics of U.S. businesses, Melvin Cole 301-457-3320
Survey of Income and Program Participation (SIPP), Staff 301-457-3242
Transportation:
• Commodity Flow Survey, John Fowler 301-457-2108
• Economic census, Pam Palmer 301-457-2811
• Vehicle inventory and use, Kim Moore 301-457-2797
• Warehousing and trucking, Ruth Bramblett 301-457-2766
Undercount, demographic analysis, Gregg Robinson 301-457-2103
Union membership, Staff 202-691-6378
Urban/rural population, Michael Ratcliff/Rodger Johnson 301-457-2419
Veterans, characteristics, Staff 301-457-3242
Veterans in labor force, Staff 202-691-6378
Voters, characteristics, Staff 301-457-2445
Voting age population, Jennifer Day 301-457-2464
Weekly earnings, Staff 202-691-6378
Wholesale Trade:
• Current sales and inventories, Scott Scheleur 301-457-2713
• Economic census, Donna Hambric 301-457-2725
• Quarterly Financial Report, Ronald Horton 301-457-3343
Women, Staff 301-457-2378
Women in the labor force, Staff 202-691-6378
Work experience, Staff 202-691-6378
Working poor, Staff 202-691-6378
Youth, students, and dropouts in labor force, Staff 202-691-6378

Census Regional Offices

Information specialists in the Census Bureau's 12 regional offices answer thousands of questions each year. If you have questions about the Census Bureau's products and services, you can contact the regional office that serves your state. The states served by each regional office are listed in parentheses.

• **Atlanta** (AL, FL, GA) .... 404-730-3833; atlanta.regional.office@census.gov
• **Boston** (CT, MA, ME, NH, NY, RI, VT) .... 617-424-0510; boston.regional.office@census.gov
• **Charlotte** (KY, NC, SC, TN, VA) .... 704-344-6144; charlotte.regional.office@census.gov
• **Chicago** (IL, IN, WI) .... 312-353-9747; chicago.regional.office@census.gov
• **Dallas** (LA, MS, TX) .... 214-655-3050; dallas.regional.office@census.gov
• **Denver** (AZ, CO, MT, NE, ND, NM, NV, SD, UT, WY) ....
  .... 303-969-7750; denver_regional_office@census.gov
• **Detroit** (MI, OH, WV) .... 313-259-1875; detroit.regional.office@census.gov
• **Kansas City** (AR, IA, KS, MN, MO, OK) .... 913-551-6711; kansas.regional.office@census.gov
• **Los Angeles** (CA southern, HI) .... 818-904-6339; la.regional.office@census.gov
• **New York** (NY, NJ selected counties) .... 212-264-4730; ny.regional.office@census.gov
• **Philadelphia** (DE, DC, MD, NJ selected counties, PA) ....
  .... 215-656-7578; philly.regional.office@census.gov

- **Seattle** (CA northern, AK, ID, OR, WA) .... 206-553-5835; seattle.regional.office@census.gov
- **Puerto Rico** and the **U.S. Virgin Islands** are serviced by the Boston regional office. All other outlying areas are serviced by the Los Angeles regional office.

State Data Centers and Business and Industry Data Centers

For demographic and economic information about states and local areas, contact your State Data Center (SDC) or Business and Industry Data Center (BIDC). Every state has a State Data Center. Below are listed the leading centers for each state-usually a state government agency, university, or library that heads a network of affiliate centers. Asterisks (*) identify states that also have BIDCs. In some states, one agency serves as the lead for both the SDC and the BIDC. The BIDC is listed separately if a separate agency serves as the lead.

Alabama, Annette Watters, University of Alabama .... 205-348-619; awatters@cba.ua.edu

Alaska, Kathryn Lizik, Department of Labor .... 907-465-2437; kathryn_lizik@labor.state.ak.us

American Samoa, Vaitoelav Filiga, Dept. of Commerce .... 684-633-5155; vfiliga@samotelco.com

* **Arizona**, Betty Jeffries, Dept. of Economic Security .... 602-542-5984; popstats@de.state.az.us

Arkansas, Sarah Breshears, Univ. of Arkansas/Little Rock.... 501-569-8530; sgbreshears@ualr.edu

California, Linda Gage, Department of Finance .... 916-323-4086; filgage@dof.ca.gov

Colorado, Rebecca Picaso, Dept. of Local Affairs ....303-866-2156; rebecca.picaso@state.co

Connecticut, Bill Kraynak, Office of Policy and Management ....
.... 860-418-6230; william.kraynak@po.state.ct.us

* **Delaware**, O'Shell Howell, Economic Development Office .... 302-739-427; oshowell@state.de.us

District of Columbia, Herb Bixhorn, Mayor's Office of Planning ....
....202-442-7603; hbixhorn@dcgov.com

* **Florida**, Pam Schenker, Dept. of Labor and Employment Security ....
.... 850-488-1048; pamela_schenker@awi.state.fl.us

Georgia, Robert Giacomini, Office of Planning and Budget ....
.... 404-463-1115; robert.giacomini@sdrc.gadata.org

Guam, Eugene Yungi Li, Department of Commerce .671-475-0205; e-mail unavailable at this time

Hawaii, Jan Nakamoto, Dept. of Business, Ec. Dev., and Tourism ....
....808-586-2493; jnakamot@dbedt.hawaii.gov

Idaho, Alan Porter, Department of Commerce .... 208-334-2470; aporter@idoc.state.id.us

Illinois, Suzanne Ebetsch, Bureau of the Budget .... 217-782-1381; sebetsch@commerce.state.il.us

* **Indiana**, Roberta Brooker, State Library .... 317-232-3733; rbooker@statelib.lib.in.us

Indiana BIDC, Carol Rogers, Business Research Center .... 317-274-2205; rogersc@iupui.edu

Iowa, Beth Henning, State Library .... 515-281-4350; b.henning@lib.state.ia.us

Kansas, Marc Galbraith, State Library .... 785-296-3296; ksstl3lb@ink.org

* **Kentucky**, Ron Crouch, University of Louisville .... 502-852-7990; rtcrou01gwise@louisville.edu

Louisiana, Karen Paterson, Office of Planning and Budget..
.... 225-219-4025; webmaster@doa.state.la.us

* **Maine**, Eric VonMagnus, State Planning Office .... 207-287-2989; eric.vonmagnus@state.me.us

* **Maryland**, Jane Traynham, Office of Planning .... 410-767-4450; jtraynham@mdp.state.md.us

* **Massachusetts**, John Gaviglio, Institute for Social and Ec. Research ....
.... 413-545-3460; miser@miser.umass.edu

Michigan, Carolyn Lauer, Dept. of Management and Budget .... 517-373-7910; Lauerc@state.mi.us

* **Minnesota**, David Birkholz, State Demographer's Office ....
.... 651-297-2360; david.birkholz@mnplan.state.mm.us

Minnesota BIDC, Barbara Ronningen, State Demographer's Office ....
.... 651-296-4886; barbara.ronningen@mnplan.state.mm.us
* **Mississippi**, Rachel McNeely, University of Mississippi .... 662-915-7288; rmcneely@olemiss.edu
Mississippi BIDC, Deloise Tate, Dept. of Ec. and Comm. Dev. ....
.... 601-359-3593; dtate@mississippi.org
* **Missouri**, Debra Pitts, State Library .... 573-526-7648; pittsd@mail.sos.state.mo.us
Missouri BIDC, Fred Goss, Small Business Devel. Center .... 573-341-4559; fredgoss@umr.edu
* **Montana**, Allan B. Cox, Department of Commerce .... 406-444-4393; jclack@state.mt.us
Nebraska, Jerome Deichert, University of Nebraska at Omaha ....
.... 402-554-2134; jerome_deichert@unomaha.edu
Nevada, Joyce M. Cox, State Library and Archives .... 775-684-3303; jmcox@clan.lib.nv.us
New Hampshire, Thomas Duffy, Office of State Planning .. 603-271-2155; t_duffy@osp.state.nh.us
* **New Jersey**, David Joye, Department of Labor .... 609-984-2595; djoye@dol.state.nj.us
* **New Mexico**, Kevin Kargacin, University of New Mexico .... 505-277-6626; kargacin@unm.edu
New Mexico BIDC, Karma Shore, Econ. Development Dept. .... 505-827-0264; kshore@unm.edu
* **New York**, Staff, Department of Economic Development ....
.... 518-292-5300; rscardamalia@empire.state.ny.us
* **North Carolina**, Staff, State Library .... 919-733-3270; francine@ospl.state.nc.us
North Dakota, Richard Rathge, State Univ. .... 701-231-8621; richard_rathge@ndsu.nodak.edu
Northern Mariana Islands, Diego Sasamoto, Dept. of Commerce ....
.... 670-664-3034; cad@itecnmi.com
* **Ohio**, Barry Bennett, Department of Development .... 614-466-2115; bbennett@odod.state.oh.us
* **Oklahoma**, Jeff Wallace, Department of Commerce ... 405-815-5184; jeff_wallace@odoc.state.ok.us
Oregon, George Hough, Portland State University .... 503-725-5159; houghg@mail.pdx.edu
* **Pennsylvania**, Diane Shoop, Pennsylvania State Univ./Harrisburg ....
.... 717-948-6096; des102@psu.edu
Puerto Rico, Lillian Torres Aguirre, Planning Bd. .... 787-728-4430; torres_l@jp.prstar.net
Rhode Island, Mark Brown, Dept. of Admin. .... 401-222-6183 mbrown@planning.state.ri.us
South Carolina, Mike MacFarlane, Budget and Control Board ....
.... 803-734-3780; mmacfarl@drss.state.sc.us
South Dakota, Nancy Nelson, Univ. of South Dakota .... 605-677-5287; nnelson@usd.edu
Tennessee, Betty Vickers, University of Tennessee .... 423-974-6080; bvickers@utk.edu
* **Texas**, Steve Murdock, Texas A&M Univ. .... 409-845-5115/5332; smurdock@rsocsun.tamu.edu
Texas BIDC, Donna Osborne, Dept. of Economic Dev. .... 512-936-0223; donna@ded.state.tx.us
* **Utah**, Lisa Hillman, Office of Planning and Budget .... 801-537-9013; lhillman@gov.state.ut.us
Vermont, Sharon Whitaker, Univ. of Vermont .... 802-656-3021; sharon.whitaker@uvm.edu
Virgin Islands, Frank Mills, Univ. of the Virgin Islands .... 340-693-1027; fmills@uvi.edu
* **Virginia**, Don Lillywhite, Virginia Employment Commission ....
.... 804-786-8026; dlillywhite@vec.state.va.us
* **Washington**, Yi Zhao, Office of Financial Management .... 360-902-0599; yi.zhao@ofm.wa.gov
* **West Virginia**, Delphine Coffey, Office of Comm. and Ind. Dev. 304-558-4010; dcoffey@wvdo.org
West Virginia BIDC, Randy Childs, Center for Economic Research ....
.... 304-293-6524; childs@be.wvu.edu
* **Wisconsin**, Robert Naylor, Dept of Administration .... 608-266-1927; bob.naylor@doa.state.wi.us
Wisconsin BIDC, Dan Veroff, Univ. of Wisconsin .... 608-265-9545; dlveroff@facstaff.wisc.edu
Wyoming, Wenlin Liu, Dept. of Admin. and Information .... 307-766-2925; wliu@state.wy.us

Glossary

adjusted for inflation Income or a change in income that has been adjusted for the rise in the cost of living, or the consumer price index (CPI-U-XI).

American Housing Survey The AHS collects national and metropolitan-level data on the nation's housing, including apartments, single-family homes, and mobile homes. The national survey, with a sample of 55,000 homes, is conducted by the Census Bureau for the Department of Housing and Urban Development every other year.

Asian In this book, the term "Asian" includes both Asians and Pacific Islanders.

baby boom Americans born between 1946 and 1964. Baby boomers were aged 37 to 55 in 2001.

baby bust Americans born between 1965 and 1976, also known as Generation X. In 2001, baby busters were aged 25 to 36.

central cities The largest city in a metropolitan area is called the central city. The balance of the metropolitan area outside the central city is regarded as the "suburbs."

Consumer Expenditure Survey The Consumer Expenditure Survey (CEX) is an ongoing study of the day-to-day spending of American households administered by the Bureau of Labor Statistics. The survey is used to update prices for the Consumer Price Index. The CEX includes an interview survey and a diary survey. The average spending figures shown in this book are the integrated data from both the diary and interview components of the survey. Two separate, nationally representative samples are used for the interview and diary surveys. For the interview survey, about 5,000 consumer units are interviewed on a rotating panel basis each quarter for five consecutive quarters. For the diary survey, 5,000 consumer units keep weekly diaries of spending for two consecutive weeks.

consumer unit (on Spending tables only) For convenience, the terms consumer unit and household are used interchangeably in the spending tables of this book, although consumer units are somewhat different from the Census Bureau's households. Consumer units are all related members of a household, or financially independent members of a household. A household may include more than one consumer unit.

1994–96 Continuing Survey of Food Intakes by Individuals This survey was conducted by the Agricultural Research Service of the U.S. Department of Agriculture to measure the food consumption of individuals. In taking the survey, a nationally representative sample of 21,700 people of all ages and 11,800 children aged 0 to 19 were asked to provide information on their food intakes for two nonconsecutive days.

Current Population Survey A nationally representative survey of the civilian noninstitutional population aged 15 or older. It is taken monthly by the Census Bureau for the Bureau of Labor Statistics, collecting information from 50,000 households on employment and unemployment. In March of each year, the survey includes a demographic supplement which is the source of most national data on the characteristics of Americans, such as their educational attainment, living arrangements, and incomes.

1994–96 Diet and Health Knowledge Survey This survey was conducted by the Agricultural Research Service of the U.S. Department of Agriculture to measure the public's knowledge about healthy eating. It was designed as a follow-up to the 1994-96 Continuing Survey of Food Intakes by Individuals, with telephone interviews placed to 5,800 individuals who had taken part in the Continuing Survey of Food Intakes about two weeks earlier.

disability Children under age 5 were identified as disabled if they had a developmental delay or a condition that limited their ability to use arms or legs or a condition that limited walking, running, or playing. Children aged 6 to 14 were identified as severely disabled if they met any of the following criteria: 1) had a mental retardation or some other developmental disability; 2) had a developmental condition for which they had received therapy or diagnostic services; 3) they used an ambulatory aid; 4) they had a severe limitation in the ability to see, hear, or speak; or 5) they needed personal assistance for an activity of daily living.

dual-earner couple   A married couple in which both husband and wife are in the labor force.

earnings   A type of income, earnings is the amount of money a person receives from his or her job. See also Income.

employed   All civilians who did any work as a paid employee or farmer/self-employed worker, or who worked 15 hours or more as an unpaid farm worker or in a family-owned business, during the reference period. All those who have jobs but who are temporarily absent from their jobs due to illness, bad weather, vacation, labor management dispute, or personal reasons are considered employed.

expenditure   The transaction cost including excise and sales taxes of goods and services acquired during the survey period. The full cost of each purchase is recorded even though full payment may not have been made at the date of purchase. Average expenditure figures may be artificially low for infrequently purchased items such as cars because figures are calculated using all consumer units within a demographic segment rather than just purchasers. Expenditure estimates include money spent on gifts for others.

family   A group of two or more people (one of whom is the householder) related by birth, marriage, or adoption and living in the same household.

family household   A household maintained by a householder who lives with one or more people related to him or her by blood, marriage, or adoption.

female/male householder   A woman or man who maintains a household without a spouse present. May head family or nonfamily households.

full-time employment   Full-time is 35 or more hours of work per week during a majority of the weeks worked during the preceding calendar year.

full-time, year-round   Indicates 50 or more weeks of full-time employment during the previous calendar year.

General Social Survey   The General Social Survey (GSS) is a biennial survey of the attitudes of Americans taken by the University of Chicago's National Opinion Research Center (NORC). NORC conducts the GSS through face-to-face interviews with an independently drawn, representative sample of 1,500 to 3,000 noninstitutionalized English-speaking people aged 18 or older who live in the United States.

Generation X   Americans born between 1965 and 1976, also known as the baby-bust generation. Generation Xers were aged 25 to 36 in 2001.

Hispanic   People or householders who identify their origin as Mexican, Puerto Rican, Central or South American, or some other Hispanic origin. People of Hispanic origin may be of any race. In other words, there are Asian Hispanics, black Hispanics, Native American Hispanics, and white Hispanics.

household   All the persons who occupy a housing unit. A household includes the related family members and all the unrelated persons, if any, such as lodgers, foster children, wards, or employees who share the housing unit. A person living alone is counted as a household. A group of unrelated people who share a housing unit as roommates or unmarried partners is also counted as a household. Households do not include group quarters such as college dormitories, prisons, or nursing homes.

household, race/Hispanic origin of   Households are categorized according to the race or Hispanic origin of the householder only.

householder The householder is the person (or one of the persons) in whose name the housing unit is owned or rented or, if there is no such person, any adult member. With married couples, the householder may be either the husband or wife. The householder is the reference person for the household.

householder, age of The age of the householder is used to categorize households into age groups such as those used in this book. Married couples, for example, are classified according to the age of either the husband or wife, depending on which one identified him or herself as the householder.

housing unit A housing unit is a house, an apartment, a group of rooms, or a single room occupied or intended for occupancy as separate living quarters. Separate living quarters are those in which the occupants do not live and eat with any other persons in the structure and that have direct access from the outside of the building or through a common hall that is used or intended for use by the occupants of another unit or by the general public. The occupants may be a single family, one person living alone, two or more families living together, or any other group of related or unrelated persons who share living arrangements.

immigration The relatively permanent movement (change of residence) of persons into the country of reference.

income Money received in the preceding calendar year by each person aged 15 or older from each of the following sources: (1) earnings from longest job (or self-employment); (2) earnings from jobs other than longest job; (3) unemployment compensation; (4) workers' compensation; (5) Social Security; (6) Supplemental Security income; (7) public assistance; (8) veterans' payments; (9) survivor benefits; (10) disability benefits; (11) retirement pensions; (12) interest; (13) dividends; (14) rents and royalties or estates and trusts; (15) educational assistance; (16) alimony; (17) child support; (18) financial assistance from outside the household, and other periodic income. Income is reported in several ways in this

book. Household income is the combined income of all household members. Income of persons is all income accruing to a person from all sources. Earnings is the amount of money a person receives from his or her job.

labor force The labor force tables in this book show the civilian labor force only. The labor force includes both the employed and the unemployed (people who are looking for work). People are counted as in the labor force if they were working or looking for work during the reference week in which the Census Bureau fields the Current Population Survey.

labor force participation rate The percent of a population that is in the labor force, which includes both the employed and unemployed. Labor force participation rates may be shown for sex-age groups or other special populations such as mothers of children of a given age.

married couples with or without children under age 18 Refers to married couples with or without children under age 18 living in the same household. Couples without children under age 18 may be parents of grown children who live elsewhere, or they could be childless couples.

median The median is the amount that divides the population or households into two equal portions: one below and one above the median. Medians can be calculated for income, age, and many other characteristics.

median income The amount that divides the income distribution into two equal groups, half having incomes above the median, half having incomes below the median. The medians for households or families are based on all households or families. The median for persons are based on all persons aged 15 or older with income.

metropolitan area An area qualifies for recognition as a metropolitan area if it includes a city of at least 50,000 population, or it includes a Census Bureau defined urbanized area of at least 50,000 with a total metropolitan population of at least 100,000 (75,000 in New England). In addition to the county containing the main city or urbanized area, a metropolitan area may include other counties having strong commuting ties to the central county.

millennial generation Americans born between 1977 and 1994. Millennials were aged 7 to 24 in 2001.

Monitoring the Future Project The MTF survey is conducted by the University of Michigan Survey Research Center. The survey is administered to approximately 50,000 students in 420 public and private secondary schools every year. High school seniors have been surveyed annually since 1975. Students in 8th and 10th grade have been surveyed annually since 1991.

National Ambulatory Medical Care Survey The NAMCS is an annual survey of visits to nonfederally employed office-based physicians who are primarily engaged in direct patient care. Data are collected from physicians rather than patients, with each physician assigned a one-week reporting period. During that week, a systematic random sample of visit characteristics are recorded by the physician or office staff.

National Health Interview Survey The NHIS is a continuing nationwide sample survey of the civilian noninstitutional population of the U.S. conducted by the Census Bureau for the National Center for Health Statistics. Each year, data are collected from more than 100,000 people about their illnesses, injuries, impairments, chronic and acute conditions, activity limitations, and the use of health services.

nonfamily household A household maintained by a householder who lives alone or who lives with people to whom he or she is not related.

nonfamily householder A householder who lives alone or with nonrelatives.

nonmetropolitan area Counties that are not classified as metropolitan areas.

occupation Occupational classification is based on the kind of work a person did at his or her job during the previous calendar year. If a person changed jobs during the year, the data refer to the occupation of the job held the longest during that year.

occupied housing units A housing unit is classified as occupied if a person or group of people is living in it or if the occupants are only temporarily absent-on vacation, example. By definition, the count of occupied housing units is the same as the count of households.

outside central city The portion of a metropolitan county or counties that falls outside of the central city or cities; generally regarded as the suburbs.

own children Own children are sons and daughters, including stepchildren and adopted children, of the householder. The totals include never-married children living away from home in college dormitories.

owner occupied A housing unit is "owner occupied" if the owner lives in the unit, even if it is mortgaged or not fully paid for. A cooperative or condominium unit is "owner occupied" only if the owner lives in it. All other occupied units are classified as "renter occupied."

part-time employment Part-time employment is less than 35 hours of work per week in a majority of the weeks worked during the year.

percent change The change (either positive or negative) in a measure that is expressed as a proportion of the starting measure. When median income changes from $20,000 to $25,000, for example, this is a 25 percent increase.

percentage point change The change (either positive or negative) in a value which is already expressed as a percentage. When a labor force participation rate changes from 70 percent of 75 percent, for example, this is a 5 percentage point increase.

poverty level The official income threshold below which families and persons are classified as living in poverty. The threshold rises each year with inflation and varies depending on family size and age of householder.

proportion or share The value of a part expressed as a percentage of the whole. If there are 4 million people aged 25 and 3 million of them are white, then the white proportion is 75 percent.

race Race is self-reported and appears in four categories in this book: Asian, black, Native American, and white. A household is assigned the race of the householder.

regions The four major regions and nine census divisions of the United States are the state groupings as shown below:

Northeast:
–New England: Connecticut, Maine, Massachusetts, New Hampshire, Rhode Island, and Vermont
–Middle Atlantic: New Jersey, New York, and Pennsylvania

Midwest:
–East North Central: Illinois, Indiana, Michigan, Ohio, and Wisconsin
–West North Central: Iowa, Kansas, Minnesota, Missouri, Nebraska, North Dakota, and South Dakota

South:
–South Atlantic: Delaware, District of Columbia, Florida, Georgia, Maryland, North Carolina, South Carolina, Virginia, and West Virginia
–East South Central: Alabama, Kentucky, Mississippi, and Tennessee
–West South Central: Arkansas, Louisiana, Oklahoma, and Texas

West:
–Mountain: Arizona, Colorado, Idaho, Montana, Nevada, New Mexico, Utah, and Wyoming
–Pacific: Alaska, California, Hawaii, Oregon, and Washington

renter occupied *See* Owner occupied.

rounding Percentages are rounded to the nearest tenth of a percent; therefore, the percentages in a distribution do not always add exactly to 100.0 percent. The totals, however, are always shown as 100.0. Moreover, individual figures are rounded to the nearest thousand without being adjusted to

group totals, which are independently rounded; percentages are based on the unrounded numbers.

self-employment A person is categorized as self-employed if he or she was self-employed in the job held longest during the reference period. Persons who report self-employment from a second job are excluded, but those who report wage-and-salary income from a second job are included. Unpaid workers in family businesses are excluded. Self-employment statistics exclude people who work for themselves in an incorporated business.

sex ratio The number of men per 100 women.

suburbs The portion of a metropolitan area that is outside the central city.

unemployed Unemployed people are those who, during the survey period, had no employment but were available and looking for work. Those who were laid off from their jobs and were waiting to be recalled are also classified as unemployed.

Youth Risk Behavior Surveillance System The YRBSS was created by the Centers for Disease Control to monitor health risks being taken by young people at the national, state, and local level. The national survey is taken every two years based on a nationally representative sample of 16,000 students in 9th through 12th grade in public and private schools.

Bibliography

Bureau of Justice Statistics
    Internet site <www.ojp.usdoj.gov/bjs>
    —*Sourcebook of Criminal Justice Statistics 1999*, Kathleen Maguire and Ann L. Pastore, eds., 1999

Bureau of the Census
    Internet site <www.census.gov>
    —2000 Current Population Survey, unpublished data
    —*A Child's Day: Home, School, and Play, 1994* (Selected Indicators of Child Well-Being), Household Economic Studies, Current Population Reports, P70-68, 2001
    —*Americans with Disabilities: 1997*, detailed tables from Current Population Reports, P70-73, 2001
    —American Housing Survey for the United States in 1999
    —*Educational Attainment in the United States: March 2000*, detailed tables from Current Population Reports, P20-536, 2000
    —*Geographic Mobility: March 1998 to March 1999*, Current Population Reports, P20-531, 2000
    —*Household and Family Characteristics: March 1998*, detailed tables from Current Population Reports, P20-515, 1998
    —*Marital Status and Living Arrangements: March 1998*, Current Population Reports, P20-514, 1998
    —*Money Income in the United States: 1999*, Current Population Reports, P60-209, 2000
    —*Population Projections of the United States by Age, Sex, Race, and Hispanic Origin: 1995 to 2050*, Current Population Reports, P25-1130, 1996
    —*Poverty in the United States: 1999*, Current Population Reports, P60-210, 2000
    —*School Enrollment: Social and Economic Characteristics of Students: October 1999*, detailed tables from Current Population Reports, P20-533, 2001
    —*Statistical Abstract of the United States: 1999* (119th edition) Washington, DC 1999
    —*Statistical Abstract of the United States: 2000* (120th edition) Washington, DC 2001

Bureau of Labor Statistics
    Internet site <www.bls.gov>
    —1990 and 1999 Consumer Expenditure Surveys, unpublished data
    —2000 Current Population Survey, unpublished data
    —*Contingent and Alternative Employment Arrangements*, February 1999
    —*Employment and Earnings*, January 1991
    —*Employment and Earnings*, January 2001
    —*Handbook of Labor Statistics*, Bulletin 2340, 1989
    —*Monthly Labor Review*, November 1999

Centers for Disease Control and Prevention
    Internet site <www.cdc.gov>
    —"Youth Risk Behavior Surveillance—United States, 1999." *Mortality and Morbidity Weekly Report*, 49, no. SS-5 (June 9, 2000)

Consumer Healthcare Products Association
    Internet site <www.chpa—info.org>
    —*Self-Medication in the '90s: Practices and Perceptions*, 1992

Gallinsky, Ellen. *Ask the Children: What America's Children Really Think About Working Parents.* New York: Harper Collins, 1999.

Higher Education Research Institute
   Internet site <www.gseis.ucla.edu/heri/heri.html>
   —Sax, Linda J.; Alexander W. Astin; William S. Korn; and Kathryn M. Mahoney. *The American Freshman: National Norms for Fall 2000.* UCLA: 2001

Immigration and Naturalization Service
   Internet site <www.ins.usdoj.gov/graphics/aboutins/statistics/index.htm>
   —*1998 Statistical Yearbook of the Immigration and Naturalization Service,* 2000

Institute for Social Research
   Internet site <http://monitoringthefuture.org>
   —*Monitoring the Future: National Results on Adolescent Drug Use, Summary of Key Findings.* University of Michigan, 1999

National Center for Education Statistics
   Internet site <http://nces.ed.gov>
   —*Digest of Education Statistics: 2001,* NCES 2001034, 2001

National Household Education Survey 1999, unpublished data
   —*Projections of Education Statistics to 2010,* NCES 2000071, 2000

National Center for Health Statistics
   Internet site <www.cdc.gov/nchs>
   —*Births: Final Data for 1998,* National Vital Statistics Report, Vol. 48, No. 3, 2000
   —*Births: Preliminary Data for 1999,* National Vital Statistics Report, Vol. 48, No. 14, 2000
   —*Current Estimates from the National Health Interview Survey, 1996,* Series 10, No. 200, 1999
   —*Deaths: Final Data for 1998,* National Vital Statistics Report, Vol. 48, No. 11, 2000
   —*Health, United States,* 2000
   —"National Ambulatory Medical Care Survey: 1998 Summary," *Advance Data* 315 (2000)

National Opinion Research Center
   Internet site <www.norc.uchicago.edu>
   —General Social Surveys, unpublished data

National Telecommunications and Information Administration
   Internet site <www.ntia.doc.gov>
   —*Falling through the Net: Toward Digital Inclusion—A Report on Americans' Access to Technology Tools,* October 2000

Sporting Goods Manufacturers Association
   Internet site <www.sgma.com>

U.S. Department of Agriculture, Food Surveys Research Group
   Internet site <www.barc.usda.gov/bhnrc/foodsurvey/home.htm>
   —ARS Food Surveys Research Group, 1994–96 Continuing Survey of Food Intakes by Individuals
   —ARS Food Surveys Research Group, 1994–96 Diet and Health Knowledge Survey

U.S. Substance Abuse and Mental Health Services Administration
   Internet site <www.samhsa.gov>
   —National Household Survey on Drug Abuse, 1999

Index